Soldier in the Downfall

A Wehrmacht Cavalryman in Russia, Normandy, and the Plot to Kill Hitler

By Baron Rudolf-Christoph von Gersdorff

Translation with Notes by Anthony Pearsall
With an Introduction by Lory Reinach, *née* von Gersdorff

THE ABERJONA PRESS
Bedford, Pennsylvania

Editor: Patricia K. Bonn
Copy Editor: Gayle Wurst, Princeton International Agency for the Arts, LLC
Cartographer: Tom Houlihan
Printer: Mercersburg Printing, Mercersburg, Pennsylvania

The Aberjona Press is an imprint of Aegis Consulting Group, Inc.,
        Bedford, Pennsylvania 15522
© 2012 Lory Reinach
English translation and endnotes © 2012 by Anthony Pearsall
Printed in the United States of America
19 18 17 16 15 14 13 12   5 4 3 2 1

ISBN 13: 978-0-9777563-4-6

Except as noted, all photos are from the National Archives, College Park, Maryland, or the Military History Institute, Carlisle, Pennsylvania. Photos from the author's collection are noted in the caption with *(Au.).* Photos from the translator's collection are noted with *(Tr.).* Special thanks to Editions Tallandier, publisher of Gersdorff's upcoming French translation, for providing digital photos from the author's collection.

Cover photo: Baron Rudolf-Christoph von Gersdorff, 1944. *(Au.)*

Contents

*He who survives a tragedy
was not its hero.*
   —Stanislav Jerzy Lec

In memory of
the most active men
in the German resistance

Hans Oster

Henning von Tresckow

Count Claus von Stauffenberg

Translator's Notes

While praising the Prussian noblemen who plotted against Hitler's life, essay-ist Clive James made the necessary point that, after all, "Aristocratic recruits to the SS were plentiful: promotion was rapid, and there were opportunities to ride horses. (Funding an SS equestrian team was one of Himmler's master strokes.) Most of the young officers who developed doubts about Hitler had friends who never developed any doubts at all."[1]

This is the story of a man— an aristocratic professional soldier of impec-cably Aryan lineage who would have certainly been welcomed as one of Him-mler's horsemen had he so chosen—who instead developed doubts and then acted upon them, despite an oath he had pronounced, despite the likelihood of failure and the contempt of those people he most valued, despite a training in obedience and loyalty that would have begun, for him, at some point before his own earliest memories.

Memories are largely what Baron Rudolf-Christoph von Gersdorff had to work with when he sat down to write his memoirs. He was by then a weary paraplegic, aging and wheelchair-bound, a dispossessed refugee from what he emphatically regarded as his eastern *Heimat* (native land) along the lower reaches of the Oder River, and limited in his research to such books and papers as might have been available to him as a private citizen of limited means and capacities, in the divided Germany of the mid-1970s. Fortunately his power to recollect was strong, and his life as a German soldier through 1947 had provided him with more memorable experiences than most.

He wrote in memory of three of the uniformed anti-Hitler conspirators whom he knew, namely Hans Oster, Henning von Tresckow, and Baron Claus von Stauffenberg—the three men whom another rare survivor of the conspir-acy, Baron Phillip von Boeselager (who will be met in the following pages) described as being respectively "the mind, the heart, and the courageous arm" of the plot that culminated on 20 July 1944.

"To save Germany was not granted to them; only to die for it; luck was not with them, it was with Hitler. But they did not die in vain. Just as we need air if we are to breathe, and light if we are to see, so we need noble people if we are to live." So wrote the German intellectual Ricarda Huch as she surveyed the ruins of her homeland in the spring of 1946. Clive James observed that Huch "was well aware that there were other and less charismatic people in the conspiracy apart from the glamorously uniformed [nobles]. . . . There were obscure commoners who had seen through Hitler in the beginning. What she meant by nobility was the sacrificial spirit that joined, in this one instance, the beautiful young men from the *Almanach de Gotha* [the genealogical bible of the German aristocracy] and the plodding minor bureaucrats from the local council."

In a much smaller way this book is the result of a similar collaboration, this one between European aristocracy and American bourgeoisie: and I would like to gratefully acknowledge Mme. Lory Reinach, *née* Lory von Gersdorff, the author's friendly and gracious offspring; Professor Emeritus Klemens von Klemperer, survivor and scholar of those violent times; Mrs. Patti Bonn, owner of The Aberjona Press, for instantly taking a chance on this book; and Gayle Wurst, Ph.D., the masterful editor of the English version, and all-around inspiration. In addition my thanks are owed to the anonymous readers who vetted the text and endnotes at the publisher's request. It goes without saying that I am responsible for any surviving errors. I am likewise grateful to my wife and daughters for their patience while I sat hunched over books and keyboards, engaged in this project.

This is a book by another man and not mine to dedicate; but if it were I would inscribe it to all those in every time and place who have risked that which they held most dear, up to and including their lives, out of what the Germans call *Zivilkourage*—moral courage.

Anthony Pearsall
Pacific Grove, California, 2012

Editor's Note: German military ranks from *Generalmajor* up are transposed to United States usage; a German *Generalmajor* will be referred to as a Brigadier General, and so on.

Introduction:
Memories of My Father

In order to describe my father, Rudolf-Christoph von Gersdorff, I must nowadays reach far back into the past. Moreover it was our fate never to live together under the same roof for longer than a few months at a time. Nonetheless, many events remain engraved in my memory.

On 9 February 1945—I was seven years old at the time—I was forced to leave Schloss Matzdorf in Silesia, together with four cousins, my uncle (my father's older brother), and my aunt. We were fleeing from the Russians. The village of Matzdorf (now known as Maciejowiec, in western Poland) lay in what was then the Prussian province of Silesia, a few miles away from the town of Hirschberg (now Jelenia Góra).

I still remember that scene, over sixty years later. In front of the manor house stood a black carriage drawn by Max and Moritz, two black horses with cropped tails, wearing dark blinkers. The snow-covered estate park, from which the Riesengebirge mountain range could be glimpsed on the horizon, was a white winter landscape. Even the chapel and the mausoleum were mantled with a thick layer of snow. Our goal was to reach Schloss Thurnau, in the Upper Franconia region in western Germany. Here there dwelled a distant aunt who was willing to take us in as *Flüchtlinge* (refugees). At the last possible moment, my father was able to get us places in a German Red Cross hospital train, a train that passed through Dresden less than a week before that city was firebombed into ruins. After two days of traveling we arrived safely at our destination.

Schloss Thurnau was a big castle, parts of which dated back to the thirteenth century, with two interior courtyards and many wings. Among the other people taking shelter there were the famous concert pianist Wilhelm Kempf and his family. Before long the castle and village were both overrun by the U.S. Army. The American occupying troops, who were mostly black men, made an enormous impression on us children. They chewed gum and had a panicky fear of the castle ghost, who was known as "the little gray man."

I can only dimly recall my father from these years. Whenever I asked somebody about him, I would be told that he was at the war, or later on, in American captivity as a prisoner of war. All the same, I have preserved a number of memories. I will never forget how one night, sometime after 7:00 P.M.—that was my bedtime, and everyone must have assumed that I was sound asleep—I became aware of uniformed men standing next to my child-sized bed in our Berlin apartment. They had crimson stripes running down the sides of their trouser legs: as I learned only much later, this was one of the distinguishing marks of army officers on the General Staff. The crimson stripes, which I noticed very markedly owing to the position I was in, lying down in my bed, were the reason why I later asked my father who these gentlemen could have been. He told me that every now and then he and his friends came into my room in the evenings. Perhaps they were exchanging secret information.

There is another story to be told from this period: an odd childhood memory, a small thing in itself. Even as a little child, I shared my father's enormous passion for the German candy called Lübeck marzipan, so whenever hunger (I was known as a "poor eater") and the craving for sweets led me to do so, I would search my bedroom for candies. My nanny Gretel knew this weakness of mine, although she nonetheless continued to serve me spinach and chopped meat. She also knew that the hiding places for bonbons and chocolate in my room were getting steadily easier for me to find, at the age of four or five. So she simply put whatever I wasn't supposed to eat out of my reach.

At around 7:00 P.M. each night, after my dinner—which often went back to the kitchen untouched, unless it was forcibly stuffed down my gullet—Gretel would give me my bath and then put me to bed. After I said my evening prayers, she would leave me, and there I would lie on my back, my eyes turned toward the ceiling. One evening, however, she wandered back in and tidied up the dresser, on top of which there lay a packet all wrapped up in paper. Little child that I was, all the imagination I possessed became fixed upon this packet. Marzipan, pralines, bonbons, chocolate! But I couldn't get at it, for I was too small. This memory has never left me. It is engraved in my mind.

Many years later when I was visiting my father one Christmas and brought him a box of Lübeck marzipan, I told him about this childhood memory. He gave me a long look and then said, "You know, Lory, those were bomb fuses that I thought would be safe on the dresser in your room." These fuses were captured English war materiel that had been dropped by parachute into France. They had the very great advantage of not making any noise after being set, and were considered especially suitable for the planned assassination attempt on Hitler. So it is that the fuses for the attempted bombings of 23 March 1943 and 20 July 1944 were for some time probably to be found in my childhood bedroom in Breslau.

Berlin had been our home until early 1942, when my mother died. My father's increasingly brief and rare home leaves had left her feeling very much alone, and news of the arrest and deportation of her Jewish friends in the neighborhood filled her with grief. Her increasing loneliness and melancholy eventually developed into a deep psychological depression. On 15 January 1942, after writing a despairing farewell note to my father, she hanged herself in the attic of a friend's house in Rehberg, a small town not far from the capital. I was barely four years old at the time and was told nothing about my mother's tragic passing.

My mother was regarded as a very beautiful woman who was in love with life. When she married my father at Schloss Matzdorf in 1934, they were thought of as the ideal couple. He was a successful young officer, a passionate horseman, slender, elegant, six feet four inches tall, and a wonder on the dance floor; she was young, gorgeous, and rich. He escorted my mother to every significant event on the social calendar. They were welcome guests at the Hotel Adlon, then (and now once more) the finest place in Berlin.

My mother came from a very well-to-do background. Her family owned some large textile factories in Silesia, as well as a number of estates and manor houses in the province. Schloss Matzdorf, where my Polish great-grandmother then resided, was considered to be the jewel in the crown. Alongside the centuries-old trees in the park were modern greenhouses filled with ripening orchids, oranges, and lemons. There was an icehouse—a rarity at the time—where champagne could be kept chilled all year round, and from that little detail one can imagine that there were some fabulous festivities at Matzdorf. By coincidence, Baron Magnus von Braun, a neighbor who was the father of the famed rocket engineer Wernher von Braun, described life at Matzdorf in that era in his book *Von Preussen nach Texas* (From Prussia to Texas).

Between 1933 and 1939, my parents lived like two people in a fairy tale, an intoxicating dream, or a movie. The things that my father subsequently had to see and do while he was serving on the Russian front stood in grotesque contrast to this earlier life. He could scarcely even describe to my mother what he had seen at the battlefront. And so she tumbled downward into her deep, dark depression and was never really able to cope with me. Instead she entrusted me to an ever-changing series of nannies.

I barely knew my father during those years; and I really began to get acquainted with him, as a conscious matter, only when I visited him in the American-run prison camp at Allendorf near Marburg, in 1947. By the time of my visit I was about ten years old. There were hundreds of German generals at Allendorf, locked up inside a barracks compound. I saw the men in their threadbare old uniforms, sitting down or stretched out in "sleeping quarters" that were for the most part nothing but bunk beds separated from one another by dangling strips of fabric. The Americans were keeping all the generals from the former Wehrmacht confined here. There wasn't much to eat. I remember my father showing me some worm-infested cheese and telling me, "You see, we get this wormy cheese, but you can get used to anything."

Later on I would realize that those months at Allendorf were among the toughest of his life. As a resistance member—for that fact about him had quickly spread around the POW camp, after an article on the subject appeared in a newspaper—he was seen by many of the men, even some of his old friends, as a traitor. A Prussian general who had attempted to kill Hitler was an unimaginable thing for many of his fellow prisoners, and morally alien to them as well. As I walked through the rows of bunks with my father, I also felt the hostile stares.

My poor father! Once again, he was caught between two camps. He must have had the same feeling at the Nuremberg trials. Brought there as a witness, he was however treated from the start like a war criminal himself. My mother had given him a gold cigarette case once; it turned out to be the last present he ever received from her. He had managed to hang on to it through everything, but an American soldier in the Nuremberg prison stole it from him. He was so enraged by this that he even wrote in protest to General Eisenhower, the Allied supreme commander. He never got a reply, and the cigarette case never reappeared.

Incidents like this left my father feeling very downcast; but he was really a sentimental fellow at heart. Underneath the hard shell that the war had required him to grow, there hid a musically inclined person who showed his feelings quite easily. He loved music very, very much. Whenever he listened to Tchaikovsky's *Symphony No. 5,* tears would fall from his eyes. On his night table there were always books of verse by renowned poets.

He always seemed to be worried about me. "Whatever will I do about my daughter? I have no home; I haven't got any money; I can't just have her living with me." Such concerns were his constant companions. So after primary school, which I attended with my cousins in the village of Thurnau, I was raised in various boarding schools.

When I was about seventeen, my father sent me away to Ashridge College, at Berkhamsted in Hertfordshire, near London. The institution was well known at that time as the site of Conservative Party congresses, and also as the place where Princess Margaret, the younger sister of Queen Elizabeth II, had held her "coming out" ball as a debutante. It was also a boarding school for young ladies from all around the British Commonwealth, headed while I was there by a woman named Miss Neville-Rolfe. When I first became a student at Ashridge, she asked me what my father's profession was. I answered that my father was an army officer waiting to be recalled to military service, and that he had played a role in the German Resistance as an assassination planner. Miss Neville-Rolfe turned away from me with the words, "So your father was a traitor, then."[1] I loved England very much, but it was as a result of this exchange that I never married my future British fiancé—her words just stuck in my mind.

Events of this sort, whenever they occurred, saddened my father. He would often repeat Henning von Tresckow's words, "The world will not forget this about us for hundreds of years." I can remember him quoting this sentence after I told him about what had happened to me in New York City. By then, in 1960, I was working for the United Nations in New York and sharing a Park Avenue apartment with two female colleagues. There was a delicatessen close to our flat. After I had brought bagels and donuts home from there twice, one of my girlfriends had to let me know that she had been told that "the German woman" was not welcome in the shop.

During the 1950s I lived with my father in Cologne for brief periods, never longer than a few months at a time. He was trying to start a new life. Every day he hoped to be called back into military service. Many influential people in politics and business wanted to intercede on his behalf, but it was all to no avail; his presence was not desired in the new armed forces.

So he got on with other things. He had rented a little apartment in Cologne's city center. Here we lived together under one roof for the first time since the war, and now I could see for myself just how successful my father was with women. The telephone never stopped ringing. Despite his worn-out flannel suits and his down-at-heel shoes, his height and lean physique caused him to be regarded as quite elegant, and it was no wonder that he very rapidly became a highly prized bachelor guest in wealthy homes. Thus I made the acquaintance of a whole series of potential stepmothers, until he married again in 1953. The woman he married was not rich, but she was beautiful— Eva von Waldenburg, another Silesian refugee. This marriage lasted for only three years, however.

I can still see my father in those days, sitting at his desk in a house on the outskirts of Cologne. At the time he was writing reports for Reinhard Gehlen, his wartime colleague, who had led the Wehrmacht's Foreign Armies East intelligence section and was by then the chief of the West German intelligence service. Arranged in a green leather frame on my father's writing table were photographs of the four men who were his role-models in life: Hans Oster, Fabian von Schlabrendorff, Ludwig Beck, and, of course, Henning von Tresckow. "The best man I ever knew," he said to me once of Tresckow.

My father earned his living by means of a great deal of hard work. Thanks to his interest in German horse racing, he found a managerial position in the League of German Amateur Equestrians in Cologne. Even after the war, he always remained a passionate horseman. He won over twenty races during his lifetime, and he would proudly note that once in Breslau he had even won two races in a single day. Each morning he arose at six o'clock and went cantering around the Cologne track on several thoroughbreds. On the weekends he spent most of his time at various German racecourses. I will never forget how important it was to him that I kissed the hands of older noblewomen whom we met at this or that racetrack. He wanted his daughter to show her good manners!

In 1963 he met the woman who would become his third wife: Irmgard, another Silesian, with a son and a daughter from her first marriage. His choice of wives showed very clearly that he could never give up the memory of his Silesian homeland. Better a poor Silesian woman than a rich Rhinelander! (As far as I can recall, such a choice was his to make.) They settled down in Munich and remained there until their deaths. Despite the tragedy that would so powerfully affect both their lives five years after the wedding, theirs was a very happy union.

One day in 1967 as he rode a horse in the morning workout at the Munich racetrack, my father was thrown from his saddle, and crippled for the last dozen years of his life. That fateful morning he lost control of a horse when it was "spooked" by a bystander's sudden movement. My father apparently lost consciousness when he hit the ground, but one of his feet was caught in a stirrup and the wildly galloping horse dragged him halfway around the track before being stopped. At the hospital in Munich, the initial diagnosis was "quadriplegia"—total paralysis. He wanted to die. His dreams turned into nightmares—always the same thing. He dreamed about his friends who had been hanged after 20 July from ropes tossed over those hooks in Plötzensee prison. Why not him as well? During his lifetime he never seemed free from a sense of guilt for being one of the conspiracy's few survivors.

I visited him in Heidelberg at the special hospital for paraplegics. While standing at his bedside, I had only one thought in my mind: hopefully he'll be able to die soon. The sight of him was so depressing. He couldn't move a single part of his body except for his lips, and so he was being fed through a straw. It was horrible. But after several months his condition improved and he was able to return to his home in Munich. Until the end of his life, this very active man was a paraplegic, unable to walk, chained to his wheelchair—but I had the chance to deeply regret my earlier wish. He lived another twelve happy years, sustained by his wife's self-sacrificing care, and before dying in 1980 he wrote the book you hold in your hands.

His Christian upbringing and his love for his fellow man lay at the roots of my father's character. This was evident from his long and often self-sacrificing work for the German Order of St. John. When Prince Oskar of Prussia (a son of Kaiser Wilhelm II, and the Master of the Order), asked my father to take over the St. John Accident Assistance during the 1950s, my father viewed this task as a moral obligation. A salary could scarcely be expected, for at that time the Order's coffers were still empty.

For years he spent his Christmas holidays out on the highways with his youthful assistants, aiding travelers who had been in auto accidents. To lead and guide young people was a true pleasure for him. He had an especially good relationship with members of the younger generation. He shared his life experiences with them, and listened to theirs as well. He thought of them as "his people," just as he had felt as an officer about recruits during the war, when his troops would have run through fire for him.

My father was an aristocrat in the truest sense of the word. "Whatever you inherit from your father, strive to make it your own"—many a time he would quote these lines by Goethe to me. His passions were women and horses. He saw loving his neighbor as his great task in life: both during the war, when he attempted to free the world from its biggest criminal, and after it, when he tried to help young people, to hear what they had to say, and (for the sake of their futures) to transmit genuine values to them, in keeping with his own passage through life. This final wish is reflected in the words he inscribed in my personal copy of these memoirs:

> If you so desire, you can learn from your father's experiences—including the mistakes he made. With love from your father, Rudolf-Christoph Gersdorff. Munich, Christmas 1979.

Lory Reinach, née von Gersdorff
Paris, 2012

Foreword

On 25 February 1947, the Allied Control Council in Berlin enacted "Law Number 46" which decreed the abolition of the state of Prussia, "the bearer of militarism and reaction in Germany." Baron Rudolf-Christoph von Gersdorff was a Prussian soldier through and through, and a deeply conservative aristocrat—yet he was neither a militarist nor a reactionary.

During the Second World War, he served in leading positions on the German eastern and western fronts, yet he managed to translate his fundamental rejection of Adolf Hitler and Nazism into action. In this memoir, he tells his own story and that of his comrades in the Wehrmacht who had the courage to plan the assassination of the tyrant.

The thesis of the "good" Wehrmacht and the "bad" Nazis has been oversold in the past. That is all the more reason for the story of the extraordinary soldiers of the German Resistance to be told. The legacy of *travailler pour le roi de Prusse* ("to labor for the King of Prussia"), had its distinctly positive aspects, and must outlast the formal dissolution of Prussia in 1947.[1]

Dr. Klemens von Klemperer
L. Clark Seelye Professor Emeritus of History,
Smith College, Northampton, Massachusetts
Author of German Resistance Against Hitler: The Search for Allies Abroad, *and* German Incertitudes, 1914–1945

Preface

A people that wishes to have no past will also have no future.
—Wilhelm von Humboldt (1767–1835)

"A Prussian general dies, but he leaves no memoirs." With this reasoning General Constantin von Alvensleben, the renowned army commander in the Franco-Prussian War of 1870–1871, rejected all attempts to persuade him to write about his military experiences and personal recollections.[1] This austere attitude was in keeping with the typically reserved behavior of the late nineteenth century officer corps, an officer corps that existed to protect the monarchist form of government, and considered itself responsible to the monarch above all else. In addition, German military regulations, just as those of Austria, Russia, France, and England, ensured that all writings published by officers underwent prior censorship and could only appear in print with formal permission. The transferal of such traditional mental fetters (as anachronistic as they had become) to the Reichswehr, as well as the "depoliticizing" of the military that was prescribed by the Military Code of the Weimar Republic, had as a side-effect the creation of the "just-a-soldier" type of officer, who in many instances—under the shield of obedience to the loyalty oath or to the command authority of the National Socialist dictator—became witting or unwitting accomplices to crime.

The epochal change that my generation experienced is a further reason for holding on to important lessons and passing them along to succeeding generations. During the first quarter of the twentieth century, I was still being taught to regard the lance as the queen of weapons, within a powerful horse cavalry. Only twenty years later the first atomic bomb fell on Hiroshima, extinguishing 260,000 human lives. Such an enormous advance in military technology was necessarily accompanied by a process of mental readjustment, not only with regard to strategy and tactics but also fundamental ethical values. As a result, the military and moral situation of modern armed forces has changed at root level. While recognizing this fact, it must also be said that many human and military fundamental principles remain intact, and coping with them can be made easier with the assistance of past experience.

Such considerations have led me to write down my own experiences. With few exceptions, I have limited myself in doing so to those events in which I personally took part, and for whose faithful depiction I can give a guarantee. This limitation in scale has consequences, for which I must beg the reader's understanding. First, it compels me to write more about myself than I would prefer. Next, it results in some gaps in the depiction of political or military situations with respect to prior events in which I had no role. Finally, in the course of studying many postwar publications, I have run into some isolated contradictions to my own version of the facts. With regard to this, I can only offer my assurance that in every case, my depiction of events corresponds to my own perceptions and judgments.

Because I was able to preserve only a few documents and notes as a man in flight from the downfall of 1945, I must essentially rely upon my own recollections in the following memoirs. Therefore, with only a few exceptions, I cannot guarantee that the dialogues presented in the form of direct quotations represent the exact form of the words used on that occasion. I can only guarantee that the *sense* of the words that were actually spoken has not been falsified in the least.

I have introduced the story of my army life with a chapter about my background and education. This seemed necessary to me, in order to give the reader an insight into my mental attitudes. Only by this means can I hope for understanding of my conduct with respect to the grave decisions that were demanded of me.

To all those who have helped me to review the accuracy of my information, my hearty thanks are due.

Baron Rudolf-Christoph von Gersdorff
Munich, 1976

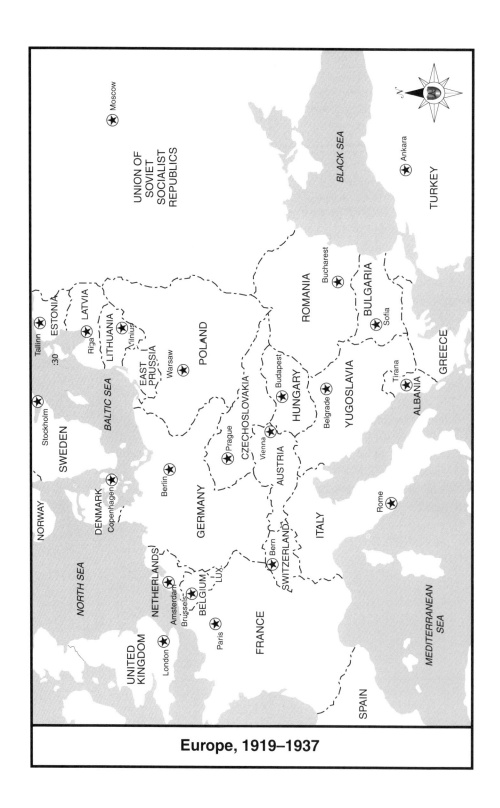

Europe, 1919–1937

Germany, 1938

Miles 0   50   100

Km 0   100

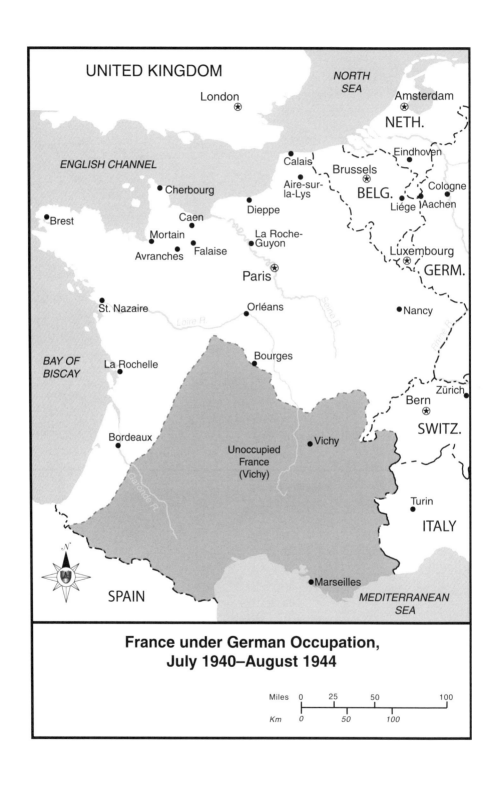

UNITED KINGDOM

London ✪

NORTH SEA

Amsterdam ✪

NETH.

ENGLISH CHANNEL

Calais

Eindhoven

Brussels ✪

BELG.

Cologne

Aire-sur-la-Lys

Liége Aachen

Cherbourg

Dieppe

Brest

Caen

Mortain

La Roche-Guyon

Avranches Falaise

Luxembourg ✪

GERM.

Paris ✪

St. Nazaire

Orléans

Nancy

BAY OF BISCAY

La Rochelle

Bourges

Zürich

Bern ✪

SWITZ.

Bordeaux

Unoccupied France (Vichy)

Vichy

Turin

ITALY

SPAIN

Marseilles

MEDITERRANEAN SEA

France under German Occupation, July 1940–August 1944

Miles	0	25	50	100
Km	0	50	100	

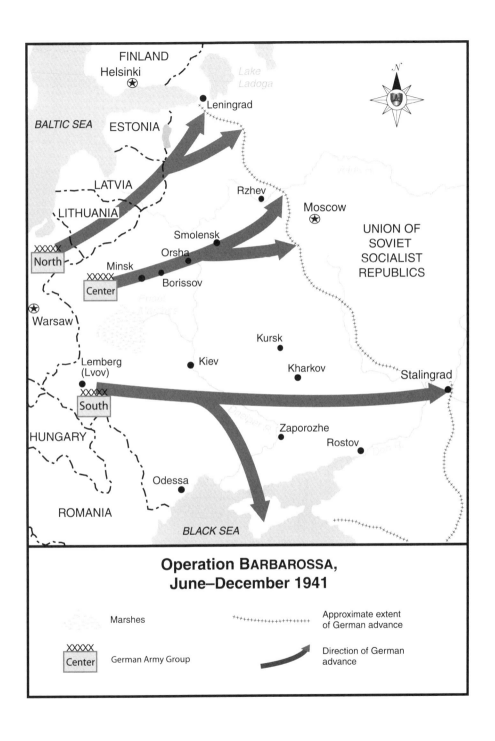

FINLAND
Helsinki ✪

Lake Ladoga

Leningrad

BALTIC SEA   ESTONIA

LATVIA

LITHUANIA

Rzhev

Moscow ✪

UNION OF
SOVIET
SOCIALIST
REPUBLICS

XXXXX
North

Smolensk

Orsha

Minsk
XXXXX
Center

Borissov

Warsaw ✪

Kursk

Lemberg
(Lvov)

Kiev

Kharkov

Stalingrad

XXXXX
South

HUNGARY

Zaporozhe

Rostov

Odessa

ROMANIA

BLACK SEA

Operation BARBAROSSA,
June–December 1941

Marshes

Approximate extent
of German advance

XXXXX
Center   German Army Group

Direction of German
advance

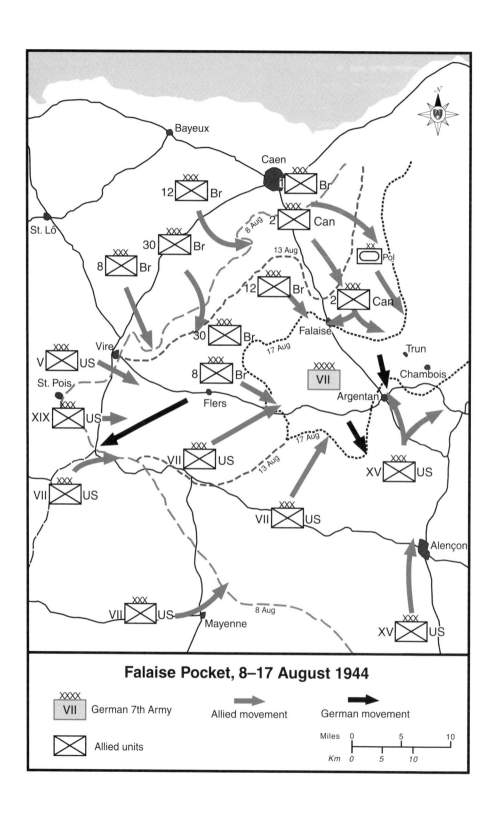

Bayeux

Caen

12 Br

1 Br

2 Can

30 Br

St. Lô

8 Aug

8 Br

13 Aug

Pol

12 Br

2 Can

30 Br

Falaise

Trun

Vire

Chambois

V US

8 Br

VII

St. Pois

17 Aug

Argentan

XIX US

Flers

17 Aug

XV US

VII US

13 Aug

VII US

VII US

Alençon

VII US

Mayenne

8 Aug

XV US

Falaise Pocket, 8–17 August 1944

XXXX
VII   German 7th Army   Allied movement   German movement

⊠ Allied units

Miles 0   5   10

Km 0   5   10

Rank Equivalents and General Staff Positions

US Army	British Army	German Army	German Waffen-SS
General of the Army	Field Marshal	Generalfeldmarschall	
General	General	Generaloberst	SS-Oberstgruppenführer
Lieutenant General	Lieutenant-General	General (der Infanterie, der Artillerie, etc.)	SS-Obergruppenführer
Major General	Major-General	Generalleutnant	SS-Gruppenführer
Brigadier General	Brigadier	Generalmajor	SS-Brigadeführer
—	—	—	SS-Oberführer
Colonel	Colonel	Oberst	SS-Standartenführer
Lieutenant Colonel	Lieutenant-Colonel	Oberstleutnant	SS-Obersturmbannführer
Major	Major	Major	SS-Sturmbannführer
Captain	Captain	Hauptmann/Rittmeister	SS-Hauptsturmführer
1st Lieutenant	Lieutenant	Oberleutnant	SS-Obersturmführer
2d Lieutenant	2d Lieutenant	Leutnant	SS-Untersturmführer

German General Staff Officers

Chief of Staff (only at corps level and above)

Ia	Chief of Operations (also: 1st General Staff Officer)
Ib	Quartermaster (Chief Supply Officer) (also: 2nd General Staff Officer)
Ic	Intelligence Officer (also: 3rd General Staff Officer)
Id	Director of Training (only at army level and above)
IIa	Chief Personnel Officer (Adjutant) (also: 4th General Staff Officer)
IIb	Second Personnel Officer (subordinate to IIa)
III	Chief Judge Advocate (subordinate to IIa)
IVa	Chief Administrative Officer (subordinate to Ib)
IVb	Chief Medical Officer (subordinate to Ib)
IVc	Chief Veterinary Officer (subordinate to Ib)
IVd	Chaplain (subordinate to IIa)
V	Motor Transport Officer (subordinate to Ib)

Others: Chief of Artillery, Air Liaison Officer, Chief of Signals, etc.

Note: The Ia, Ib, and Ic were almost always members of the armed forces General Staff per se. Other positions, including but not limited to those involving technical or professional specialties such as law, medicine, or the chaplaincy, were typically held by non-GS officers in staff assignments.

I

Background and Education

Noblesse oblige!

The breed of counts, barons, and gentlemen sharing the name of von Gersdorff may be traced, with a probability bordering on certainty, to certain men
by the name of Gero who belonged to the German dynastic aristocracy of the
ninth and tenth centuries. Their most important representative was Gero III
(890–965) who, as the Count of Oberlausitz (Upper Lusatia) under the Holy
Roman Emperor Otto I, conquered, Christianized, and defended the southern
portion of the Ostmark, early medieval Germany's eastern borderlands. He
figures in history as one of the paladins of Emperor Otto the Great. He resided
southeast of Quedlinburg at Burg Gersdorf (*Geros Dorf*; Gero's Village), a
fortress built by his father Gero II; its ruins have been preserved to this day.

The first bearer of my family name, Rudolf Gersdorff, is referred to in a
document from the year 965 as the lord of the castle and the heir of Count
Gero. He was expressly described as a *cognatus* (blood relation) of Gero III.
The fortress of Gersdorf remained in the family's possession until the end of
the thirteenth century. Subsequently the family's then-living members moved
on to Upper Lusatia as colonizers. There, a *dominus Christianus advocatus
provinciae Gorlicenis dictus de Gerhardisdorf* (the Christian lord advocate
of the province of Görlitz, called von Gerhardisdorf) appears in a document
dated 25 April 1301. In the fifteenth century the landholdings of the Gersdorffs were said to include 196 manorial estates in Upper Lusatia alone. On
4 June 1572, two hundred Gersdorffs assembled in the town of Zittau for the
first family reunion.[1]

Many members of the family joined the Order of the Teutonic Knights,
to fight for Christendom in the Holy Land or in the Ostmark. The knight
Georg von Gersdorff fell in the battle of Tannenberg on 15 July 1410, as the
Order's standard bearer.[2] His statue stands—or stood—in the high tower of
the Order's citadel at Marienburg in East Prussia.

1

In the course of centuries, Gersdorffs also settled and acquired estates in Silesia, the Baltic region, and Denmark. But it is a striking characteristic of the family that its members were by no means limited merely to being estate owners and landlords. Along with civil servants and military officers, the clan has repeatedly produced scholars, scientists, authors, and artists. From the sixteenth century, for example, one reads of Hans von Gersdorff, a celebrated surgeon and specialist in wounds. At the end of the nineteenth century, Baron Karl von Gersdorff (1844–1904) was a close friend of Friedrich Nietzsche; their correspondence has become part of literary history.

Among the numerous distinguished men and women of my family, two people stand out. The first was Karl Friedrich Wilhelm von Gersdorff (1746–1829), *Generalleutnant* [equivalent to a major general; subequent occurrences of this rank will use Major General] and chief of staff in the army of the Kingdom of Saxony and a military historian; he was a friend of Napoleon I, who made him a Grand Officer of the Legion of Honor. The other prominent personality was Hermann Konstantin von Gersdorff (1809–1870), who fell in the front line at the battle of Sedan as a Prussian major general and the deputy commander of XI Army Corps. He was posthumously honored when the 80th Fusilier Regiment, stationed in Wiesbaden and Bad Homburg, was granted the name "von Gersdorff." Thirteen Gersdorffs died defending their fatherland in World War I, and another twenty in World War II. From 1914 until 1917, Gersdorffs from the Baltic region also died fighting on the Russian side.

I was born on 27 March 1905, at Lüben in the Prussian province of Silesia, as the second son of Baron Ernst von Gersdorff. He was at the time a *Rittmeister* (Cavalry Captain) and squadron commander in the 4th Dragoon Regiment (1st Silesian), also known as the "von Bredow" Regiment. Later he became a *Generalmajor* [equivalent to a brigadier general; subsequent occurrences of this rank will use Brigadier General]. My mother was by birth a Countess von Dohna-Schlodien. She belonged to one of the oldest German noble houses, one that had ruled the county of Meissen before it passed to the Wettin dynasty in 1100, and whose members later settled for the most part in East Prussia and in Silesia.[3]

For my siblings and me, our parents were and remain our most influential role models. Both of them were distinctive personalities, aristocrats in the best sense of the word, people with a strong sense of political and social responsibility. Together and separately, they performed their great tasks in life with thoroughness. Universally cherished and highly regarded by people from every walk of life, my father and mother died in 1926 and 1944, respectively. As a result they did not have to endure the loss of their beloved eastern German homeland. Their graves were cared for after the war by a German family that remained behind in Lüben.

Tolerance and a cosmopolitan outlook were as characteristic of my parents as their love for and loyalty to their homeland and the hereditary reigning dynasty. They were Prussian folk, in the philosophical sense of "Prussianism." Justice, charity, and responsibility toward God and man were combined with a dutiful pride in their family traditions, a distinct historical consciousness, and an inclination toward art and nature.

They were Lutheran Christians, ever humble before God but tolerant toward members of other faiths, and full of respect for human worth. They may not have been without human flaws, but I am not in a position to name any that could cast a shadow upon the portrait of their characters.

My father was a superb soldier, but at the same time the exact opposite of a militarist or a crude army man. It had been my grandfather's desire, on account of my father's above-average intellectual gifts, that he should study law and embark upon an academic career. But on 1 April 1884, after a few semesters at the University of Leipzig, he joined the 1st Life Guard Cuirassiers Regiment "Great Elector" (1st Silesian) as an *Avantageur* (officer candidate). I assume that he was led to this decision by his love for a profession in which he could be a leader of men, by his desire for soldierly camaraderie, and, not least, by his love of horses and his passion for riding. How else could he have been able to awaken and keep alive in me the same passion, despite war and revolution? From my many discussions with him, I learned his opinions about the military ethos and about the tremendous responsibility that is placed upon the officer profession.

My father was regarded as an Anglophile by many of his acquaintances. During my youth he was often in England for long stretches of time, and his penchant for the British "way of life" certainly derived from this. In civilian clothes, which he preferred, he looked more like an English aristocrat than a Prussian officer. Above all, he expressed the "English gentleman" concept in his personal behavior. He always knew just what he could do, and what he could not do under any circumstances. He was far from desiring merely to copy the English prototype externally. It was more a matter of this prototype permeating his entire approach to living. Even while on horseback, he favored the elegant British equestrian style over the Prussian military method—something that often brought irritation his way within the service. In his youth he rode in horse races, and he was an excellent cross-country rider all his life.

My mother was extraordinarily beloved by everyone with whom she came in contact. She was known as one of those few originals who were already becoming increasingly extinct. Her originality lay chiefly in her saying exactly what she thought, always and to everyone. She did not concern herself about whether anyone occasionally took this the wrong way. She was uncommonly bold, and mastered life's trials the same way that she did the toughest jumps in the mounted hunts of East Prussia and Silesia. She rode the most difficult horses—always on a side-saddle—and under her light hands they quickly became, for the most part, excellent and obedient mounts.

It may surprise many readers that I highlight my mother's riding abilities in this description of her character. But to begin with, horseback riding was to a remarkable extent an expression of her entire nature. And besides that, my first real memory of my mother is one of riding by her side, on a pony that she was guiding with a long lead. I must have been barely four years old.

For her whole life long, my mother was always "present" for other people. I have seldom seen love and charity toward one's neighbor more ingrained in anyone than it was in her. Her vitality and unbending courage in facing life lifted her above her surroundings and always endowed her with a mighty circle of friends. Her first name was Christine, and all of Silesia knew who "Tina" was. The memory of her was still alive thirty years after her death. She was especially loved and looked up to by the simple folk and all the inhabitants of Lüben. When she left Lüben in 1932 in order to move to Breslau and be near her sons, she was celebrated in the little town like an honorary citizen.

Although my mother was an enthusiastic Silesian, she never forgot her East Prussian homeland, which was simply a part of her being. To her children she passed along her fundamental Prussian attitude, and a certain toughness in the face of life's unavoidable setbacks. Later on I often found this to be a great help.

If someone were to ask me whether my parents had raised me in an authoritarian or anti-authoritarian manner (to use a modern phrase), I wouldn't even know how to answer. They were such strong personalities that their authority went without saying. I can't recall ever being struck by my father, or hearing harsh words from him. My parents' effect on us was above all due to their example, their image. They were always there for us but never pressured us.

My father shared with us his comprehensive learning in every subject, but with rare exceptions it never occurred to our parents to help us with our school homework. From our earliest childhood it was made clear to us that each of us had to do our own duty, and that was that. We were neither forced into a template nor kept tied to apron strings by means of constant admonitions. With our parents' good example before our eyes, it was far more a matter of our growing up with great personal freedom. We could seek out our own playmates and friends from among the neighborhood children and our schoolmates. But as much as our ages permitted, our elders took us along with them to social and sporting events, so as to present us with examples of the way of life they found preferable. Since it was their practice to criticize openly, we were also prompted to think critically, but without ever being permitted to veer off into arrogance or being disrespectful to others. I can never forget how my parents always taught us to be especially concerned for poor, sick, and disabled people.

Our rearing was decidedly simple; in fact, Spartan. This was not only by design but out of necessity, because our parents had to live on a fixed officer's salary. So we had neither costly toys nor expensive clothing. We boys mostly wore our father's old clothes, altered to fit us. Money was scarcely mentioned in our parents' home, even if we sometimes observed very clearly how little of it there was around. But because the value of money was never overemphasized, and other values were emphasized by contrast, we developed an inner lack of dependence on cash and luxury that I have preserved for a lifetime. The values our parents imparted to us were modesty and good conduct. My spiritual and physical development bore the stamp of my parental home far more than that of my school.

I progressed smoothly through elementary school and then the Lüben *Real-gymnasium* [the modern-curriculum high school], all the way to my diploma. Today I am grateful that my transfer to a boarding school was obviously never a topic for consideration; for had that occurred, it would have affected my development, above all where the spiritual and social atmosphere of our own house and our family traditions were concerned.

Historical consciousness, and love of our homeland, of music, and of sport, were the most important things for us and were the decisive factors in my own life. I cannot remember ever reading a single Karl May western, or any similar adventure yarn.[4] By contrast I devoured history books for young people; naturally those concerning the history of Prussia and the German Reich interested me the most.

My father's universal learning and my parents' tolerant attitudes were enough to ensure that I did not develop into a one-sided nationalist. For one thing, ever since my earliest childhood there had always been a French governess living with us. By design, French was frequently spoken in my parental home, so that soon enough I knew it fluently. A young Belgian woman even lived in our home during the entire First World War, and we all loved her very much. Her national pride, which despite Belgium's occupation by German troops never permitted her to harbor any doubt about her king's final victory, impressed me greatly.

Very early on, I came to the decision to make my life as a soldier in the service of my fatherland. My grandfather Gersdorff once said to my father that it was not the duty, but rather the privilege, of the nobleman to fight and die for his fatherland. This attitude of *noblesse oblige*—which even in my childhood had become, for me, something that went without saying—had to a large degree shaped my patriotic consciousness and my sense of responsibility.

Moreover, in my Silesian homeland I was constantly confronted by Prussian-German history, within which the varied history of my own family had the effect of forestalling any narrowly nationalistic type of thinking. During the Silesian War between Prussia and Austria, Gersdorffs had fought on both sides. Under the banner of Frederick the Great there was a "von

Gersdorff" infantry regiment and a "von Gersdorff" hussar regiment, while on the Austrian side yet another Gersdorff—then the commander of a regiment of *pandour* cavalry—actually captured and burned down my birthplace of Lüben.[5]

For me, Silesia was and still is Germany's most beautiful and richest region. The population, the culture, the landscape, and the local customs were purely German; one could detect a healthy blend of Austrian charm and Prussian discipline. The best of Prussians were the so-called "Water Poles" of Upper Silesia, who also proved themselves to be the best of soldiers in war and peace. As in all border regions, there also existed in this region—surrounded as it was by Poland, Hungary, Austria, and Bohemia—family and social connections to the neighboring countries. This was particularly the case for the Catholic nobility in Upper Silesia.

But my Protestant family also had close ties to Poland. We spent almost every holiday on the estates of my grandparents and my father's siblings in the former province of Posen [now Poznan in Poland]. I never experienced any kind of hostility toward us Germans, whether from the neighboring Polish aristocrats, from the Polish townspeople, or from the farm workers. At Parsko in the Schmiegl district, my grandfather's estate, there was not a single other German apart from my family. As children we played with the children of the Polish employees. Close and warm friendships existed with the Polish owners of the neighboring estates. My grandmother was by birth a Countess von Strachwitz and a Catholic. The simple Polish folk regarded her as one of their own: *"Babuscha Catholic, Babuscha Polish."* This identification of religion with Polish nationality was widespread and is still not without significance today.

I experienced the so-called "Warthegau" region both under German and—following the Great War—under Polish administration, and could never have imagined any essential change in the coexistence of the Germans and Poles there.[6] For German landlords, the conditions of the 1920s in Poland were for the most part better than in the German homeland, hard-pressed as it was by its economic crises. For the Germans in the districts turned over to Poland after 1918, life went on in the normal way, without any meaningful restrictions or even threats. The decisive worsening in German-Polish relations only began when the National Socialists came to power in Germany.

Just as I never regarded the former province of Posen as being German territory, the idea of a possible Polish claim on Silesia, apart from some small border districts in eastern Upper Silesia, never even occurred to me. Everything of an economic or cultural nature that had been developed in Silesia over the centuries was the work of the Germans. There was nothing Polish in this land, not even any Polish tradition. That fact cannot be altered by the current Polonization of the German place-names. On the contrary, Silesia had belonged for a long time to the kingdom of Bohemia. Since the days of Emperor Barbarossa, the Piast dukes had been princes of the German Reich, and it was they who had invited German settlers into the Silesian region.[7] The German farmers came into a thinly inhabited, underdeveloped country, and with tenacious labor turned it into one of the most thoroughly cultivated landscapes in Central Europe. That made the occasional reports in the Silesian press, according to which hundreds of letters from the western end of the Reich arrived each year in Breslau addressed to "Breslau, Poland," all the more shocking. Even then there was an imaginary "border" at the Elbe River.

Music played a big role in my family home. My father, my mother, and all of my grandparents were highly musical people, so it was no wonder that from our earliest days we children also took pleasure in good music. My mother's salon was dominated by the big Bechstein grand piano. She could play the piano bewitchingly, although without attempting really difficult pieces. From his own youth my father had preserved the memory of a small repertoire of Chopin's compositions. My older brother Ernst-Carl and I took piano lessons without ever really becoming proficient. The reason we both increasingly suspended our own musical exercises was my younger brother Hubertus—who as early as his fourth year revealed himself to be a musical child prodigy. He had perfect pitch, and could play every melody that he heard with a lovely touch and with as much technique as his little hands permitted. I have never forgotten with how much skill and earnestness my father knew how to guide and promote this natural-born talent. My brother's musical development raced ahead so rapidly that even in his youth he was a successful concert pianist. We family members were passionate listeners.[8]

Every good and experienced horseman knows that horses are musically inclined, and that as a result there is a close connection between riding and music.[9] So it was for me: my equestrian and music-loving passions developed in tandem. My love of horses was something innate. The stables out in the back were an organic part of my parental home, and three or four of my father's thoroughbreds were always stalled there. It was my favorite stopping-place. A little brook called the "Cold Stream" ran directly past our house and stables. The horses often stood for hours in the cold water, and I was proud to be allowed to hold one or another of them there at the end of a long rein, under the watchful eye of a guardian. At the racetrack my father often purchased broken-down thoroughbreds for bargain prices, healed their injured tendons chiefly by means of the massaging action of the flowing water, and then won a whole string of races with a recovered convalescent. He trained his horses at the military exercise grounds close to our home.

But at the beginning, my favorite horse was the little pony Taube (Dove) on which I had first been mounted when I was four years old. In a sailor suit with the trouser legs pushed up, stockings to my knees, and a big straw hat atop my head, I sat on the pony saddle—which had no stirrups, but handles in the front for clinging to. They were extremely necessary, for "Dove" did no honor to his name. His spirits were particularly excessive when he first came out of the stables, and so my brother and I were thrown off his back countless times. But even when we were hurt, we had to get back in the saddle immediately. Today I know how much this training helped us in life; helped us to endure setbacks and failures and to stick things out.

Very soon, however, I felt secure on the pony's back, and I was allowed to accompany my mother when she went riding out in the countryside. She would guide my pony at the end of a long leather lead, and in this fashion I trotted alongside her big horse. When my mother wanted to ride faster or to jump, she tossed the lead to me. Taube often used this opportunity to race back to his home stables, certain of his direction even over great distances.

From 1914 on, my older brother and I took our riding lessons on full-sized horses. Soon enough, Dragoon Sergeant Major Endorf became our instructor, after being so badly wounded by Cossack lances in the early months of the war that he was no longer capable of campaigning. This fundamental training in horsemanship was completely supervised by my mother. After my father sent his three thoroughbreds back from France to Lüben around the end of 1915, because he had taken over an infantry regiment and could no longer give the horses sufficient attention due to the demands of trench warfare, we were able to ride daily. A mare called Kvas became especially dear to my heart. Before the war she had won six races.

From these equestrian beginnings grew my life spent on and with horses. Until 16 August 1967, when a bad riding accident at the Munich racetrack left me paralyzed from the waist down, there were not many days in my life, including during the war years, when I failed to ride, usually on several horses. They have truly given me "the greatest joy on Earth." Even now, in a wheelchair, my love of horses and equestrian sports remains unchanged.

My youth as a soldier's son in a little garrison town, my constant connection with soldiers and horses, and my early awakening love of nature and for my homeland were the decisive factors in my life. Other notable experiences during the first nine years of my life, however, left their lasting and decisive impressions as well. Two events from before the outbreak of World War I may be singled out here.

In the autumn of 1911, my father took my older brother and me for an excursion in the Riesengebirge mountain range. From Krummhübel we ascended over the Riesenbaude to the Schneekoppe, where we spent the night.[10] The next day it was on to Spindelmühl on the Bohemian side. From there we went up the Elbgrund to the Schneegrubenbaude. On the third day we wandered along the mountain crest back to Krummhübel, from whence we returned to Lüben by train. Besides the magnificent natural vistas (which my father supplemented with talks about history and natural science), I remember the hard climbs up icy-smooth, zigzagging paths; the frozen water in the washbasins of the Koppenbaude; an incomparable *Kaiserschmarren*— the famous mountain dish of Austrian-style pancakes packed with sugar and raisins, ripped to shreds and topped off with fruit compote—in Spindelmühl; and the strange impression that the deep snow-filled hollows made upon me.

Although I was but six years old, I could never forget our wandering through this legend-shrouded region, the domain of the mountain-spirit Rübezahl of whom so many tales were told. The experience of these three days in the then-still-wild and therefore especially beautiful Riesengebirge, our little adventure, and the togetherness with my father and my brother gave a strong impetus to my personal development. My unchanging love for my Silesian homeland, my joy in everything that nature gives us, and my drive for a free and active lifestyle all go back to this youthful experience. I could never have borne a life spent chained to a desk, an existence of physical restrictions and spiritual dependency; and thus the cornerstone was laid for an adventurous soldier's life. In later years the beauty of the Silesian mountains drew me back again and again. Once, as a young officer, I made a Riesengebirge expedition on horseback with my regimental comrades, during which we ascended the "Koppe" with great difficulty, and then rode along the crest of the entire range.

In 1913 we spent the Pentecost holiday with my Dohna grandparents in Potsdam, the imperial residence-city of the Hohenzollerns. I had my first visit to a theatre during this trip. At the Royal Theatre in nearby Berlin we saw Ernst von Wildenbruch's impressive drama *The Quitzows*.[11] The possibility of resistance to authority was put before my eyes for the very first time in my life. My private sympathies lay with the rebel, Dietrich von Quitzow. Incidentally, we sat in a court box which had been placed at our disposal by my aunt and godmother Claire von Gersdorff, lady-in-waiting to Her Majesty, the Empress Augusta Viktoria.

Several days later I was allowed to visit my aunt in Potsdam at the New Palace. When I entered the palace, I thought that the first uniformed footman we met was the Kaiser himself. My disappointment at learning that he was not was generously washed away with hot chocolate and cookies in my aunt's private salon.

On Pentecost Sunday, however, we were supposed to be able to see the imperial couple at point-blank range. The so-called *Schrippenfest* took place on the great parade ground in front of the New Palace. In accordance with an old tradition, each year the Kaiser invited the members of the Infantry Training Battalion to a meal. Along with a grand entourage, the imperial couple came from the New Palace to the tables and benches set up on the parade grounds, where the long bread rolls that Berliners call *Schrippen* would be served. We sat on a small platform reserved for guests of honor, and could see everything well. I can still recall very well how jolly and expansive, without losing his dignity, the Kaiser appeared, the way he sat down in the midst of the soldiers and had a lively conversation with them. Simultaneously there was a musical concert by the mounted trumpet corps of the Life Guard Hussars, the only Prussian cavalry regiment to feature a "Moor," a black man from North Africa, as its kettle drummer. The whole magnificent sight—the glittering, colorful uniforms, the splendid horses, and the musically so very lovely cavalry march-tunes—made an indescribably beautiful impression on me, one that reinforced my fundamentally monarchist beliefs.

We spent the summer vacation of 1914 on the Pomeranian estate of one of my father's sisters and at Danzig-Langfuhr on the Baltic coast, from whence we went daily to bathe in the sea.[12] In the town of Zoppot I witnessed our mare Kvas's last racing victory, which came in an officers' steeplechase. In the course of a very stormy steamer voyage across Danzig Bay, I nearly received my first slapping when I said to my father that it would be splendid, all the same, if we were to be blown off-course all the way north to Bornholm Island, which lies in the middle of the Baltic Sea near Sweden.

Then at the end of July we had to travel back to Lüben in all haste, because World War I was standing outside the door. Even now, I can well remember the mass enthusiasm when the Lüben Dragoons went marching off to the front—an enthusiasm that stood in stark contrast to the seriousness at the outbreak of World War II. My father, however—by that time a major on the regimental staff, who did not move out along with the active-duty regiment but only several days later, now as the commanding officer of the 3rd Reserve Dragoon Regiment—told us on the day Great Britain declared war against Germany that he considered the conflict to be lost. Able to judge the British Empire's might better than many another person, he did not share in the general euphoria.

In the first days of the war the famous "gold autos," which were purportedly criss-crossing between Russia and France, played a big role for us children. In the immediate vicinity of our house, sentries armed with carbines and drawn sabers stood on the highway from Lüben to Polkwitz and Glogau, assigned to halt and inspect each—then quite rare—automobile. In case an auto did not halt, the sentries were first supposed to try to slash its tires with their sabers. If this failed they were under instructions to use their firearms.

Officers in the Russian Army often wore uniforms with white coats. When an acquaintance of my parents who was passing through Lüben while wearing the white peacetime uniform of the Life Guard Cuirassiers was halted on the road and treated with suspicion, he came into our house in order to request my father's assistance. On this basis the *Landrat* [local government administrator] who lived across the way from us was informed that a Russian agent had entered our home. Due to this grotesque report the *Landrat,* who was a friend of my parents, wanted to put both the alleged spy and my father under arrest. Although naturally the whole business was quickly cleared up, the rumor persisted in Lüben for many days that a Russian agent had been with us, bearing an incredible fortune in gold. This anecdote shows the enormous agitation that reigned among the people at that time, which in many places led to shooting incidents that had serious consequences.

When my father got to come home on leave for the first time in May 1915, we fetched him from the train station at Liegnitz.[13] There we all waited in the station restaurant for the train back to Lüben. I have never forgotten how my father suddenly remarked that he marveled that artillery shells were not constantly landing near us.

Immediately after the beginning of positional warfare in the fall of 1914, my father was assigned to be the commander of the 6th Reserve Infantry Regiment. This regiment was sent into action in all the flashpoints of the western front: on the Verdun front for the longest period of time, then in Champagne, on the Hartmannsweilerkopf, in Flanders, and on the Somme.[14] We heard again and again about how calmly and resolutely, and with how much personal valor, my father led his regiment. He earned high decorations and was regarded as a magnificent combat soldier.

My mother was active throughout the war in caring for the wounded at the Lüben volunteer hospital. We were often allowed to accompany her. The encounters with the horrors of war that we experienced at the bedsides of severely wounded, blinded, or crippled men left an indelible impression on me.

Then in the latter wartime years the war began to affect us children directly; food-related hardships became greater and greater. We boys were frequently sent out into the countryside on "scrounging" missions, and often enough we came back empty-handed. In the early morning when we walked to school, there were often some crows dangling from the knocker on our front door. Wounded officers on garrison duty had shot them. Back then we devoured crows prepared in every possible manner.

Although we had been prepared for it by my father (whose opinion of the overall situation had remained unalterably pessimistic through all the ups and downs of the conflict), the end of the war in 1918 still hit us hard. In a single day, the end of the monarchy yanked out from beneath the aristocracy and the upper middle class the foundation upon which they had constructed their entire prior lives. Not only my father's professional career, but his very right to receive rations, appeared to be at least endangered by the revolution. In addition, the loss of the province of Posen caused us at first to be cut off from the estates of our kinfolk there.

Thirteen years old at the time, I did not grasp the entire situation. Today it is clear to me that November 1918 was an even bigger dividing line for my parents' generation than May 1945 was for us. Aside from the effects on individual lives, the end of World War I set off revolutionary processes throughout the world, processes which meant nothing less than an epochal change. I will note here only the most important: the end of the great dynasties in Russia, Austro-Hungary, and Germany; the founding of the first communist regime, in the Soviet Union; the enhanced influence upon Europe of the United States of America; the beginning of the dissolution of the great colonial empires, and the related formation of a Third World; and the decisive impetus which technology received as a result of the war, which significantly accelerated progress in many areas, particularly air travel.

At the time, the abdication of the "Kaiser and King" made a bigger impression on me than the loss of the war, or the fact that my second homeland—the province of Posen—now belonged to Poland. When an older student at my high school founded a "Youth League of Kaiser Loyalists," I enthusiastically joined the organization. True, the League never attained a large membership and was never able to wield any influence worth mentioning, but it molded my own political position. My belief in monarchy and my love for the German fatherland became the decisive factors in my life.

In the little city of Lüben, which had no industry aside from a small piano factory, everything went along relatively quietly. Demonstrations and brawling only occurred, at the most, when revolutionary-minded workers from neighboring places came into the town, which was the capital of the local district. Socialist election rallies found little resonance in our town's middle class. My mother, who attended such events many times, usually had the laughter on her side as she wittily heckled the speakers.

With our hearts ablaze, we followed the news of the defense of Silesia's borders. My father was in action for a long time with the *Grenzschutz,* the volunteer border-protection force. Many of our close relatives and family friends took their stand in the battle for Upper Silesia, which was under threat from Polish insurgents. Mostly they fought in self-contained units alongside their own household servants and farmhands, as well as the farmers from their villages. At that time, just after the loss of the war, the unifying idea of the German nation lived on, an idea which everybody, most especially the young people, supported even at the risk of their lives. In those days, in contrast to the post-World War II era, longings for the satisfaction of material desires took second place to love for the fatherland.

There was an exciting incident during the Kapp Putsch.[15] The top soldier involved in this luckless enterprise, General Baron Walther von Lüttwitz, was a blood cousin of my father's. In 1920 my father had just become the commander of the Lüben-based 29th Cavalry Regiment, a Reichswehr unit pieced together from squadrons of the 4th Dragoons and other old cavalry outfits. After the collapse of the putsch a close relative, Richard John von Freyend, turned up at our house. On the basis of the two cousins' striking resemblance, he asked for my father's passport. He got it, and with this passport my Uncle Lüttwitz really did get away over the border to Slovakia unhindered. This event was the final cause of my father's retirement from the army, which coincided with his promotion to brigadier general.

When I look back now on my early youth, I see that it was infinitely happy in spite of war, revolution, and an outwardly modest lifestyle. My parents' examples and the training they instilled in us left their mark on me to such an extent that I was able to commence my professional life with well-founded views and solid moral foundations. I have never had to alter them in principle.

II

Soldier in the Reichswehr

Don't carp at the soldiers' jolly ways; let them hug, let them kiss—
for who knows when they will have to die.
—Old military saying

After getting through my diploma exams with good results, I entered the 7th (Prussian) Cavalry Regiment on 1 April 1923. The regiment was headquartered in the Cuirassier Barracks in Breslau-Kleinburg, with its headquarters staff, the signals platoon, a machine-gun platoon, and the 1st and 2nd Squadrons; the 3rd and 4th Squadrons and another machine-gun platoon were based in Lüben; and the 5th (Training) Squadron was in Breslau-Carlowitz. The 1st Squadron carried on the traditions of the 1st Life Guard Cuirassiers "Great Elector" (1st Silesian), in which my father had passed his lieutenant years and which he always regarded as his military home. The 3rd Squadron preserved the heritage of the 4th Dragoon Regiment "von Bredow" (1st Silesian), to which my father had been transferred as a squadron commander in 1900, and whose last commander he had been immediately after the war ended.

Actually I should not have been allowed to become a soldier, for at my induction physical I was marked down as unsuitable due to being severely underweight. Just turned eighteen, I was already almost six feet three inches tall, but weighed—like my father, who was still slightly taller at the time—only about 125 pounds. The then-commander of the 3rd Squadron, Major von Reinersdorff, didn't worry much about this, however, because he, too, had been underweight when he entered the service. As a successful competitive jockey before World War I, he had won a whole string of races, including some on horses that belonged to my father. For me he became the riding instructor from whom I learned the most by far.

In 1923, a high school graduate was still not an officer candidate when he started his military service. He could be designated as such only after serving in the ranks for twelve months. Even then, he remained on the same level as the other recruits and enjoyed no special privileges at all. The only difference was that his training was harder and more multifaceted. Not until their promotion to *Gefreiter* (private first class) were the officer candidates generally grouped together and provided with specialized training. In their third service-year they attended the Infantry School as *Fahnenjunker-Unteroffiziere* (cadet-corporals), and finally, attended the Cavalry School as *Fähnriche* (ensigns). During this two-year period they needed to pass the cadet-corporal, ensign, and officer examinations, as well as many intermediate tests, before returning to the troops as *Oberfähnriche* (senior ensigns). There they would wait for their promotion to officer status, which was granted in accordance with their numerical rank on the officer examination.

Four years of steady training before becoming an officer was a long time; but still, it would be ideal if such a thorough, fundamental formation were possible for the young officers of modern armed forces. This is unfortunately not the case whenever the need for young officers is great. After our four-year training period, nobody could put anything over on us. We had learned the soldier's life from the ground up. We could really put ourselves in the place of the ordinary trooper, from our own experience. We also knew about every possible form of harassment, and pointless grinding-down by commanders of every rank.

I was able to grasp the great value of the prolonged training period as soon as I became a recruit trainer myself, but I understood it even more later on, when I was a squadron commander. In 1925 the then-current head of the army, *Generaloberst* (Colonel General) von Seeckt, issued instructions pursuant to which the severity of the training of officer candidates was softened somewhat.[1] That may well have been justified, but for me, who no longer had a personal stake in the matter by that point, becoming familiar with the soldier's hard life had not been harmful but helpful.

In every Reichswehr unit during the 1920s there were old *Obergefreite,* lance corporals functioning as acting corporals, who had been through the latter years of the war. The same was true for almost all of the officers and NCOs. They were all typical war veterans, some of whom had never experienced any peacetime training. This was noticeable above all in the case of the old lance corporals. As if they were Turkish pashas, they had themselves waited on by the young recruits, and they took the slightest opportunity to smash a mighty "signature" onto someone's face. But then, by contrast, they could also be extremely comradely and ready to help, the way they had learned to be at the front during the war. Despite this other side, the senseless grinding down of trainees is, in the final analysis, only a sign of the trainer's own incompetence. You can achieve the same toughness in military training using sensible activities whose value for real-life situations can be explained.

During the first half-year of my military service, I was in the 5th (Training) Squadron in Breslau-Carlowitz, along with all the regiment's other new recruits. Our training officer was Cavalry Captain Seel, a former sergeant in the Life Guard Cuirassiers, who had been raised to officer's estate for valor in the face of the enemy. He was, in keeping with his name, an excellent soul (*Seele*), even if he handed us no presents. The "old man" in my barracks bay was Corporal Artur Wanke, who in later years was promoted to officer rank, and came back from World War II as a lieutenant colonel and a regimental commander. We young soldiers owed much to his care for us and his good instructions.

Two other memories remain unforgettable: one was my first night as a soldier, when I lay on the blue-and-white-checked army cot, unable to sleep from sheer excitement, and heard the sound of the "Cavalry Retreat" blown by a bugler at the compound gate. This splendid trumpet signal from the Grand Tattoo has accompanied me for a lifetime since then. I hope it will be played one last time by my casket. The second thing was quite a different matter: in 1923, we experienced the high point of the great postwar inflation. From millions of marks, it became a matter of billions and trillions. We received our pay weekly at first, then every few days, and at the end daily. You had to move fast in order to still be able to get something for the monstrous sum of paper money.

From 1 September 1923, I was stationed in Lüben with my permanent squadron, the 3rd. There were about ten of us recruits, of whom I—the lone high school graduate—was the only one who could hope for an officer's career. The next half-year was my hardest time as a soldier. Aside from our actual duties, we young soldiers were thoroughly subject to the whims of the old lance corporals. We instinctively banded together in strong comradeship. This tight, loyal friendship would last for a lifetime. Today most of the lads from back then are dead, but the few survivors are bound together in old camaraderie, whether a man ended his military career as a staff corporal or, like me, as a general. We still use the familiar *du* and our first names whenever we talk to one another; we fall into one another's arms whenever we meet again.

The outdoor training was hard, the indoor training even harder; and when we were done for the day, we cleaned the boots and gear of the old lance corporals and the non-commissioned officers, scrubbed out the barracks bays and the latrines as well, and were just happy whenever somebody let us go to sleep. I made up for the strenuousness of the physical demands (to which I was even less accustomed than my comrades) by eating enormously. I caused vast quantities of army rye bread, margarine, and artificial honey to disappear, together with every other kind of food that the older soldiers were happy to leave for me. The result was that I very rapidly lost the jockey weight that had still been mine as an eighteen year old. Later I would often lament that fact.

All these adversities were compensated for by my joy in riding and in being with horses. My squadron commander, Major von Reinersdorff, who knew about my "pre-service" equestrian training, soon let me ride in the section for young remounts, the newest cavalry horses. That caused a sensation because this section contained the most talented riders in the entire squadron. He put me on his own horse and rode with me through the countryside. His riding style resembled my father's, so my equestrian concepts progressed and developed along the same lines. This opportunity to do extra riding and thereby receive enhanced training was the only advantage that I enjoyed. Even the fact that my father, a retired brigadier general and a former commander of the regiment, lived only a few hundred meters from the barracks earned me no privileges.

The most enchanting thing besides the individual horseback riding was squadron-level cavalry drill on the vast training grounds. Until 1927 these exercises were still conducted just as they had been before World War I, that is to say, in rigid mass formations. It was soon clear even to me that this method of training for mounted combat simply made no sense in view of the steady development of weapons technology. I'm glad to this day, however, that I was able to experience the last five years of the real and genuine cavalryman's lifestyle. (Even if there were still several "swarming attacks" by cavalry during the Second World War, above all during the Polish campaign, nevertheless after 1927 the horse was only a mode of transport for a weapons-carrying soldier in an infantry-type assignment.)

Mounted drills in platoon and squadron columns and, better yet, in platoon and squadron lines, gave everyone who was able to participate an indescribable feeling of pleasure—especially when performed at full gallop. However, in the course of such maneuvers, one could land in truly unpleasant situations. Since the flanker-corporal had the task of pressing inward so that the closed ranks of the formation could be perfectly preserved, he rode pressed up tightly against the horse and rider to his side. The neighboring rider's weapons dug into his thigh and leg and could cause tremendous pain. Sometimes the flanker-corporal was lifted completely out of his saddle by the rider beside him, and he felt as if he were hanging in the air. Then it was a matter of getting oneself back down into the saddle, for in such circumstances a tumble could put one's very life in danger.

Each cavalryman carried a carbine in a leather holster at his side, and every platoon carried a light machine gun along with it: but the "queen of weapons" was still the lance. The long, heavy, sharp-ended iron rod—from whose upper end the black-and-white pennon fluttered—was very difficult to handle, and it took a lot of practice to master the use of this already long-outmoded weapon. But when young cavalrymen were veering off in the wrong direction, flankers could use their lances to bash them on the steel helmet or in the gut, so as to get their attention and correct them.

As we galloped across Lüben Heath in those days, we had no idea that we were riding over the richest copper deposits in eastern Europe. They were discovered during World War II and are presently being exploited on a grand scale by the Poles. The expanded Lüben cemetery now includes the area where the trail once ran that we rode along to reach the training grounds. That's where the graves of my parents are.

With my promotion to private first class on 1 July 1924, my status changed to officer-candidate and I was transferred to Breslau-Kleinburg, where I met up again with the four other candidates. First in the 2nd Squadron, then in the 1st Squadron, I experienced the same joys, fears, and trials that I had gone through in Lüben. But now we were given more specialized training in subjects such as heavy machine guns and the different types of signal equipment. We were introduced to the armory and to the blacksmith shop. In the smithy we also learned how to shoe horses.

During this time I was able to put my first riding successes on the books. I finished in first place in the young remounts race at a regimental sports festival, riding the East Prussian Cramon, out of Dankl XX.[2] This horse Cramon would play a special role later on in my equestrian life. On the occasion of a big riding tournament in Breslau, riding Vielfrass (Big Eater), I was able to win a fairly easy hunter-jumper event, coming out ahead of General Hasse, the commander of 2nd Cavalry Division, who was mounted on General, a then-famous jumper. General Hasse and I both got through the whole course without incurring any penalties. He remarked that the oldest rider and the youngest rider had done the best work.

After my next promotion on 1 November 1924, to cadet-corporal, like others of my rank, I had to eat my lunches and dinners in the *Kasino* (officers' club). Located in a wing of the old Life Guard Cuirassiers barracks, the club was very beautifully furnished, largely with gifts from various Prussian monarchs to the officers of their cavalry guard regiment. The most valuable items were the paintings, some of which were by renowned masters like Antoine Pesne, as well as the battle trophies accumulated during the long history of the world's oldest cavalry regiment.[3] Included in the collection were the silver kettle drums and silver trumpets captured from the French cuirassiers at the battles of Oudenarde in 1708 and Malplaquet the following year.

Inside the Great Hall there hung nothing but a portrait of the Great Elector, Friedrich Wilhelm I (1620–1688), after whom the old regiment had been named, and beneath it a painting of Kaiser Wilhelm II in his younger years.

In addition to these paintings, the walls of the Gothic-style passageways and Great Hall were bedecked with the coats of arms of all the officers who had ever served in the regiment. Scarcely a single one of the emblems of the old Silesian noble houses was missing. The arms of the Gersdorff and Dohna clans were represented many times over.

Amid these surroundings, rich in tradition and almost luxurious as they were, we lived with a notable modesty and simplicity. The officer corps of that era dined from stoneware plates on the same lunches and dinners that the mess hall served to the enlisted men, which was good, solid fare but naturally included no delicacies. There was much less drinking than in the smaller provincial garrisons, since Breslau, with its rich cultural life, offered so much variety that one seldom had to spend long nights in the *Kasino*. But when the evening had gone on for an exceptionally long time—and of course we cadet-corporals had to hold out until the last officer had departed—then our enlisted comrades took care of us, making sure we didn't sleep through morning stable duty or our other assignments. Without too many words being spoken, let alone any actual instructions, we were gradually schooled from the example the regimental officers set for us in the style of thought and conduct appropriate for the officer corps. We were given constant attention, without ever being pressured or made to feel restricted in our personal freedom.

On 1 March 1925, the ensign training course began at the Infantry School. This was located at the Ohrdruf training facility in Thuringia, and the course took place after the so-called Hitler Putsch in Munich. Included in the class were the infantry cadets who, for the most part, had been involved in the Munich putsch [which has also been labeled the "Beer Hall Putsch" because it began in the famous Munich Hofbrauhaus].

Soon after our arrival at Ohrdruf, the head of the Reichswehr, Colonel General von Seeckt, visited the Infantry School. Beginning days before his arrival, there was a hubbub that could not have been exceeded for a visit from the Kaiser prior to 1918. Uniform inspections, barracks inspections, and practice drills followed hard upon each other. We experienced something of the powerful influence that emanated from Seeckt's personality. During his speech, he turned toward the cadets with the words that became famous: "For the first time in my life, I stand before common mutineers. . . ." Though I had not been involved in the putsch, Seeckt's talk made a huge impression on me. I can still seem to hear it even now. There has probably never been another German general since Seeckt who enjoyed as much respect and who radiated as much personal charisma.

My time at the Infantry School was less significant for the military training than for the large number of friends I made outside of my regiment. Here at Ohrdruf, one could really see what made the Reichswehr so unique up until

1934: everyone knew everyone else, and with few exceptions, everyone was bound together in a special spirit of camaraderie. In our limited free time, we enjoyed the beauty of the Thuringian landscape, most of all in Oberhof, Friedrichsroda, Gotha, and Eisenach.

The camaraderie grew even tighter around the beginning of November 1925, when after passing the ensign examination at the Infantry School, we cavalrymen were transferred to the Cavalry School at Hanover. Many aspiring officers had already been washed out by the intermediate tests or the ensign exam. Even a fellow cadet-corporal from the 7th Cavalry had had to doff his uniform early.

At the Cavalry School, so rich in tradition (it had been the Military Equestrian Institute in the imperial era), we felt the "cavalry spirit" to a high degree, and likewise the powerful sense of solidarity that had distinguished the cavalry for hundreds of years. As the direct descendants of the mounted knights of the Middle Ages, we preserved the chivalry of former times even more than did other branches of the service. This, however, altered nothing about our professional training, which was modern and suited to our own times.

Our class supervisor and tactics instructor was the future *Feldmarschall* (Field Marshal) von Kleist, who already displayed his brilliant abilities as a major in the General Staff.[4] I am grateful to him for laying the foundation for my own capabilities in staff work. He taught us the most current strategy and tactics. He was therefore all the more shocked when, during the critique session after a tactical field exercise conducted by the Hanover-based 13th Cavalry, a highly experienced staff officer once called for the introduction of a special attachment to be fitted over the end of a lance, with which snipers in trees could be speared from below! Kleist simply told us to forget what we had heard as quickly as possible. This rather amusing incident demonstrates, however, just how strongly tactical and technological notions dating from the turn of the century still endured.

The equestrian training at Hanover was a disappointment to me. With my passion for equestrian sports, I had hoped to experience everything that a horseman's heart could dream of, here in the Mecca of riding, from the school stables, which housed the finest dressage horses in all of Germany, to the renowned hunts on the Leinewiesen. However, the emphasis in our training was (quite properly) on tactics and leadership. The riding instruction, while good enough, was a secondary matter. We got to mount the dressage horses in the school stables only once, in order to get a feel for the techniques of "High School" riding, such as *Piaffe* and *Passage*.

In our off-duty hours we officer-candidates were in demand as dancers. In this connection I experienced the obvious distinction between Welfs—people of the former kingdom of Hanover—and Prussians, which still affected life even as late as the Weimar Republic.[5] Only after much difficulty were we Prussians allowed to attend Welf social events. Before leaving, we were admonished not to display our "Prussianness" too much. But the city of Hanover had such close ties to its Cavalry School that we were welcome guests everywhere.

The conclusion of the Cavalry School course was the officer examination, which I passed near the top of the class. On 1 October 1926, we senior ensigns returned to duty with the 7th Cavalry Regiment. I was assigned to the 1st Squadron, the "Life Guard Cuirassiers" squadron. This filled me with a tremendous feeling of joy, because it was here in the barracks of the Breslau Cuirassiers that my father had also begun his military career.

Everything was still the way it had been back in 1884. In the middle of the barracks courtyard still stood the incomparable statue of the Great Elector, crafted by the sculptor Christian David Rauch. (I shall return to its eventual fate.) In the *Kasino,* I sat in a chair that had my family's coat of arms carved into the backrest, and I could dine with silver cutlery that my father had had engraved with our crest. To clean and make up my modest bachelor officer's flat in the barracks, I hired the daughter of "old lady Feuerstein," who had served my father in the same capacity. This daughter, who was now sixty years old herself and named Frau Kruber, was a real character whose tales and anecdotes could have filled another book.

My regimental commander was *Oberstleutnant* (Lieutenant Colonel) von Felbert, former member of the old Krefeld Hussars. He was uncommonly vital, energetic, and wiry: in short, a splendid soldier, who was loved and feared in equal measure by his subordinates. When he asked me one day in the club whether I had selected my own charger yet, I informed him that I was still looking. Felbert replied, "Then go on over to the stables—your horse is standing there." And there I found the East Prussian Cramon, progeny of the thoroughbred Dankl XX—the same Cramon I had ridden to win the prize in the young remounts race while I was a cadet-corporal. The commander, who had taken this horse as one of his own service mounts (considering him to be one of the best in the regiment), had put him at my disposal.

On the day I was promoted to *Leutnant* (lieutenant)—20 December 1926— my father died, completely unexpectedly, of an acute lung infection. At his military funeral in Lüben, while wearing my lieutenant's uniform for the very first time, I carried the glass-topped display case that held his decorations. In the midst of the greatest sorrow in my life up to that point, I had but one thought: to try to follow in my father's footsteps, and to attempt to be what he had been, a cavalryman and a gentleman.

During the next few years my duties claimed me entirely. My squadron commander, Cavalry Captain von Obernitz, was a really excellent soldier who demanded a lot from his officers. At the latest, my service day began at 6:00 A.M. during the winter. It continued without interruption until the end of the officers' riding practice at 1:00 P.M.; but then my afternoon duties commenced immediately and went on until five or six o'clock. When the squadron's first lieutenant, Karl-Wilhelm von Schlieben (who stood almost six and a half feet tall) noticed once that after the officers' riding practice I only bolted down a hasty sandwich, he went to Obernitz and asked him to give me at least half an hour for lunch. When Obernitz observed in reply that as a lieutenant in the old 10th Lancers at Züllichau, *he* had never had time for the noon meal, Schlieben, who incarnated the old-school *Premierleutnant* of the Kaiser's army, answered plainly and spiritedly, "By that hour of the day the 10th Lancers were probably always drunk!" Obernitz laughed and granted me the half-hour.[6]

At this point, I will make several general observations about the Reichswehr. After initial difficulties regarding its inner direction, which as a result of the lost war were probably unavoidable, the Reichswehr developed under Seeckt's leadership into a superb military force. Despite the restrictions on manpower and equipment imposed on it by the Treaty of Versailles, it is my conviction that the Reichswehr, in its organization and esprit de corps, was then the most modern, cohesive, and reliable army in the military history of the entire world.

This bold claim is based on the following four points. It was clear from the start to *Reichspräsident* Friedrich Ebert and his Reichswehr minister, Gustav Noske, that they could "win the revolution only *with* the Reichswehr and its officer corps."[7] They saw that they were dependent on the officers and noncommissioned officers from the old royal armies of Prussia, Bavaria, Saxony, and Württemberg. Both men acted like statesmen, not like political party functionaries, when they handed expansive authority over the army to Colonel General von Seeckt.

Seeckt combined magnificent General Staff and organizational abilities with the highest degree of practical leadership skills. He was himself a political soldier, who saw his mission as the salvation of the values of the Prussian-German soldierly tradition of a different era. He was so successful at this that these values remained intact and are still in effect in our time, even if not one of his successors down to the present day was so great a man. Seeckt understood so well how to enhance his position and his prestige that he was able to rule almost like an absolute monarch—but one who was always distinguished by his elevated awareness of political responsibility. Because it suited his reconstruction project, he mounted no resistance to the firmly established depoliticizing of the Reichswehr in the Military Code. By this means he warded off outside influences that would only have hindered the Reichswehr's development into a reliable and loyal force.

Despite many who think otherwise, the royal armies of the German Reich were already well in advance of the armed forces of other countries, in terms of their training and spirit. Leadership deficiencies such as I observed in the U.S. Army during World War II had long since been overcome and eliminated in the German armed forces. Because the officer corps (as well as the non-commissioned officer corps) of the Reichswehr had been formed by the most severe selection of personnel from the enormous manpower pools of those older armies, modern-style thinking and leadership were so pervasive as to transform the Reichswehr into a true elite force. Nowadays every state that can financially afford to do so prefers to maintain professional armed forces. The Reichswehr showed that a professional army is superior in training and mentality to all armies that are put together on the basis of universal military service. A unit comprised of volunteer soldiers who remain together in the same place for years on end can achieve far more than a conscript force that is beset by constant personnel changes and never really manages to achieve true cohesion.

With all of that having been said, a professional army of this type also has its drawbacks. Above all, these lie in a certain isolation of the army inside the society: the Reichswehr turned more and more into a state within a state. However, this did not concern us too much at the time; basically, we were scarcely even aware of it.

In fact we felt so good about everything, within our solid circle of comrades as well as in our off-duty private lives, that to this day I look back on my period of soldiering from 1923 until 1933 as the happiest days of my life. I admit that our regiment's homogeneity and its Silesian locales were largely responsible for this feeling. Our most important "heritage regiments," the Life Guard Cuirassiers and the Bredow Dragoons, had been so-called exclusive regiments; they had only admitted aristocrats as officers.[8] The natural result was that the 7th Cavalry's officers came almost entirely from Silesian noble families and were to a very large extent actually related to one another. There were times when I was serving alongside five of my Strachwitz cousins and two of my Lüttwitz cousins. This "cousin society" was often criticized from the outside. I can only say that our sense of togetherness had positive professional effects. The feeling of kinship also gripped our non-commissioned officers and enlisted men; not only the officer corps, but the entire regiment, formed one big family.

An essential element for the regiment's esprit de corps and its superior standard of training was the fact that during all the years of its existence, each commander was even better than the one before him. Colonels von Thaer and von Roeder, who had built up the regiment and assembled its officer corps at the beginning of the 1920s, were succeeded by Colonel von Felbert from western Germany, who with his tremendous verve had elevated the training program to a state of near perfection. Afterwards, Colonel Baron Kress von Kressenstein and Colonel von Gossler particularly promoted the tactical and equestrian programs. At the end, Colonel Count von Seherr-Thoss and Colonel von Prittwitz knew how to preserve and improve upon the already high standard of training. I owed an infinite amount to every single one of these commanders.[9]

I also had the great good fortune to find within the regiment the best friend I ever had. The Borussia (Latin for "Prussia") fraternity at Bonn University sent us its members at regular intervals, so that after their fraternity time they could spend several weeks absorbing some military training with us.[10] As a result, the fraternity's "Fox Major," Count Adrian von Pückler, turned up in our midst during the fall of 1926.[11] He had actually intended to go into business as a horse-breeder, but he was so enchanted by his brief stint of soldiering that he decided to become an active-duty officer. Even while I was training him we became good friends, and after he returned from the Cavalry School in 1930 and became an officer, we were almost inseparable. In Silesia they called us "Castor and Pollux." We lived together in an officer apartment above the *Kasino,* had identical interests, and did everything together.

Adrian von Pückler was an extraordinary person in every respect. He was much influenced by his parental home at Branitz near Cottbus, where his ancestor Prince Hermann von Pückler had laid out what was probably his most beautiful park and had spent the evening of his life. The spiritual inheritance of this man, who was as restless as he was spiritual, had definitely left its traces on my friend. I have never since encountered a man who combined the courage and strength for life with as much spirit and charm. Wherever he arrived, the atmosphere turned electric. The degree to which people of every class adored him, both old and young, women and men, was absolutely unique. Whenever he entered a riding tournament to compete in a hunter-jumper event, the promoters always highlighted him in their advertising. They knew that if they did so, many more spectators would show up to cheer on their favorite, even if he was already out of the running by the second or third obstacle. The soldiers under his command would ride themselves to pieces for his sake, because they knew that they could count on him in everything. Despite so much spoiling and despite great success in both his professional and private lives, Adrian von Pückler remained modest, serious, even introverted at times. He hated superficiality and banality, but he was able to overcome every obstacle in his path because of his boundless lust for life. When he was killed in action as a Panzer commander on the Eastern Front a few months before the collapse in 1945, a great and joyous life came to an end.

The inception of Adrian von Pückler's active officer career was personally approved, in a most peculiar way, by the new chief of the *Heeresleitung*

(Supreme Army Command). In mid-October 1926, Colonel General von Seeckt, the creator of the Reichswehr, was replaced by Colonel General Heye.[12] The latter man visited my regiment on 14 January 1927, in the Cuirassier Barracks at Breslau. In Seeckt's time, such a visit would have gone off just like a parade for the Kaiser, but now we were exposed to the glaring difference between Seeckt and Heye.

In accordance with our precise preparations, the regiment stood in parade formation in front of the Great Elector's statue in the courtyard of the compound. While the band played the "Presentation March," the commander, Colonel von Felbert, presented the regiment to the new chief of the *Heeresleitung*. Instead of the anticipated bawling of commands at the head of the formation, a speech while we stood at parade rest, and a concluding parade, Heye immediately halted the music and ordered "at ease!" and "ground your weapons!" We stood around feeling completely at a loss, with no idea of what was to follow.

What followed was unique. Heye immediately ordered that day's birthday boys to report to him. After prolonged hesitation two corporals stepped to the front; one could see that they were plainly ill at ease. The chief of the *Heeresleitung* now had three glasses of schnapps brought from the canteen, and he drank to their health. Finally he summoned up every possible combination of soldiers: war veterans, married men, non-swimmers, eyeglass-wearers, and so forth. Among these groups he had the officer candidates come forward, and at this point he said to Pückler, "You may be a count, but all the same I'll approve your enlistment. But I won't set you free again until you're a general." Someone exclaimed loudly and disrespectfully, "I'd make sure to get that in writing!" When cadet-corporal Hans von Helfritz admitted in response to questioning that he received a monthly allowance of fifty Reichsmarks from his father, Heye said, "So, you're quite the Farmer Moneybags!" The whole thing ended informally in a general discussion.

The year 1927 became a time of great military achievements for my regiment. Inspections, maneuvers, and field training exercises, during which "the regiment with all the aristocratic officers" was graded with particular severity, resulted in splendid successes thanks to the inspiring leadership of Colonel von Felbert and to the fine training of the previous years. The regiment's inspection at the Jüterbog training facility by the "cavalry-eater" General von Tschischwitz, which was almost completely restricted to infantry-type combat maneuvers, concluded with his enormous praise.[13]

That evening all the squadrons celebrated. Felbert, whom the troops had long ago nicknamed Fritzchen, delivered a marvelous speech. When he had finished, Senior Corporal Müller from the 1st Squadron—the so-called "Black" Müller—leaped onto the table upon which Felbert stood, embraced

him, and with the words "your pardon, *Herr Oberst,* I can do no other!"—
gave him a kiss.[14] That was the signal for all the officers to be lifted high on
shoulders, and for the squadrons to form up and then parade past the beloved
commander "at the gallop." These proceedings show, once again, some of the
spirit that reigned in the Reichswehr in general and the cavalry in particular.

But 1927 also saw our farewell to the lance. However justified this was, it
put the end of the old-time cavalry right before our eyes. As a result, discussions about the lance were very controversial in this period. When, during the
course of a critique session after some training maneuver, Colonel General
Heye asked all the officers of our regiment for their opinions on the subject,
he received a variety of responses. At the very end he asked me, as the junior
lieutenant, whether I was in favor of abolishing the lance or preserving it.
When I spoke up loudly and clearly for its preservation, he smugly replied,
"You presumably learned all about lances in your schoolroom?" I retorted
proudly, "No, *Herr Generaloberst,* I've ridden with a lance for three years."
Although I soon realized how stupidly I had reacted (with all my twenty-two
years!), I could then have had no idea that fifty years after the abolition of
the lance, I would be listening to discussions about the abolition of nuclear
weapons.

My attendance at a chemical weapons defense course in 1927 and a course
in smoke camouflage reminded me of the ceaseless progress of military technology. In the summer of '28 I spent several weeks attached to a mechanized
smoke platoon, whose equipment, however, was still quite primitive. Despite
our observance of every precautionary measure, during a field exercise at the
Neuhammer training facility we came within a hair of setting an entire forest
ablaze.

During our training-area interludes and military maneuvers in those years,
we were often visited by delegations of Soviet officers. (Once one of these
guests was General Tukhachevsky, later executed by Stalin.)[15] The following
experience was an unforgettable one for me: on the occasion of an especially
smooth and rapid river crossing exercise on the Oder, I asked the Russian
guests, through an interpreter, how they had liked it. The answer came back,
"Very pretty, but far too slow." In response to my astonished inquiry as to how
one could do it any faster, they said, "Our divisions close ranks—then they
ride in on one side of the Volga and out the other side. We don't have any
lifeboats or ferries, or all that other stuff." I asked how many horses and riders were typically left behind in the river using this method, and received the
laconic response, "Sometimes over a hundred!" This was my first encounter
with the utter ruthlessness of the Soviet leadership, which I would come to
know very well indeed during World War II.

One evening Soviet officers were our guests in the *Kasino*. The trumpet corps was playing a concert for us, and right after the meal ended I went over to the musicians, as I usually did, to tell them which marches to play. One of my favorites was the "Cherkassy March" by Tchaikovsky, in the middle of which one hears the splendid notes of the old Russian national anthem, "God Save the Tsar." Without even thinking about the Soviet guests, but full of musical enthusiasm, I directed the band to play this beautiful tune. By the time I got back to my place the Soviet guests had silently risen from their chairs, and with some slight bows they all left the hall. We did not see them again. I expected to get a severe dressing-down from my commander, but Fritzchen Felbert only raised his glass and drank to me, saying, "You did a good job there! Now at least we're by ourselves." Although at that moment I was happy to have gotten off so neatly, I remained conscious of my unintentional tactlessness.

During those carefree lieutenant years, apart from our military duties we lived chiefly for equestrian sports. Due to my height and weight, I had specialized from the outset in hunter-jumper events. At Silesian tournaments I succeeded in placing high in a number of such contests and in winning several competitions. But racing increasingly became my main passion. Felbert had tapped some little-used regimental funds to have thoroughbred horses purchased in Berlin, which were then trained by a well-known Breslau trainer. In 1927 I had received my first thoroughbred, the stallion Sarazener (by Santoi out of Rahana). I was able to ride him daily at the morning workout before the service day began, and soon I took part in my first race. Since the error had been made of purchasing eight cheap thoroughbreds instead of two or three really good ones, the regiment's racehorses were only suited for middling, provincial-level competitions. My own Sarazener was no exception, so we were quite happy when we began to win some prizes in small races.

Our shining example was my comrade and friend Gero von Götz. In May 1926, riding one of the regiment's good half-blooded horses, a mare named Amsel, he had surprisingly won two officers' races in Mannheim and received a thoroughbred as the grand prize. Gero, with whom I had used to daydream about racing horses when we were still back in Lüben, quickly developed into one of the best and most successful gentleman jockeys of the inter-war era. He was the champion of all the gentleman jockeys in Germany in 1928, with forty-one racing victories. Another regimental comrade blessed with a light bodyweight, Friedrich-Wilhelm von Mellenthin, won a large number of races, too. I was always handicapped owing to my weight, but over the years I also had a string of victories, chiefly in Breslau, but also in Frankfurt am Main, Hanover, and Berlin.

Mounted hunts, which unfortunately occurred only in the fall, were special pleasures. True, we had no pack of hounds, but the hunts in the difficult
countryside around Breslau were still a lot of fun. I learned about managing
such events from our masters of the hunt, Cavalry Captain von Obernitz and
Cavalry Captain von Hülsen. I succeeded them in turn as the hunt master, and
rode at the head of the field on my horse Cramon. Only someone who has
ridden in many hunts over fair ditches and hedges can understand the pleasure
of this sport.

Sports were not our only source of happy hours. I still recall the stag dinners and the mixed-company dinners in our *Kasino*. The high point every
year was 2 December, when the veterans' society of the Life Guard Cuirassiers remembered the attack at Loigny-Poupry. During its long history the
regiment had ridden in many important assaults, but the anniversary of this
relatively bloodless charge in the 1870–71 war had been made into the annual
regimental day. I participated in this memorial ceremony as a full member of
the Life Guard Cuirassiers because (like some of my other comrades) I had
been admitted to the veterans' society as a Cuirassier's son.

We entered the great hall amidst the notes of the "Great Elector March,"
composed by Count Kuno von Moltke, himself a former Life Guard Cuirassier.[16] Two sergeants wearing the black-and-white colors of the old regiment
were posted at the door. The most senior man present, *Herr* von Ruffer (over
ninety years old), made the first toast to the colonel-in-chief of the regiment,
lifting his glass and crying out, "To the King!" Before the chairman of the
society, Major General Count von Schmettow, began his speech, he turned,
raised his glass, and bowed slightly to the portrait of the last Kaiser.[17]

These ceremonies might be dismissed today as theatrical and reactionary.
At the time they made a great impression on me. In honoring great traditions
there lay an infinite amount of chivalry and pride, which, considering the regiment's three-hundred-year history, was completely justified.

The balls that took place at our *Kasino* were the high points of Silesia's
social season. The Crown Prince and his wife were usually there, as were the
Grand Duchess of Saxe-Weimar and the wife of Prince Friedrich-Sigismund
of Prussia. And if polonaises, quadrilles, and cotillions were still danced just
as they had been a hundred years earlier, these parties were by no means stiff
or boring. The regimental trumpet corps could put together a superb dance
band, which played all the modern dances. Adrian von Pückler and I were the
lead dancers. As such, we were responsible for the conduct of the balls, and
also had to ensure that no wallflowers remained in their seats. Although of
course we all danced energetically to contemporary dances like the tango and
the Charleston, nonetheless in Silesia—so saturated in Austrian traditions—
the Viennese waltz was our greatest favorite.

During the cotillions, two little Russian ponies with black and white ribbons attached to their saddlecloths would carry baskets of flowers into the hall, where the prettiest young ladies present would distribute ribbons and flowers to everyone. These officer parties had culture and style, perhaps for the last time in an era that was drawing to its close.

Another custom seems to me to be worthy not only of mention, but of imitation. At the beginning of the 1930s we accepted a sizable quantity of male university students as regular paying guests in our club. The immediate impetus for this action came when the *Kasino* budget ran into red ink, owing to the relatively small number of members and to deficient fiscal management. Although we had always had some steady individual guests, the significant enlargement of our circle was a blow to the traditional intimacy of the club, a place where one could say anything without fear of indiscretion. Therefore we only invited friends and close acquaintances, who also had some kind of pre-existing connection to the regimental officer corps, to dine with us at lunch and dinner. As soon as we noticed that any of these men did not wish to conform to our style or held different fundamental opinions, we parted ways.

Based on the foregoing premises, the coexistence of soldiers and civilians was a complete success. Since the students represented various university departments ranging from law and economics to agriculture and medicine, the subject matter of our discussions was rapidly enriched. Now we no longer mainly discussed professional military or equestrian topics—or, as we ourselves ironically put it, "Alma the mare's inward-turning back hoof"— but also issues in their various fields of study. The intellectual level of our expanded circle was noticeably enhanced.

The presence of our civilian guests also led to a stronger interest in political questions. The complex of issues designated as "the Reichswehr and politics" was legally regulated by the Military Code of 23 March 1921. In Section 36, paragraphs 1–3, it was stated among other things that, "Soldiers may not engage in political activity [. . .]. Membership in political organizations or participation in political rallies is forbidden for soldiers. The soldiers' right to vote in national, state, or local elections, or referendums, is hereby suspended."

The depoliticizing of the Reichswehr, firmly established by the foregoing regulations, led to our becoming less and less concerned with domestic political developments in our own country. The Reichswehr's position within the state, and therefore our own position, was clear. After the post-war tumults which had occasionally required the deployment of the Reichswehr had all been overcome, the only missions remaining to us were to train the soldiers entrusted to us into a combat-ready, self-sufficient force, and to indoctrinate them in such a way that they presented no threat to internal security. The presidency of Field Marshal von Hindenburg, who was simultaneously our commander-in-chief, appeared to be the guarantee for the preservation of our soldierly principles.

Naturally we stayed informed from newspapers about developments in domestic politics and foreign policy; but we only rarely discussed them. After the putsch of 1923, the up-and-coming National Socialist movement aroused our interest only once, on the occasion of the Ludin-Scheringer trial.[18] This passive attitude toward politics only began to change at the beginning of the 1930s, when the SA (*Sturmabteilung*; Storm Troops) and the SS (*Schutzstaffel*; Security Group) started to make the Nazi Party increasingly noticeable in public life.

Their pseudo-revolutionary rowdiness, which was particularly manifest in the person of Edmund Heines, the SA chief in Silesia, was as alien and repulsive to us as it could possibly be.[19] On top of that, there were more and more altercations and even violent brawls between soldiers from our regiment and SA and SS men. Once when one young officer ventured to say something positive about the National Socialist movement inside the *Kasino,* he was set straight again, and very sharply at that. The attitude of the officer corps spread out across the whole regiment. I do not recollect a single instance of a Nazi cell being formed among the NCOs and the enlisted men.

At least in my regiment, an order to proceed against the Nazi movement would have been obeyed without argument. The Reichswehr's leadership had the troops firmly in hand. We officers were convinced that, in keeping with our soldierly responsibilities, the high command would take the necessary steps firmly and at the appropriate time. At our own level, we didn't take Hitler seriously enough. We were more likely at first to find the agitator from Braunau merely laughable.

During these years I was personally influenced by my older brother Ernst-Carl, who had recognized the criminality of National Socialism from the very start.[20] He was one of the very few people who never had the slightest doubt about their attitude toward Hitler and their opinion of the movement, and he often surprised my friends when he predicted the Reich's downfall, even at the height of its triumphs, if nobody overthrew the dictator. From 1929 to 1930, my brother played a leading role, along with politicians like the former cabinet minister Treviranus, Ambassador Hans Schlange-Schöningen, and the conservative political leader Count Kuno von Westarp, in founding the conservative "German People's Party," which wanted to stem the rising tide of Nazism.[21] But this early attempt to mount a resistance foundered not only due to the lack of funds, but also due to a widespread failure to comprehend the problem, not least on the part of the German National Party. An attorney in private practice in Breslau, my brother put himself steadfastly at the service of his Jewish colleagues after the Nazi Party came to power, and even during the war years he continued to defend and represent the interests of his Jewish fellow-citizens. The Gestapo was naturally familiar with his opinions, and beginning in the mid-1930s he seemed to be under surveillance. But despite being arrested three times by the Gestapo, he managed to outlive the Third Reich—in the otherwise highly dubious safety of the Wehrmacht.

On 1 April 1930, I was reassigned to the regimental staff as *Ordonnanz-offizier* (aide-de-camp) to the commander. This assignment meant that I was being groomed for the post of regimental adjutant, which I took over in 1933. But even if I was now chained to my desk for many hours a day, I kept in close touch with field service through my riding and my additional duty as the supervisor of our training program for non-commissioned officers.

III

Soldier in Opposition

Obedience is the principle; but the man stands above the principle.
—*Count Helmuth von Moltke (1800–1891)*

On 31 January 1933, in my capacity as the deputy regimental adjutant, I suggested to the commander, Colonel Count Theobald von Seherr-Thoss, that he might give the officers a clear statement about the political events in Berlin. I knew of his harsh attitude against National Socialism, and wanted to use his authority in order to nip in the bud any possible shift of opinion that might occur among the younger officers amid the general euphoria. Count Seherr was of one mind with me. However, he declined to use the notes that I had prepared for his talk. The following lines, reconstructed from my memory, correspond to the sense of what he actually said then. The last two sentences were his exact words:

> Gentlemen! I need not provide you with any further explanations about what took place yesterday in Berlin. You were all able to keep up with that. But I would like to share with you my opinion concerning the governmental change that has occurred. The National Socialists, who now hold the deciding power in the government, have repeatedly stressed that they developed their ideology from the spirit of the front-line troops in the war. If that were accurate, then we soldiers could only be glad of it. But I cannot conceal my skepticism. I will also tell you why: *This Hitler, in my opinion, is no gentleman, but merely a rogue. And for that reason, sooner or later his movement will fall to pieces.*

When the commander had left, I requested the officers not to let a word of this speech become public knowledge, or we would probably lose our commanding officer very rapidly. Needless to say, none of it got out.

Count Seherr's conclusion did not mean much to me at the time. In fact it seemed primitive. Only long afterwards did it become clear to me that he had instinctively recognized the actual, the essential, point. For all his—criminal—genius, Hitler remained a petty product of the petty bourgeoisie, who in dealing with the type of real gentleman embodied by the army's senior officers always felt an inferiority complex.

Not much changed for us at first in our military ghetto. For the time being, the cavalry branch remained undisturbed by the military reorganization that was rapidly set in motion. But outside our "service life" we were more and more powerfully confronted with the actions of the SA and the SS, which took on a particularly repulsive form in Silesia due to SA leader Heines and his cronies.

Soon afterward I became the regimental adjutant. With the complete agreement of my commander, and also that of my deputy, Count Adrian von Pückler, I regarded it as my assignment to guard the officers, non-commissioned officers, and men against the new *Zeitgeist,* or spirit of the time, and therefore to constantly promote a soldierly and comradely spirit.

For example, two very junior officers gave us the impression that they harbored a certain sympathy for National Socialism. We were able to get rid of them both in the course of a mandatory levy of officers to mechanized infantry units. A lieutenant who had transferred to us from the 9th Infantry Regiment was quickly set straight. When he turned up at the officers' club one night in civilian attire, wearing the swastika-emblazoned Nazi lapel pin for military men, Count Seherr took it from his coat, and with the words "this kind of thing isn't worn around here," hurled it outside through an open window. When the lieutenant wanted to complain to someone about the commander, it was made clear to him that it was not our custom to wear such an item. Either he would have to adapt to the style of our regiment, or he would need to request a transfer out. He chose the former, and became a much-loved comrade.

Two events in 1933 really made the dawning of a "new era" plain to me.

The *Grenzschutz,* or paramilitary border guard, so important for my Silesian homeland, was taken over by a special command group from the Reichswehr, for which our regiment had to supply instructors and supervisors. Now all sorts of high-ranking SA men suddenly appeared in the Breslau *Generalkommando* (General Headquarters), making shameless demands for positions on the basis of their prior work with the *Grenzschutz.* In contrast to several overly timid staff officers at the Breslau military headquarters, I argued against these rowdies in the sharpest possible manner, and preserved the unrestricted authority of army men as opposed to SA members.

One day a very senior civil servant from the Reichswehr Ministry in Berlin arrived in my office, in order to listen to our desires regarding improvements and renovations for the Cuirassier Barracks, which had been built in 1870–71.

We had been engaged in a prolonged battle for central heating and to get the latrines and baths fixed up. Now these really urgent wishes were to be granted immediately. When he then inquired about any additional improvement plans we might have, I hesitated to respond; I was still in the clutches of fundamental Prussian thriftiness. Then the senior official said to me, "I need to tell you one very basic fact. *Money is absolutely no obstacle anymore.* I've even been authorized to approve the total demolition of your old compound and the construction of a new one."

His words left me speechless. Within a few more minutes, the construction of a large riding-track had been ordained, as well as a string of other new building projects. At the end of the meeting the official mentioned that he would order the construction of tennis courts in the little garden of our *Kasino,* although nobody had ever even asked him for that. When the civil servant from Berlin had left my office, it was clear to me that Prussian professional officialdom, as it had developed over the centuries, was now dead and gone.

Still, I have to admit that there were several things about the new regime that pleased every one of us, despite all our distaste for National Socialism. One of the most important of these things was the restoration of the black, white, and red national colors. We had never been able to resign ourselves to the Weimar Republic's black, red, and gold. On the day that the change of colors was announced there was a conference going on in the Great Hall of the *Kasino,* attended by over a hundred officers and civil servants from the headquarters of the *Wehrkreis,* our local military district. Their caps were all hanging in the cloakroom; naturally they all still bore the black, red, and gold cockade. We lieutenants had ourselves some fun by removing the emblem from every cap, so that their wearers were forced to go home as "privates second class" (without a cockade). Not one man took any offense at this particular lieutenants' prank! Understandably, we also welcomed the plans for the reorganization of the Reichswehr into a modern Wehrmacht, something we were hearing more and more about.

But the SA's ever-growing struggle against the Reichswehr guaranteed that despite all the benefits the armed forces were deriving from the new regime, their disdain for it constantly received fresh nourishment. The perversely inclined Silesian SA leader Edmund Heines and his adjutant, who was generally known in Silesia as "Fräulein" Schmidt, behaved like Asiatic usurpers.[1] It was no wonder that their subordinates followed their examples. Disorderly drinking bouts, fistfights, and shootings were all on the daily program. My friend Adrian von Pückler and I had a set-to ourselves with "Fräulein" Schmidt in a Breslau tavern, during which we were able to separate him from his bodyguard and give him a frightful beating. Instead of the anticipated official complaint or criminal charges, the next day we received a formal apology from the SA command.

During this period the Nazis still pulled back whenever they encountered massive resistance. When Heines demanded that the commander of the 2nd Cavalry Division, General von Kleist (my old tactics instructor from Hanover, later a field marshal), give him the name of a suspected military spy on the staff of the SA regional command, Kleist was said to have replied, "You'll get that name just as soon as you give *me* the name of the man in your entourage who stole two top-secret documents from my desk the last time you came over for a visit." The embarrassed Heines said not a word.

In June 1934, the struggle between the SA and the Reichswehr reached new heights. From our civilian guests in the club, who as university students had connections in SA units, we learned all about the plans of the Silesian SA leadership. Then on 30 June, the whole thing finally culminated in Hitler's purge of the SA, in the course of which Heines and Schmidt were both murdered.

During those days the regiment was kept confined to quarters and in the highest state of alert. It so happened one day that I overheard a loud argument at the compound gate between our sentries and a number of SS men. When I got there I encountered the commander of the Silesian SS, Udo von Woyrsch.[2] He vociferously complained that the guards had not let him pass through the gate with several trucks and numerous SS members. I forbid him to employ the tone he was using with me, and let him know that the sentries had done their duty. Woyrsch then demanded several hundred pistols along with a corresponding quantity of ammunition. Because we actually had received an order from the *Generalkommando* to supply the SS with all the weapons they wanted, I sent for the sergeants in charge of the squadron armories, so we could work out how many pistols we could give away.

Naturally all this took too long for Woyrsch, and when the Model '08 (Luger) pistols—about seventy-five of them—had been stowed away in his automobiles, he wanted to roll out immediately. I planted myself in front of his car and demanded that he sign the official receipt that had been prepared in the meantime. In a wild haste he scrawled something with a pencil across the entire sheet of paper. When I mockingly asked him if that was his signature, he furiously shouted *"Ja!"* and then drove off at top speed. I could not have suspected that on that day and in the days that followed, the SS would execute many people by shooting, among them a certain Baron von Wechmar and a Herr von Grolmann, who were well known to me.[3] The exact number of people murdered at that time in the 30 June purge was never ascertained.

If at the time we were unable to grasp the full extent of the so-called "cleansing action within the National Socialist movement," it was nonetheless clear for the first time to us soldiers with what ruthless violence the new men in power knew how to sustain themselves, and how much the rule of law had been shaken. The murders of Generals von Schleicher and von Bredow were a clear sign of the dangers that were approaching the army.[4]

Within my regiment, at least, hostility to the regime was constantly on the increase. In the first place we were unable to adequately judge the whole situation, given the existing state of communications; and there was something else as well: all of us were too used to waiting for orders. The fact is that only the high command of the Reichswehr—Blomberg and Fritsch—could have undertaken effective countermeasures.[5]

Just over a month later we were shaken up by another event. On 2 August 1934, *Reichspräsident* Paul von Hindenburg died. One or two days later, the entire Breslau garrison was ordered to assemble on the great square by the Centennial Hall. On one side of the open quadrangle stood my regiment, on horseback—the three Breslau-based squadrons, lined up side-by-side in parade formation. The future Field Marshal von Rundstedt took the commanders' reports and then delivered a brief and honorable eulogy for the dead president.[6] The band played the farewell tune *"Ich hatt' einen Kamerad."*[7] As soon as it had finished, Rundstedt abruptly commanded, "By regiments—raise the right hand to take the oath!" Nobody had told us anything beforehand about a new swearing-in. Above all, not a single word of the oath had been made known to us. Since we could only assume that we were to renew the oath we were already familiar with—to Germany and the German people—we unsuspectingly lifted up our right hands. (Because we cavalrymen were holding our swords in our right hands, the regimental commander had to quickly order, "Sabers in your rein-hands!") Then Rundstedt recited the new oath, line by line, while the entire garrison repeated the words after him in chorus.

Up until that moment the following pledge had applied to members of the Reichswehr: "I swear by God this sacred oath, that I will at all times serve my people and fatherland, faithfully and to the best of my ability; and that as a brave soldier I will be ready to give my life for this oath at any time." By contrast, the wording of the new vow was like this: "I swear by God this sacred oath, *that I will give unconditional obedience to the Führer of the German Reich and people, Adolf Hitler, supreme commander of the Wehrmacht*; and that as a brave soldier I will be ready to give my life for this oath at any time." The difference was glaring; but even if someone had grasped it immediately, he was as a practical matter not in a position to avoid taking the oath. I must confess that I, too, only realized what had happened after the oath-taking was already over and done with.

As we rode back to our compound I talked with a number of officers about the oath's new formulation. When I asked them whether they were aware that an entirely personal vow to Hitler had been slipped in, they at first stared at me uncomprehendingly. Only when I had reconstructed the words of the oath did they even understand my question.

The whole thing was extremely uncomfortable for us, because we had—and in a good Prussian-German military fashion—bound ourselves to a man who in our eyes was both alien and bizarre. But who could have known at the time that Hitler would ever use this oath to compel the performance of criminal orders? The consequences of the subtlety and devilishness with which Hitler had bound the soldiers of the German Wehrmacht to his own person were not yet apparent.

During these first two years of National Socialism I had been quite consciously concerned about political developments, but without ever imagining in the least what would actually happen later. Those of us soldiers who disapproved of the new regime still had high confidence in our top-ranking superiors, that is, in the army's senior generals. Without exception, we saw ourselves not only as good soldiers but as absolute "gentlemen" who would never permit the armed forces to be sucked into the vortex of upheaval and criminality—the first rumors were cropping up about concentration camps at Oranienburg and Dachau—that was steadily emerging.

We could not imagine anything other than that at the right moment, the high command would make the proper decisions. So for us at present, the only thing to do was to keep the units entrusted to us reliable, and their competency as high as possible, so that they would be completely prepared for every possible mission—including being called out against the regime. I believe to this day that this goal was completely achieved within the 7th Cavalry Regiment. Even after the so-called *Machtergreifung* we would have had no serious obstacles to overcome, either among the officers, the NCOs, or the enlisted men, if we had been ordered into action against the Nazis.[8] I am not certain, however, whether the response would have been the same in a number of other Reichswehr units.

Aside from my concerns about political developments, the years 1933–34 were especially happy ones for me. In my military assignment as regimental adjutant, I was able to put some real successes on the books. However, I had managed so well to dodge the military-district examination that would have led to my assignment to the *Kriegsakademie,* the General Staff College, that I was able to remain with the troops.[9] I never wanted anything else. Along with my passion for riding, my desire to command a cavalry squadron for as many years as possible kept me within my beloved regiment.

In February 1934, I became engaged to Renata Kracker von Schwarzen-feldt.[10] Her father had been a member of the Life Guard Cuirassiers. Both of her parents were dead. The wedding took place on 25 August 1934, at the estate of Matzdorf in the district of Löwenberg, which belonged to her grandmother Emma von Kramsta. I was able to have almost all my regimen-tal comrades attend, along with their wives if they were married; and so there was a grand and joyful celebration in the mansion designed by the renowned eighteenth-century architect Karl Friedrich Schinkel.

I had my brightest successes as a rider during these years. With the best thoroughbred that I ever owned, Caesarion (by Diadumenos out of Circe), I won many a steeplechase. Riding the Hanoverian mare Nosoza II belong-ing to my friend Pückler, I won many hunter-jumper events at tournaments. On a September day in Breslau in 1934, after I had won two races and was headed for the scales on Caesarion following my second victory, my promo-tion to Cavalry Captain was announced over the public-address system. The commander of the 2nd Cavalry Division, who was present at the track, had arranged for the announcement to be made ahead of schedule. At the celebra-tion in our apartment that evening, my friend Baron Konrad von Wangenheim wrote in the guest book, more or less, "Just once I'd also like to have as much luck!" Two years later as a member of the German army equestrian team, he won a gold medal at the Berlin Olympics.[11]

In the meantime my wish to command a squadron had been granted. It was the custom in our regiment for the adjutant to be a bachelor, so that he would be better able to stay connected with the younger officers. Therefore on 1 November 1934, I turned over the adjutancy to my friend Adrian von Pückler, and took over my regiment's 2nd Squadron.

For most officers, commanding a troop unit is probably the best job in their entire military careers. Some 150 men and a like number of horses were entrusted to a squadron commander. He was solely responsible for every single squadron member and every single horse. I saw it as my principal task, amidst all the tough training, to win the trust of my subordinates and to cre-ate a comradely unity within the squadron, which would in turn enable me to truly fulfill my commanding role the right way. I sought to become informed about the life and family of each individual man, so that in cases of need I could be involved for advice or support. I was happy about each sign of con-fidence that I received in return.

When at the end of November 1934 I led a great field of riders over the typ-ical Breslau-area drainage ditches as master of the hunt, I had no idea that this would be the very last hunt that the 7th Cavalry would ever host. In January 1935, we got the first rumors that my regiment was going to be transformed into a Panzer unit. I was never able to discover whether the first choice fell on the 4th Cavalry in Potsdam and the 7th Cavalry in Breslau because of their especially high standard of training—or because it was desired by this means to "level out" the two cavalry regiments that had especially high proportions of aristocratic officers. At the time we assumed the latter.

My commander, Colonel Count Seherr-Thoss, fought personally and with every means at his disposal against the proposed reorganization. In this quest he received the support of the Breslau *Generalkommando*. But it soon became clear that the decision reached by the Ministry in Berlin was unalterable. As zealous cavalrymen, we were very hard-hit. All the same, we decided to resign ourselves to the situation and to maintain the solidarity of our officer corps under all circumstances. With the exception of one officer (who had to be sent to the 18th Cavalry at Cannstadt with a squadron levied from every component of our regiment, along with all of our best horses), we all vowed to go along with the bitter change from horses to tanks. But in actuality, the regimental officer corps would be completely torn apart in the course of further army reorganizations.

Without my having anything to do with it, fate had also laid out a different path for me. I took part in an officers' hunter-jumper event in Berlin at the end of March 1935, in order to train for a better-class steeplechase in Hanover that I badly wanted to win aboard Caesarion. When I noticed in the home stretch that I had a good chance of winning, I probably took the last jumps too hard. Caesarion, who had never fallen before, ran straight into one of these obstacles and somersaulted like a shot hare. I rolled in front of him and was then pinned beneath him. Caesarion had broken a leg; he had to be shot then and there. I had stood up, stroked his neck while he was being put out of his misery, saluted my dead horse, and then walked into the dressing room. Only there, beneath a cold shower, did I emerge from a blackout. I had done everything while I was unconscious, even agreeing to ride in another hunter-jumper event to take place three days later at the same course! I actually did make that ride, despite a concussion, several broken ribs, and knocked-out front teeth.

During my stay in Berlin I spoke frequently with the chief of the army's central office for thoroughbred breeding and racing, Count Wolff-Metternich.[12] I told him that nothing could be done about the mechanization of my regiment. As a result, he might wish to see to it that all of its racehorses were transferred to the 8th Cavalry, the other Silesian cavalry regiment, so that unit could keep supporting horse racing in Breslau, which had a lot of trouble in that regard owing to its geographical location. Metternich asked me whether he shouldn't also arrange for my own transfer to the 8th Cavalry. I turned down this well-meaning offer and urgently requested him not to undertake anything on my behalf.

By the time I got back to Breslau, however, my transfer to the 8th Cavalry Regiment in Brieg had already been ordained; and, in addition to taking command of the next squadron that became free there, I was also to take over the regiment's racing stable as the trainer.[13] His intervention in my military career would later have a decisive effect on the course of my life. I would probably never have come to the General Staff from the armor branch, and as a Panzer leader I would perhaps not have survived the war.

At the beginning of May 1935, the regiment gave up its last horses. It was a heartbreaking farewell. The officers, NCOs, and enlisted men parted from their best comrades. On the night of 14 May there was a foot march from the Cuirassier Barracks to the Breslau-Freiburg train station, from whence the regiment's component units were to be transported initially to the Neuhammer training facility. For the sake of secrecy, the time and date of this troop movement had not been publicly announced. But somehow the word had gotten around, and when the squadrons marched out of the compound gate, all the streets from there to the station were covered with people, despite the midnight hour. The inhabitants of Breslau gave their regiment—their *Kürassieren*—a touching farewell.

Beforehand, my comrade Christoph von Kospoth, as the oldest officer in the regiment, had made a gripping speech in the barracks square in front of the Great Elector's statue, during which he once again invoked the spirit of the old regiment. He said, "We'll take this spirit along with us, and it will light up every place we come to, no matter where!" For the regiment, whose future post was to be at Eisenach in Thuringia, this departure also marked its farewell to its Silesian home. Nobody dreamed that this farewell, and the words spoken on this occasion, would take on their final meaning a mere ten years later.[14]

The famous memorial statue of the Great Elector was transported by special train to Eisenach, where it was installed amid celebrations. But shortly before the war began it was moved once again, to the Silesian town of Sagan, because the traditions of the Life Guard Cuirassiers Regiment had been transferred to the 15th Panzer Regiment that had just been formed there.[15] Who would ever have thought that the statue that Kaiser Wilhelm I had presented to the officers of his guard regiment would endure such travels—only to vanish at last in the inferno of 1945?

The departure from my beloved regiment (which always remained my military "homeland") was infinitely hard for me. It meant physical separation from my best friends. On top of that, my reception in the new regiment was remarkably unfriendly. The commander in Brieg was a Colonel Faber du Faur from the state of Württemberg, who in the first place didn't want any Silesians, and in the second place, was furious that the personnel office in Berlin had ordered that I be made the trainer in the regimental racing stables.[16] When I first reported for duty he declared that he would give me neither a squadron nor the stables. But then he returned to his senses and surrendered, probably recognizing the uselessness of his complaints.

I took over the 1st Squadron from my year-group comrade Eduard Barth; in its esprit de corps, level of training, and all-around horsemanship, it was a model unit. In the racing stables I got the 8th Cavalry's own thoroughbreds and the horses that had come over from my old regiment and, in addition, a growing number of thoroughbreds that the officers of this regiment, who were passionately involved with equestrian sports, purchased on my recommendations. At any given time I was thus the trainer for a racing stable that housed some twenty-five horses. During the racing and tournament season, the stable operation naturally was switched to the racetrack in a Breslau suburb. That meant that in the small hours of the morning every day, including Sundays, I had to drive about fifty kilometers to Breslau with two or three lieutenants to supervise the racehorse training, and then be back at the garrison in Brieg in time for the opening of the service day. My alarm clock went off at 3:30 A.M. at the latest!

The officer corps of the 8th Cavalry was not as homogenous as that of my old regiment. This also had something to do with the fact that in the 7th Cavalry, with the exception of the well-to-do regimental commanders, all the officers had had similarly limited financial means, while in the 8th Cavalry, there were varying degrees of wealth. But I also felt very good in Brieg about our military activities and our camaraderie.

One thing was just like in Breslau: the general disdain for the Nazis and their methods. The chief of the horsemanship section, Major Baron Heinrich von Lüttwitz, put up with nothing from the party functionaries.[17] He fought fearlessly and effectively against the ever-increasing claims of the party "organs." He provided evidence of his anti-Nazi position later on during the war when, following 20 July 1944, he sent Robert Ley a formal protest against Ley's public statement concerning "the blue-blooded swine."[18]

Most of the young officers of the 8th Cavalry also held a critical attitude toward the regime. This went so far that, shortly before the war broke out, a number of the lieutenants staged a pistol-marksmanship contest inside the *Kasino,* with their target being the portrait of the "Leader" that hung there in accordance with regulations. At the end of all this, the painting—shot full of holes—was buried in the club garden. This incident, which did not remain a secret, cost the commanding officer his job. In view of the war that was about to commence, the lieutenants got off with relatively light punishments.

For me, the years between 1935 and 1937 were, in both the military and sporting senses, the last carefree times in my life. I could still enjoy in full measure my Silesia, with its social and cultural advantages, and all the enchantments of a cavalry soldier's life. We didn't see, and we probably also didn't wish to comprehend, that the end of this idyll had long since been ordained.

In 1937 there came a second turning point in my life. On the occasion of a formal dinner at the home of my uncle Baron Walther von Lüttwitz (the military commander of the Kapp Putsch), my wife was escorted into the dining room by the chief of staff of VIII Army Corps, Colonel in the General Staff Erich Marcks.[19] He asked her whether she wouldn't rather live in Berlin than in Brieg. When she innocently answered yes, he remarked that he had become irritated by my nonchalant attitude about taking the Wehrkreis-level examination for the *Kriegsakademie.* Therefore he would take pains to see that I attended the General Staff course at the *Kriegsakademie* in Berlin anyway.

Soon afterward, I was ordered to take part in a corps-level General Staff ride, in which all the staff officers of the divisions, headquarters, and other commands within VIII Army Corps's zone had to participate.[20] The "Initial Situation" that was sent to us before the beginning of the trip caused me some real terror; for naturally it dealt with strategic issues, while up until then I had only ever had to concern myself with tactical problems at the level of a reinforced regiment. I did a brief and "school-style" job on the "situational assessment and conclusion" that we needed to hand in before the exercise began, without getting into the assigned problem in much depth.

Before the staff ride began in Bunzlau, many General Staff officers— among whom was Rudolf Schmundt, Hitler's future army adjutant and officer personnel chief—told me that in dealing with Colonel Marcks, one always needed to have a "non-school-style" solution.[21] Therefore I was rather worried when I was the first man called on to present my assessment of the situation. Now my shame would be public. But Marcks announced after I had finished that in his opinion, and that of the commanding general, my solution was the only possible correct one.

At the very same time, my regiment was at the Neuhammer training facility. There my own squadron was to be reviewed by the inspector-general of the cavalry, General von Pogrell.[22] Because the date of this inspection (which could no longer be altered) coincided with the last day of the General Staff ride, my then-commander, Colonel Count Rudolf von Schmettow, attempted to get me released to my squadron ahead of time.[23] The corps headquarters rejected the proposal. Then my commander hit upon the idea of holding the inspection at night, by having me brought from Hirschberg (the last stop on the staff ride) in a fast car and then brought back to Hirschberg punctually the next morning.[24] I arrived at Neuhammer only half an hour before the inspection began, and had to get out of the car and ride at full gallop on my waiting horse to reach my squadron on time. The first agenda item was a difficult night tactical exercise, which I was fortunately able to manage satisfactorily. The squadron's formal mounted maneuvers, which in those days were still always the high point of an inspection, were reviewed in the early morning hours—it was already twilight. My squadron did so well here that Pogrell said in the critique session that he regretted that all the squadron commanders in his cavalry had not seen what was, in his opinion, the best of all.

After this triumph I went racing back to Hirschberg, where my people had fixed up a decent breakfast for me. I reached the Hotel Drei Berge at the very moment when Colonel Marcks and the General Staff officers were getting into the cars that would take them to the final session in the countryside. Rudolf Schmundt asked Marcks to grant me some time for breakfast. Marcks curtly rejected the request. So all I did was go from one car into another. During the ride out, Schmundt instructed me about the supplemental information that had been put out during my absence, and told me his own assessment of the situation in a summary fashion. As he and I had both anticipated, I was the first person that Marcks asked for an assessment. I responded with what Schmundt had just told me, more or less. That evening at the end of the General Staff ride, Marcks declared to me in thc presence of the corps commander, General von Kleist, that I had shown that even after an entire night in the saddle, I could still think reasonably well. As a result VIII Army Corps would advocate my assignment to the *Kriegsakademie.* It was probably a very rare thing for a line officer to come to the General Staff the way I did.

But first, in December 1937 I was transferred to Berlin to be the adjutant in Senior Cavalry Officer Department 1. This office supervised the equestrian training of all the units in Military Districts I (Königsberg), II (Stettin), III (Berlin), and VIII (Breslau). Together with my new boss, General Stumme, I saw in the course of our work almost every garrison in eastern Germany.[25] By this means I got a representative impression of the spirit and training level of what had become the newly organized Wehrmacht. Compared to the Reichswehr, the highly negative development of the new-style army was apparent everywhere. In contrast to the cavalry, which was dwindling in both numbers and strength, I could detect in the other army branches, which had tripled or quadrupled in size, only traces of the esprit de corps that had permeated the Reichswehr. The majority of the officers were reactivated reservists or former members of the state police; for the most part they were enthusiastic Nazis.

Inside the (often brand new) barracks and officers' clubs, tasteless busts or oil paintings of the "Leader" stared me in the face. (In my old *Kasino* in Breslau, we had succeeded in avoiding this type of thing until 1935.) The style and the manners of the officers no longer corresponded to the image of the old-regime Prussian officer that we had still preserved in the Reichswehr.

Even the level of troop training had altered greatly, and to its detriment, as a result of the overly rapid reorganization.

These negative impressions deepened when I started my assignment at the *Kriegsakademie.* I became the "elder" in a class of twenty-five captains, of whom only about one-third had Reichswehr backgrounds. All the others had come from the state police or were reserve officers called back to active duty. The tough classroom competition, which required the greatest possible diligence, allowed the divisions within the class to remain dormant—at first! But they emerged with utter clarity after *Kristallnacht* (the Night of Broken Glass).[26]

On 10 November 1938, the day after *Kristallnacht,* I came to the class-room later than usual, straight from training for a horse race. I walked into a very fierce discussion about this anti-Semitic "action," which had obviously been directed by the Nazi Party. I decided to make a statement in my role as class elder, and said something like the following: "In my opinion what happened last night is a disgrace to the German people. I am ashamed that something like this would be possible in my fatherland. We soldiers should hold ourselves strictly apart from such unbelievable events. I can only hope that justice will be done for the victims." Before the sluices could open for the infuriated responses, our class leader and tactics instructor, Major in the General Staff von Reuss, entered the room and said, "Gentlemen—I over-heard your elder's last words, and I am completely and utterly in agreement with him."[27] The discussion ended there, but from that day forward there was a split within the class that could never be bridged. Only about eight of the twenty-five men shared my opinions. During a field trip to Vienna we visited St. Stephan's Cathedral. One of the top Nazis in the class grew loudly upset about how the Catholic believers knelt down in front of the monstrance. I requested him to leave the cathedral.

The most depressing event I experienced was a few days before the march into Czechoslovakia, which occurred 15 March 1939. A large collection of officers from the *Kriegsakademie* were ordered to attend a reception and din-ner at the Reich Chancellery. As one of the oldest students I was part of this group, as was my 7th Cavalry comrade Baron von Wangenheim, the victor in the Olympic games. He and I were placed together at a large, round table; Adolf Hitler was also to be seated there. Naturally I was tense about meeting this man for the first time. While we sat around for a long while, the wait-ers, some of whom were former imperial footmen, noticed my name on the place-card and immediately asked me about my aunt and godmother Claire von Gersdorff, who had been the Empress's lady-in-waiting for so long.

Then Hitler appeared. After a curt greeting he sat down slouchingly in his chair, tugged nervously on his fingers, and was at first incapable of opening the conversation. Only after his military adjutant Schmundt, who had been delayed, made his appearance, recognized a situation that was becoming painful, and suggested to Hitler that he say something about the ongoing political problem of Czechoslovakia, was the man able to shake off his awkwardness. He now commenced a lengthy lecture about the Reich's relationship to Czechoslovakia, in the style I was familiar with from the radio; it was clear that neither responses nor questions were anticipated.

At the conclusion of his increasingly impassioned talk he said, almost word for word: "Czechoslovakia is a stake in Greater Germany's flesh. Therefore I have decided to put an end to this situation, which is unbearable in the long term." Then he whipped himself up about the strategic dangers that Czechoslovakia's geographical situation posed for his plans for a greater German Reich. Because of this, he would have to consider how to eliminate the existence of the Czech race within the greater German zone. When he had finished, he wiped the sweat from his brow, leaned forward on his elbows and noisily slurped up his vegetable soup. Then he left the table, without any conversation having ever begun.

The whole impression I got of Hitler was that of a repulsive, jumped-up proletarian. I had as little sense of greatness or significance as I had of any mystical influence. On the basis of his monstrous statements about the Czechs, I was more inclined to regard him as mentally abnormal. After we had risen from the dining table, Konrad von Wangenheim came over to me and said, "This fellow's completely crazy—he needs to be put in an insane asylum." But sadly, I had the feeling that all the others at our table had been impressed.

Soon after the dinner was over, Hitler left the Reich Chancellery. The officers from the *Kriegsakademie* were allowed to look at all the chambers in the building, which had recently been constructed by Albert Speer.[28] What struck me about Hitler's office were the sheer size of the room, the portrait of Bismarck by Lenfeld, and (standing all alone on his desk) a statuette of Frederick the Great, which was a copy of the memorial statue on Unter den Linden. The French ambassador, André Francois-Poncet, had presented Hitler with the statuette. Next there occurred a scene that was unforgettably repulsive: a great swarm of officers fell upon the green desk-blotter, tore it to pieces and tussled over shreds of the paper, wanting to take them away as souvenirs. I went home with several like-minded friends, depressed and feeling ill.

I took part in the occupation of Czechoslovakia in my mobilization assignment as 3rd Aide-de-Camp in the Ic/AO section of 5th Army Group headquarters (Vienna). The army group headquarters—the commander of the group was the future Field Marshal List—switched its location from Vienna to Brünn (Brno) in Czechoslovakia for about a week. I did not get to see much of the occupied country, with the exception of this city. What has stayed in my mind is the glum resignation that had overcome its entire population. The people of Brünn paid us scarcely any attention, and we made an effort to walk around outside as little as possible. There were no protests or acts of resistance worthy of mention. What struck me particularly was the unhappy role that had been forced upon the Czech soldiers. While one army unit's horses were being led through the streets of Brünn on their way to the freight station, probably for shipment to Germany, the same unit's officers were sitting in full uniform in a café in the city, mocking their faithful four-legged friends with a kind of gallows humor. The whole effect was macabre and unpleasant.

I was in Vienna again during the last days before the war broke out. The staff of 5th Army Group, now renamed as 14th Army, was supposed to conduct the operations of the right wing of the German attack on Poland. One night while I was working in our headquarters building on the Stubenring, General Alfred Jodl walked into my office.[29] As far as I can recall, he was returning from leave and wanted to make a telephone call to the War Ministry in Berlin while en route. As he waited for the telephone connection, he talked with me about the threatening military and political situation. In the course of our conversation he asserted himself critically, almost disparagingly, about the political leadership. But mostly he lamented having to take up such a responsible position in the *Oberkommando der Wehrmacht* (OKW; Supreme Command of the Armed Forces). According to him, he would much rather have taken command of a line unit.

At the time he gave me the impression of a "just-a-soldier" type, almost frightened of the political responsibilities that awaited him in his position in OKW. Six years later I would see him again, this time as one of the principal defendants in the Nuremberg war crimes trial. I do not deny the guilt that Jodl earned for himself during the war years, owing to his pliability and his weakness towards Hitler and Keitel. But he was obviously only a soldier who in his position at OKW had been handed more than he was able to deal with in both personal and political terms. I therefore believe that in contrast to all the other death sentences, his was unjustified.

The mood in what was now 14th Army headquarters was serious and downcast. Up until the last moment (but above all after the postponement of the attack caused by Mussolini's intervention) every man hoped that it would still not come to war. I was unable to detect any kind of enthusiasm for war in this higher staff.

The attack by 14th Army, situated on the German right wing, did not encounter strong Polish resistance anywhere. After only two days we relocated the command post from Vienna to Krakow, and then later to Rzeczow.

One of the most interesting experiences of my work in the intelligence section came about in this fashion: on the fifth or sixth day of the campaign I got a telephone call from my former commander in the 1st Squadron of the 7th Cavalry, Heinrich von Hülsen.[30] He was now the commander of his division's reconnaissance section, and he was calling from his own command post. His people had taken captive the chief of staff of the Polish "South Army," General von Morawski.[31] Hülsen said that this man had been his own battalion commander in the 4th Guards Infantry Regiment at the end of World War I. He had passed him along to the staff of XVII Army Corps, and I could take him from there.

After this I traveled by car to Lanczut, where the corps staff had halted at the castle of Count Potocki.[32] Once inside this almost fairy-tale palace, I was conducted to the dining hall. There, sitting at one long table, were the corps commanding general, his chief of staff, other General Staff officers, the host, and the captured Polish general, all eating lunch together. The last-named individual was seated next to the lady of the house, while his German escort officer had been placed at the low end of the table. The chief of staff of XVII Army Corps, Colonel in the General Staff Rendulic, who had come into the German army from the Austrian *Bundesheer* (federal army), was on terms of intimate friendship with the Polish general, and showed himself to be very concerned about his well-being.[33] Only after the meal had ended, and coffee and cognac had been served around, was the prisoner of war handed over to me for transportation to the army headquarters.

Morawski had been a Royal Prussian Army lieutenant in the Life Guard Cuirassiers prior to World War I, and then during the conflict he had been assigned to the Guards infantry. His sister Countess Pivnicka was a friend of my parents. He described himself to me as a good friend of my father's brother, Rudolf von Gersdorff. During the first few days of this war, the Poles had arrested this uncle of mine at his estate of Parsko in the former province of Posen. During a long march towards the east, he had been gunned down by a Polish lieutenant. When I told Morawski about this, he was deeply shocked. He severely criticized his own countrymen and declared that a country where such a thing could happen would justly go under. Then, during his formal interrogation at Krakow, he readily answered every question he was asked. In view of the military situation, one could hardly be critical of him for doing so.

Before being transported to a prisoner of war camp, Morawski asked me to return a leather purse containing a quantity of very valuable diamond stars to his friend Count Potocki. According to him, Potocki had given him the jewelry so that he would not be without financial means in captivity; but he had learned in the meantime that he could have money sent to himself from

his bank in Warsaw. I took on this task most unhappily, and drove to Lanczut again the very next day in order to get rid of these gems (whose value I
assessed as being at least 50,000 Reichsmarks) as quickly as possible. But
Count Potocki declared to me that the jewelry didn't belong to him; that he
had never seen it before; and that he refused to accept it.

Now for the first and last time I had to play the occupation officer. In the
presence of my escort officer, I compelled the count to take the jewelry into
his possession and give me a receipt for it. I never heard anything else about
the matter, and to this day I don't know to whom the mysterious gems really
belonged. Either Potocki—who on the one hand represented himself to be
one of Goering's hunting companions, and who on the other hand, as a Polish
patriot, both concealed and gave provisions to Polish soldiers on the run—
wanted to protect himself; or else these were Morawski family jewels that the
Polish general wanted to safeguard by this means.

When I then asked Potocki to receive in his palace a group of about 100 to
150 ethnic Germans from Lemburg (Lvov), who had fled before the advancing Soviets, he initially refused again. In doing so, he referred to purported
assurances from Goering that his palace, together with its enormous and
especially beautiful park, would be safeguarded from potential military operations. I explained to him that Goering was by no means in command here;
therefore, he would preferably agree voluntarily, rather than be forced to take
in these refugee families. Since all of the estate's cattle had been requisitioned
to feed the thousands of Polish prisoners of war, Potocki gave me a hunting
rifle, and together within an hour we had shot so many pheasants that at least
the initial provisions for the refugees were assured.

One event during the Polish campaign provided a clear hint of the crimes
that were yet to come. Without ever having requested it, 14th Army had been
assigned a sizable SS detachment under the command of the head of the SS
in Silesia, Udo von Woyrsch. He was given the mission to comb through the
villages and forests behind the fighting troops in search of Polish soldiers
who had been overrun, and to deliver them to prisoner of war camps. We were
quickly realized that the SS unit was by no means on the trail of dispersed
soldiers, but was instead arresting Jewish civilians and, to some extent, shooting them. The army command reacted with an energy and swiftness that still
went without saying at the time. The army commander, Colonel General List,
demanded the SS detachment's immediate withdrawal and the punishment of
the guilty parties. At least the first item was completely accomplished.[34]

Shortly after the Polish campaign, the staff of my army (now renum-
bered again, this time as 12th Army) was transferred to the Western Front,
to the town of Mayen in the Eifel. Here the splits within the high command
concerning the further prosecution of the war emerged in their full clarity.

The *Oberkommando des Heeres* (OKH; Army High Command)—meaning Brauchitsch and Halder—in opposition to Hitler and OKW, maintained that the German combat forces, given the status of their training and equipment, were not yet in a position to undertake an offensive war against the western Allies with the prospect of success.[35] In connection with this, OKH dispatched General Staff officers who were assigned to report on the morale of the troops and the commanders' assessments of the situation, all in order to assemble counterarguments against Hitler's intention of attacking France, Belgium and Holland as quickly as possible.

By order of my army commander, I escorted Captain in the General Staff von Pezold, who had been sent to 12th Army on this assignment, to all of the army's subordinate corps and divisions, so that I would be able to learn the result of these inquiries at first hand.[36] The reports that had already been delivered (in the most open and vociferous fashion) by senior and junior commanders and their General Staff officers were overwhelmingly confirmed by every corps and division staff that we visited. Among the troops there was also no enthusiasm of any kind for war, even after the victory over Poland that had been won in such a short time. Training and equipment were both inadequate for a grand offensive in the west. Everyone who was asked warned expressly of the consequences that must follow from asking the troops to do too much. Many people at this time were of the opinion that an attack would lead to a catastrophic defeat.

On 1 November 1939, I was reassigned as 3rd General Staff Officer (Ic/AO) for XII Army Corps, which with its component divisions occupied the section of the West Wall on both sides of Saarbrücken. Here I could directly confirm the justice of the troop commanders' assessments of the situation regarding our human and material resources.

Shortly before Christmas, the corps received an order to prevent any encounter within its area of operations between Hitler and the chief of OKH, Colonel General von Brauchitsch. One man was traveling along the Western Front from north to south, the other one from south to north. Due to their respective schedules, there was a possibility that the two antagonists might run into one another in or near Saarbrücken. The order to absolutely forestall any such meeting obviously represented a nadir in the relationship between Hitler and OKH.

While with XII Army Corps I saw how imperfect a thing was the West Wall, so highly touted in our propaganda. Even here it was still far from ready, and above all else it was insufficiently armed and manned, although the construction and fortification work in the Saarbrücken sector had been carried out on a preferential basis. Altogether the West Wall at this time was nothing but a successful bluff.

A few days before the start of the French campaign, on 10 May 1940, I was assigned to be 1st General Staff Officer (Ia) in the 86th Infantry Division, a second-wave assault division that had just concluded its initial formation and training at the Grafenwöhr training facility. On 10 May, I had to report in Coblenz to the Ia of "Army Group Rundstedt," Colonel in the General Staff Blumentritt, in order to be briefed on the mission of my new division.[37]

In the Ia's anteroom I met the man who would decisively affect the whole rest of my life: Henning von Tresckow, a General Staff major at the time.[38] I was immediately impressed by the sheer force of his personality. One could avoid his gaze just as little as his clearly stated questions. When he wanted to know just what I thought about the upcoming campaign against France, I told him in plain language that I foresaw an unbearable risk in undertaking such a grand offensive with such unready troops. On purely military grounds, Tresckow appeared to be of a different opinion; but from his words I detected that he had grave concerns about Germany's political future.

In any case I was deeply impressed by our relatively brief conversation, because I instinctively realized that I had spoken with a man who combined an outstanding intelligence with an elevated sense of responsibility, a great love for the fatherland, and the Prussian spirit. From that very first moment on, he incarnated for me the type of man who compelled my respect and my trust, both from his resemblance to my father and from his own entire demeanor. When, at the end of our discussion, he asked me without any pre-liminaries whether I would be prepared to work with him someday when he could use me, I answered "yes" without hesitating. I did not suspect that with those words an alliance had been formed both in life and death.

During the Polish campaign, I had merely received my baptism of fire during numerous visits to the front. In the course of the French campaign I really became acquainted with warfare. Two situations have remained in my memory with particular clarity.

In the early hours of 9 June 1940, my division was set to attack across the Aisne River near Rethel (in 12th Army's area of operations), in order to open up a breach for General Guderian's waiting Panzer units to penetrate the French lines and reach the open country.[39] We knew that strong French forces in prepared defenses were somewhere to our front. But we knew neither the axis of their main line of defense nor the strong point of their artillery emplace-ments. Both intensive reconnaissance and a long, effective, preparatory bar-rage had been prohibited by Hitler's express command, so as not to jeopardize the surprise-effect of our own attack. This proved to be a capital error, how-ever. The attack in our division's sector was especially tough, because due to a partition, or rather canalization, of the Aisne, there were practically two rivers to cross instead of one. On the basis of passive observation, we believed that the French main line of defense lay on the tongue of land between the two streams, an assumption that later proved to be false.

At first our attack went in without a sound. It immediately triggered the heaviest possible defensive fire from artillery and machine guns, but our own artillery could not adequately respond since (due to the lack of reconnaissance) it had no registered targets. Nevertheless, our infantry succeeded in getting across the first branch of the river and reaching the spit of land in the middle—but from that point any further advance was impossible. The French troops fought extremely well. Once again it was shown that next to the German soldier, there was no better fighter in the world than the French *poilu*. We suffered heavy casualties, particularly among the officers, so that the situation became more and more critical.

When I went up front with a single aide-de-camp in order to get a personal impression of the situation, we were met on the left wing of the division sector by swarms of soldiers from the infantry regiment on that side. Some had thrown away their weapons, and all displayed every sign of panic. Their officers and NCOs had all remained at the front line. With our pistols drawn, my aide Count Merveldt and I put ourselves in the way of the backward-flowing clusters of men.[40] Then we spoke to them as if to children, and made it clear that the artillery barrage was even heavier to our rear. We were successful in turning most of the soldiers around again and moving them back to their positions. I had no doubt that any further attack from this location would be both impracticable and senseless.

Next we proceeded through heavy fire to the regiment on the right wing, which was composed of troops from Westphalia. Here there were no signs of disintegration, in spite of their heavy losses. But to me it only appeared possible to continue with our attack if our third regiment, which was being held in reserve, were to be sent in at this location. With the intention of presenting this idea to the division commander, I returned to the division's forward command post. There they had just received word that everything had gone better in the neighboring division's sector, and that Guderian's armored units had already gone into action on that part of the front. After their breakthrough, the entire French line gave way. The French had to abandon their positions in front of our division as well. I do believe to this day that without Hitler's stupid order to limit reconnaissance and preparatory fire to the slightest possible amount, much blood would have been spared.

After the breakthrough on the Aisne, all that most of the division needed to do was keep marching forward. A powerful vanguard detachment, consisting of our reconnaissance battalion and several mechanized infantry companies and artillery batteries, fought twenty or thirty kilometers out in front of the bulk of the division.

One day while on my way up from the division to this advance force, I drove over a battlefield on which, several hours earlier, French spahi cavalry—all of whom had been mounted on white Arabian or Berber horses—had attacked our machine guns.[41] The fallen spahis and the white carcasses of their noble steeds still lay everywhere. An especially beautiful and noble Arabian without a rider walked along the road in my direction, its head hanging down and its reins trailing on the ground. One could tell from the saddle and bridle that this was the horse of a dead or wounded officer. As an enthusiastic horseman and cavalryman, I was very deeply affected by the horrific sight of this battlefield. I would have preferred to stay there, to search for wounded men and gather up the many horses that were running all about. Nevertheless, I had to keep on going. Suddenly, I heard over my vehicle radio that the French head of state, Marshal Pétain, had asked for negotiations, and that a ceasefire order could be reckoned on within a short time.[42]

But then when I reached our vanguard, its artillery was still firing away with every barrel. The adjutant, First Lieutenant Baron Phillip von Boeselager, told me that the force had run into strong resistance and as a result it needed to get things ready for a systematic attack.[43]

I ordered the artillery barrage to cease immediately, and decided to drive over to the French side as a negotiator, in order to bring about the cessation of military operations in light of the latest news. With the utmost speed a white bedsheet was stretched across the hood of my auto, and a white French nightshirt was fastened to a broomstick. Then a soldier volunteered for the mission, too, telling us that as a former huntsman he could blow signals on an old French trumpet. Boeselager attached himself to me. In his youthful enthusiasm, he brought along several bottles of champagne to toast the ceasefire with the Frenchmen. I also had a captive French officer, who promised to vouch for the honorable nature of our proposal and ride along with us as an interpreter.

We drove in the direction of the French front line, using extreme caution since we had to reckon at every moment with land mines that might have been laid on the road. At first we came into a completely shot-up village, which the French troops had already vacated. Civilians crept up out of the cellars; they burst into tears when we shared the news of the war's approaching end. We drove cautiously onward. With all the power in his body, the trumpeter blew every horn signal he knew: "Stag Dead," "Fox Dead," "Hunt Over," "Greetings to the Prince," and so on.

All at once we were surrounded by the French. I requested them to ask the most senior officer they could find to come to us. After a short while, there appeared a splendid-looking French colonel. He halted ten paces away from me. We saluted one another. Then I said to him that after Marshal Pétain's proposal of a ceasefire, it seemed to me to be my primary duty to avoid all possible further bloodshed. I offered him an honorable capitulation. He explained to me that he knew nothing about any ceasefire request, and appealed to me, on the basis on my own honor as an officer, to understand that he had to carry out his orders to hold the position. I replied that I had enormous respect for his attitude, but that I begged him, in view of the hopelessness of the position in which his troops found themselves, to accept my offer. In a short time, an entire division would be standing by to assault his position. However, he refused again. Therefore I asked him to seek instructions from his higher headquarters. I granted him two hours' time for this. If he had not come to our lines by then, we would attack. We parted from one another with every military courtesy. The champagne remained untasted, and back we drove.

I told Boeselager that I had to leave immediately to tell my division commander what had gone on, and asked him to be responsible for preserving the grace period that the French had been granted. While I was on my way to the division commander, the commanding officer of the division's leading infantry regiment appeared at the vanguard's command post. Boeselager reported to him about the military situation and the negotiations with the French. The colonel nonetheless declared that he would go on the attack with his regiment immediately. When he was still unwilling to alter his decision even after Boeselager had remonstrated with him several times, this young man drew his pistol, pointed it at the colonel's chest, and told him in no uncertain terms that if need be he would use his weapon to insure that the word of a German officer was upheld. The regimental commander was so impressed by this conduct on the part of the scarcely-twenty-year-old lieutenant that he pronounced his approval of it.

When the grace period had expired and no Frenchman had reported to us, the attack went on according to plan. The French positions were taken with almost no resistance. The French colonel with whom I had parleyed was found dead in the village street. He had obviously taken his own life.

This incident shows how, despite war and battle, chivalry had not yet died out during the campaign in France. But above all it shows how a young lieutenant with a lot of character can even prevail over a high-ranking officer, if his conscience and his sense of responsibility drive him on.

From September 1940, my division was stationed on the demarcation line between occupied and unoccupied France. We were in the neighborhood of Bourges and Orléans. The division staff was billeted in a very pretty château. When I arrived at the place to accept the handover from a Württemberg division and I asked about the owner of the château, the division Ia explained to me that for security reasons he had housed the young count and his wife in a horse stall. Without waiting for my division commander's opinion, I immediately had the château owner, who had just been discharged from the French army, and his wife, who was expecting her first child, removed from the horse stall; and then arrived at a solution by means of which we could all share the château without disturbing each other. He was very grateful to me that his first son could be born within the château of his forefathers. With few exceptions, we exerted ourselves in those days to deal with the whole population not like victors and oppressors, but like gentlemen. I could give many other examples of this. Despite all personal distance, there was thus a good relationship between the Wehrmacht and the French population, one which—in contrast to the French people's relationship with Nazi Party officialdom and the SS—is still acknowledged as having been such.

One day my division commander received an order to pick up Marshal Pétain and his Minister-President Pierre Laval at the demarcation line in our sector and escort them to Tours.[44] They were both coming from Vichy. It all had to do with the historic meeting between Pétain and Hitler on 24 October 1940. We received the French statesmen with full military honors. At the marshal's desire, he and my division commander rode in the marshal's car, while Laval rode with me in my commander's car. Laval was very pleased with this arrangement, because now he could finally have a smoke. He appeared to be convinced that the meeting with Hitler would bring about the final reconciliation between France and Germany. He dreamed aloud of a Europe under joint German and French leadership; and during the journey, which took hours, he enthused about the resulting political possibilities. My division commander later told me that Pétain had been not nearly as optimistic, and had expressed his grave reservations. The dignity that the French head of state radiated deeply impressed me.

In the middle of April 1941, I was reassigned to the staff of Army Group Center as 3rd General Staff Officer (Ic/AO). Tresckow was the 1st General Staff Officer (Ia) there. Obviously, in putting together his command section he had recalled our conversation in Coblenz the day before the beginning of the French campaign, and had got me put on his staff through his good connections with the army's officer personnel chief, General Schmundt. (They had been fellow-lieutenants in the Reichswehr 9th Infantry Regiment in Potsdam.)

An automobile belonging to the Army Group, which had carried my successor as Ia of the 86th Division (Major in the General Staff von der Groeben) to Bourges, was now at my disposal for the journey to the Army Group headquarters in Posen by way of Berlin.[45] During the ride to Germany, I made a stop in Nancy in order to visit my 7th Cavalry regimental comrade Friedrich-Wilhelm von Mellenthin.[46] As we rode around the Nancy racetrack on French thoroughbreds, Mellenthin confided to me that Hitler had decided to attack Russia.

I felt as if someone had struck me on the head. In contrast to Mellenthin's optimistic attitude, I immediately had a bad feeling. My very first thoughts were of 1812 and Napoleon. I also knew all I needed to know about the immense human and material resources that the Soviet Union could draw upon. It was likewise plain to me that by starting a war in the east we would get into the same two-front situation that we had faced in World War I.

I was also afraid that Hitler would inject himself into strategic planning more and more, due to his having been proved right against the generals by the victory over France. It was here in France that Hitler's reputation as a war leader had really been established; yet even in this campaign he had already made enormous errors in command, as a consequence of which the British were still secure on their island, with their fighting strength still unbroken. Hitler's interloping into military command during the battle of Dunkirk had led directly to the escape of the mass of the British forces. Apart from that, at the end of May 1940 I had personally experienced how the 12th Army was abruptly halted and had to establish a front facing to the south, by Hitler's personal order; because he had been worried, more or less baselessly, that the left flank of the German advance was too threatened. Specially appointed General Staff officers were sometimes needed to compel the performance of "Führer Orders," because the line commanders and troops simply could not comprehend the instructions they had been given. (Later on during the Russian campaign we would frequently observe Hitler's sensitivity about flanks.)

I was able to pause in Berlin for two days to see my family again. My wife told me about the harassment of Jews that she had witnessed in the streets of Berlin. She was deeply shocked. She asked me for the first time why the army hadn't done anything to put a stop to the ever-more open crimes of the Nazis.

In my various assignments up to that point, I had only been able to mount a resistance against the overreaching of low-level, individual Nazis. I could affect the big picture as little as anybody else could. It was clear to me that I couldn't come to grips with them alone. Where were the men in responsible positions who were determined to take action?

Deep in such thoughts, I rode onward to Posen—to meet my destiny.

IV

Soldier in the Resistance

A man must either resist, or else turn himself into an accomplice.
—Ignazio Silone (1900–1978)

After my arrival at Posen on 20 April 1941, I reported to the man who would be my immediate superior from then on: Henning von Tresckow. Once again, just as during our initial encounter in Coblenz, I was immediately impressed not only by his personality, but also by his charm and personal magnetism. Even during this first meeting in my new post, I sensed the powerful authority that Tresckow radiated. I had the feeling that I either had to surrender myself to his leadership, or see about getting a transfer out as quickly as possible. This man would never have tolerated a compromise. But even without my knowing Tresckow any better than I did at that time, he always gave me the sense of his utter nobility and his tremendous strength of character. As a result I never hesitated for a moment to subject myself to his authority.

During this first meeting, Tresckow told me without delay that I would soon learn that the Army Group staff was run in a certain style. He expected me to trust him completely and to be completely open with him. Depending on how the Ic/AO section was managed, it could be worth absolutely nothing or worth a very great deal. He hoped for the latter from me.

That same day, Tresckow sent me to see his closest colleague, Berndt von Kleist, who was an important member of the command staff as the O-4, but who was impressive above all else as a career soldier and the "master of all he surveyed." Kleist—who, like Tresckow, was a former member of the imperial 1st Guards Infantry Regiment—received me with great kindness, if rather like a reigning monarch. He was the "rock of bronze" on the Army Group staff, occupying a completely unique position there, owing to his powerful personality and his flawless character.[1]

It was soon apparent to me that Tresckow's aide-de-camp, Lieutenant Fabian von Schlabrendorff, also occupied a unique position. He had been

Tresckow's closest confidant since the summer of 1939. He played the role of a counselor, and even of a participant, in the making of the tough decisions that led first to active resistance and then to the preparation of assassination attempts and plans for a coup d'état.[2] Tresckow's leading role was incontestable, however, while Schlabrendorff, for his part, used his many domestic and foreign connections to build up the resistance organization at home and abroad. We other men were not made privy to these mysteries at first, for Schlabrendorff was probably the most close-mouthed conspirator of them all. He revealed himself to those who felt the same way he did only by means of ironic remarks and merciless sarcasm. Tresckow, Schlabrendorff, and Kleist formed the nucleus of the resistance organization that came together within the command section of the Army Group.

The commanding officer of Army Group Center, Field Marshal Fedor von Bock, was a cousin of Tresckow's.[3] From his outward appearance alone, Bock cut an impressive figure. During the campaign in Russia, I also had the opportunity to become acquainted with the marshal's strategic abilities. I do not hesitate to grant that as a military commander, he was brilliant. More than once I witnessed how in some almost hopeless situation, when none of his advisors knew what to propose, he would state the only correct solution with just a few words. In doing so he would seem almost sympathetic toward those who were unable to strategize and make decisions as rapidly and as clearly as he could. At such times, a surplus of vanity and arrogance became apparent in him, traits which darken his portrait. Tresckow recognized his close relation's genius as a military strategist, but increasingly turned away from him because of the weakness of Bock's character: despite his internal opposition to the National Socialist regime, he never once dared to take an uncompromising stand against Hitler.

Within my Ic/AO section, I found my deputy chief (O-3), Reserve Major Schach von Wittenau, to be a thoroughly clever and pleasant man. We very quickly established that we were as one in our fundamental views, and above all in our political opinions. He disapproved of Hitler and National Socialism as doggedly as I did, so that we never needed to be cautious with one another. When he had to leave the front in 1942 due to a steadily worsening heart condition, I had the good luck to find in his successor, Reserve Major Baron Andreas von Knigge, a colleague who was similarly one with me in his political opinions and other basic beliefs. Among the other officers of my section, another aide-de-camp (O-6), Reserve First Lieutenant Conrad, particularly caught my eye. He was extremely intelligent, as decent as the day is long, open and honorable. To say the least, he was very critical toward the ruling regime. And where our military duties were concerned, he would develop into one of my most valuable colleagues.[4]

A counterintelligence team from OKW's office of foreign counterintelligence (*Amt Ausland/Abwehr*) had been attached and subordinated to the Ic/AO section. Like that department, which played an important role at OKW under the leadership of Admiral Canaris, this local group was divided into three sub-groups: *Abwehr I* (Intelligence Procurement), *Abwehr II* (Sabotage), and *Abwehr III* (Security and Counterespionage). Among this group's numerous officers, *Abwehr I*'s chief, Colonel Herrlitz, stood out as an especially reliable and sympathetic colleague. He eased my introduction to what was, for me, completely new territory.

I had already gotten to know the great "gray eminence," Admiral Canaris, during the Polish campaign. Without many words having been spoken (which was in keeping with his personality), a mutual sympathy grew up between us that lasted until his tragic end. He always showed complete faith in me, and expected my absolute frankness in turn. The same was true of his closest colleague, Colonel in the General Staff Hans Oster.[5]

Including the *Flugverbindungsoffizier* ("Flivo"; air liaison officer), the interpreters, the officers in charge of troop political indoctrination, and so on, the Ic/AO section had about thirty officers and *Sonderführer* (specialist leaders in various subjects), so that for the first time I was in charge of a big "department" that combined a wide variety of activities. It goes without saying that the mission of producing intelligence about hostile forces had the top priority.

I got my first important assignment on 10 May 1941, when Field Marshal von Bock sent me to Berlin in his airplane in order to uncover the background to Rudolf Hess's sensational flight to England. In OKW and OKH, I ran into either total ignorance or a wall of silence. Not until I tried a good connection in the Foreign Office did I succeed in getting the necessary information: plainly, nobody in the political and military leadership, including the Führer, had reckoned on such an impulsive act by the Deputy Führer. It could be said with real certainty that all suspicions of some possible tacit approval of Hess's adventurous decision by Hitler, or by any other authority, were false. High anxiety and bewilderment were the rule among those in responsible positions. Everyone had hoped to the last that Hess's solo flight would end up by crashing into the sea, and therefore that Hess would never reach England. Only the famous Luftwaffe general Ernst Udet had credited Hess with having enough flying ability to potentially reach England or some other destination. (Studies have shown that Hess had made his decision while in contact with Albrecht Haushofer and that gentleman's father, but that he had let no one else in on the secret.)[6]

My next interesting experience was a conference hosted by the OKH Quartermaster General in Zossen, which I was assigned to attend along with the Army Group's Ib, Major in the General Staff Günther Gericke.[7] To our amazement, a large quantity of high-ranking SS officers took part in the conference. In the course of general preparations for the Russian campaign in the area of technical logistical issues, the Ia of the Quartermaster General's office, Major in the General Staff Schmidt von Altenstadt, announced that so-called *SS-Einsatzgruppen* (task forces) would perform special missions within the operational areas of the army groups.[8] These *Einsatzgruppen* would not be subordinate to the military commanders, but would only be assigned to us for logistical purposes, and under general instructions to cooperate with us. The senior military commanders would have the right to require the withdrawal of the *SS-Einsatzgruppen* from their operational areas, if they "disturbed the operations of military units." We received only vague explanations about the tasks of the *Einsatzgruppen.* They were summed up, in a general way, as police-type missions for security and order. The word "Jew" was never once pronounced during the meeting. However, we immediately suspected that these *Einsatzgruppen* could also be employed for "actions" against the numerous Jews in western Russia.

Einsatzgruppe B was to be assigned to Army Group Center's area of operations, under the command of an *Oberführer* [an SS rank roughly equivalent to "senior colonel"] whose name escapes me. When I reported this to Tresckow after my return to the Army Group, he immediately got in touch with every possible authority to get Arthur Nebe, the director of the *Reichskriminalamt* [the national police center for crime detection and criminology] and also an *Oberführer* in the SS, named to command *Einsatzgruppe B* instead.[9] Tresckow knew Nebe as a determined opponent of the Nazi regime, as a police criminologist with an international reputation, and as a decent man. Therefore he was very pleased when his efforts proved successful. Next he assigned me to permanently maintain the closest possible connections with Nebe and his staff; and, as far as possible, to find out about everything that happened or was supposed to happen with the *Einsatzgruppe.* These precautionary measures (which were omitted in Army Group North and Army Group South) proved themselves to be very useful, even if they could not prevent every crime.

Another assignment, this time to a war game in Brussels in furtherance of the teaming of Army Group Center with *Luftflotte 2* (Air Fleet 2) of the Luftwaffe, is only worthy of mention because it was my opportunity to encounter for the first and—God be praised!—last time the almost grotesque extravagance and high living of the air force. Each of the three officers from Army Group Center who had been ordered to attend the war game was assigned two automobiles, as well as a purser and one or two "Blitz Girls," who picked us up as soon as we had landed at the Brussels airport.[10] We received unlimited foreign exchange notes and clothing-ration cards. It was plainly expected that we would buy all the fabric, jewelry, and furs that we could use. I was regarded as a lunatic for turning down all the currency and the ration cards and only taking a per diem allowance. Our accommodations and meals, in what was at the time the finest hotel in Brussels, were more luxurious than anything I had ever experienced before.

On the occasion of a gourmet farewell dinner in the Taverne Royale restaurant, Kesselring asked me how I had liked the meal.[11] I answered guardedly, but could not deny that it had all been exquisite. To which the field marshal replied, "Well, now, get a load of this—*Reichsmarschall* Goering just said to me, 'Kesselring, I'm not coming around to see you any more; the food's not good enough! It's a whole lot better at Sperrle's place, and at Richthofen's'."[12] Once more it was clear to me that the Prussian virtues were dead. When I confided this to the man seated next to me, the fighter pilot Colonel Mölders, who was later the victim of a mysterious airplane crash, he understood me completely, but he was the only one.[13]

By far my most significant experience during those weeks before the commencement of the Russian campaign took place at the beginning of June 1941.

One day there were two orders lying on my desk (copies, sent only for informational purposes): the order to limit the jurisdiction of military courts-martial, and the so-called *Kommissarbefehl* or "Commissar Order." The first order provided that Wehrmacht soldiers who committed crimes against the civilian population in Russia would not be automatically court-martialed and sentenced, as had been the practice up until then. The prosecution of this sort of crime, which was also supposed to be punished in accordance with international law, was left instead to the discretion of the responsible court-martial convening authority—of a division commander, for example. The commander could choose to do absolutely nothing, or could merely issue an administrative punishment; particularly when the case involved a battle-tested and, if possible, a decorated soldier. In practical terms this order meant that it was open season on the Russian people, who were no longer protected from murder, robbery, or rape. But the Commissar Order explicitly decreed that all political commissars of the Soviet armed forces who fell into German captivity were to be singled out and on the order of any officer invested with disciplinary authority, such as a line-unit captain or lieutenant, immediately shot without trial.

I did not know at the time that these unambiguously criminal orders went back to the special guidelines that Hitler had presented orally to the senior commanders of the three components of the Wehrmacht, when they had all gathered at the Reich Chancellery on 30 March 1941. These "Guidelines for Special Areas," which also dealt with the projected use of the *Einsatzgruppen* and the "Night and Fog Decree," had been heard out by the senior commanders without any open protest.[14] Afterwards, however, OKW and OKH had attempted unsuccessfully to either weaken Hitler's directives or, at least, to not let them be put in writing. The commander-in-chief of the army, Field Marshal von Brauchitsch, and his chief of the General Staff, Colonel General Halder, had particularly exerted themselves to this end. When they remained unsuccessful, OKH promulgated an order (on 24 May 1941) for the "preservation of military discipline"; it was intended to combat the effects of the criminal orders.

Even without knowing any of this background, I was immediately conscious of the monstrosity of these orders. For the first time the Wehrmacht had been expressly commanded to commit crimes, although Hitler, in his earlier addresses to the army generals, had always emphasized that he would never require such things of the soldiers.

I went to Tresckow, but we were both aware that we could have no further influence on the transmission of the orders to the troops, since the Quartermaster General's office had already distributed them to the armies and army corps assigned to Army Group Center. Tresckow got on the telephone with the adjoining army groups, North and South, and also ordered that our commander's personal aircraft be made ready for departure. Then we walked over to see the field marshal, who lived in a small villa only a few hundred meters away from the staff building.

On our way there we passed through a narrow little park. Suddenly Tresckow stood still and said to me: "Gersdorff, if we don't succeed in getting the field marshal to fly to Hitler immediately and compel the reversal of these orders, *then the German people will bear such blame that the world will not forget this about us for hundreds of years.* This blame will be placed not only on Hitler, Himmler, Goering, and their party comrades, but also, and just as much, on you and me, on your wife and my wife, on your children and my children, on that old lady who's walking into the shop across the way, the man riding past us on the bicycle, and the child playing over there with his ball. Think about what I've just said."

I was struck by these words, which he spoke with such deep earnestness; however, I must admit that it was only later that I understood them in their full significance. But I never forgot them, and even now it is as though I heard them only yesterday.

Field Marshal von Bock, who as a participant in the 30 March 1941, senior commanders' conference in the Reich Chancellery, really must have anticipated orders of this kind, acted highly astonished when I began my presentation. He tore the documents from my hands and read them himself. Then he pounded the table with his fist several times while exclaiming, "This is truly unbelievable! This is absolutely frightful!" At any rate, he also seemed to clearly recognize that we were dealing with commands of a criminal nature.

"Now what can we do about it?" asked Bock.

Tresckow answered, "Fedi, I've had your airplane prepared for takeoff. You'll have to fly to Hitler immediately. Not alone, though, but along with Rundstedt and Leeb [the commanders, respectively, of Army Group South and Army Group North].[15] You have to point a gun at his chest and secure the immediate reversal of these orders. Hitler has broken his word to you. If you threaten to resign, he'll have to give in." Then Bock asked, "And what if he throws us out?" Tresckow replied, "Then at least you'll have made a decent exit in the eyes of history." To this, Bock responded, "Hitler will send you Himmler as my successor." "We'd soon be done with him," replied Tresckow.

Then Bock had us wait in his anteroom, where his aides-de-camp were seated: Count Carl-Hans von Hardenberg and Count Heinrich von Lehndorff, both of whom had long since made up their own minds in favor of resistance.[16] All four of us heard the field marshal pacing rapidly back and forth in his office. Then he called Tresckow and me back in.

"Gersdorff," he said to me, "get aboard my airplane right away, and fly to OKH. Once you're there go to General Eugen Müller, and tell him that Field Marshal von Bock has lodged the severest objection to these orders, and desires that they be countermanded immediately.[17] If Müller can't say yes to that, then ask for a meeting with the commander-in-chief of the army, Field Marshal von Brauchitsch, in my name and as my personal representative."

When Tresckow agitatedly exclaimed, "But Fedi, there's no point in all that. What exactly can General Müller say to Gersdorff? You need to go to Hitler yourself—and right now, for that matter—together with Rundstedt and Leeb."

"No," Bock declared, "I have made my decision, and that's the way it's going to be."

Half an hour later I sat down in the airplane and flew to Berlin, where General Eugen Müller, already known to me as the former commanding officer of the *Kriegsakademie,* was still in his office. I recited my assigned words to him.

He answered, "My dear Gersdorff, what do you think we've been trying to do about this already? We look upon these orders the same way your army group does. Field Marshal von Brauchitsch has tried to get them taken back, or at least modified, in many face-to-face meetings with Hitler. It was all useless. On his last visit, he had an inkwell thrown at him. He's not going back to the Führer about this. The only thing we could do was to put out our own order to preserve military discipline. Nothing else can be done for the time being, even with the best will in the world."

After additional urgings, I requested, in accordance with my assignment, to be permitted to discuss the matter with Field Marshal von Brauchitsch in person. Müller explained to me, however, that the head of OKH was out with the troops on an inspection tour and wouldn't be back for about a week. I couldn't wait for that long. Doing so also seemed pointless to me.

And so I flew back to Posen the same evening, and after landing I immediately took a car to Field Marshal von Bock's villa. I was ushered into the dining room, where Bock, General Hans von Greiffenberg (the Army Group's new chief of staff, who had only arrived that day), Tresckow, and Bock's two aides were sitting down for the evening meal.[18] As soon as I walked in, Bock called out to me, "Now then, what did you arrive at?" After I had reported to him about the utter failure of my mission, there was a general silence at first. Then, glancing around the room almost triumphantly, Bock said, "Gentlemen, I will emphasize this: Field Marshal von Bock *did* object." At that moment I had to think of the words of Pontius Pilate: "I wash my hands of guilt."

It is indeed true that in the following days, the high command of Army Group Center and the commanders of its component armies made the greatest exertions to hinder the performance of the criminal orders, or even, as far as possible, to soften them. The unanimous disapproval of these orders by all the top commanders created a common front, so that at least within our operational area the worst could be prevented. It was unavoidable, all the same, that the content of the orders become known all the way down to the companies—at least by word of mouth. The Soviet commanders and troops very quickly got the whole picture from statements by captured German soldiers. That whipped up the Soviet units' will to resist to the highest possible level; and this, in turn, cost German troops infinite amounts of blood.

But aside from those effects, Tresckow and we, his trusted confidants, were also convinced by this affair that the military leadership had wasted one of its last chances to break from its dependence on Hitler's insane ideology. If the field marshals, following Tresckow's suggestion, had closed ranks and presented clear conditions to Hitler so soon before the attack against the Soviet Union, he would have had no other option but to give in to them. At that point, he could not have afforded to make command changes in these vital positions. But the fact that, in the end, the high commanders went along with everything besmirched the honor of the German armed forces while simultaneously turning them into accomplices; on the other hand, the generals' capitulation meant a tremendous prestige victory for Hitler, who knew now that he could permit himself almost anything in dealing with the high commanders.

A few days before the attack began, Army Group Center transferred its headquarters from Posen to Rembertow, near Warsaw. Here for the first time I met the head of the SS unit assigned to our army group's operational area,

Einsatzgruppe B. In contrast to the majority of SS leaders, Arthur Nebe and his adjutant, *SS-Standartenführer* (SS-Colonel) Schulz, made a thoroughly professional impression, like army officers.[19] Their behavior was modest and courteous. They gave assurances that they would always keep me informed about all the missions and operations in their purview in a full and timely manner. (When I stubbornly inquired about the details of their overall assignment, they were nevertheless not very forthcoming.) We agreed that Nebe and I would meet together at least once a week, and that as often as possible, Nebe would be present at the daily briefing for the field marshal or the chief of staff and the Ia.

This first meeting was a time for cautious probing, because Nebe, quite apart from his ignorance of my own political position, couldn't know exactly what I knew about his attitude toward National Socialism. But within the first few weeks of the Russian campaign our relationship became one of complete openness and confidence, an attitude that also extended to his adjutant, to whom Nebe was obviously very close.

The "enemy situation" for Army Group Center's front that had been assembled by the Foreign Armies East intelligence section at OKH was comprehensive, and its correctness was largely confirmed during the initial engagements along the frontier. Less clear were the strategic plans the Soviets had been pursuing with the buildup of forces on their western border, something that had been on the increase ever since 1939. From the organization and equipment of their units, as well as later statements from prisoners of war, it was apparent that in the long run they were preparing for an offensive in the direction of East Prussia and Poland and therefore, at the very least, for an aggressive defense of their western boundaries.

On the other hand, it was established that as of June 1941, the Soviet armed forces were not prepared to make any large-scale attacks. At that point they were in a period of reorganization and equipment conversion. Cavalry divisions were to be changed into armored units, and all armored units were to be equipped with motor vehicles and the newly developed T-34 tanks (which were superior to all German tanks). It is hard to say when the Soviets would have progressed so far as to be able to mount a grand offensive of their own. In contrast to some postwar publications, which claim that the Soviet attack would have had to be reckoned with as early as August 1941, I held the opinion at the time that this would not have been possible, for both organizational and equipment-related reasons. I am still of the same opinion today.

In view of the enormous Soviet troop buildup, however, Hitler could claim the necessity of a preventive war with a certain amount of justification, even if there could also be no doubt that he had always wanted a war with the Soviet Union as part of the framework of his geopolitical goals, and that he had started this war at a moment that seemed favorable to him. He plainly calculated that Stalin, for his own part, would also breach the Soviet-German pact, depending on the political "big picture" and the status of his own preparations for a military offensive.

Despite many warnings, Stalin simply did not want to believe in a German attack. Although a whole series of secret reports had given notice of an immediately impending German offensive, and although Richard Sorge, the German-born spy working for the Soviet Union in Tokyo, had on 12 May and 15 May 1941, reported to Moscow the exact invasion date of 22 June, the German armed forces met with an utterly surprised foe.[20] It is true that the oft-cited fact that freight trains were still rolling across the border carrying Soviet shipments to Germany at the hour the attack began could be explained away as a deceptive measure. Apart from that detail, however, there are many other proofs of the successful surprise. For example, in the early morning hours on the day of the attack, the chief of staff of the Soviet 3rd Army (based in Grodno) had driven off to the countryside on a fishing trip. Soon German soldiers ran into Soviet cavalry divisions that had already given up their horses and had not yet received their tanks. Immobilized and armed only with light weapons, they put up only slight resistance.

It is absolutely the case that during the first battles along the frontier, the combat strength of the Red Army was generally less than we had anticipated. Deficient leadership and inferior armament, together with the effect of surprise, led in most places to the swift collapse of the Soviet resistance. On top of this, the morale and fighting spirit of the Soviet armed forces were both at a low ebb in the summer of 1941. Spectacular exceptions like the heroic defense of the border stronghold at Brest, which persisted until the leading German attackers had already reached the Dnieper, were rare affairs.

Towards the end of the battle of Minsk, the commanding officer of Panzer Group 3, Colonel General Hoth, sought the removal of the *SS-Einsatzgruppe* operating in his army's sector of the front because it was disturbing the operations of his line units and, more than that, because it was creating unrest among the troops.[21] Nebe immediately acted on our requests to pull back all of his teams, but afterwards he let us know repeatedly that Himmler was continually pressuring him to send his *Einsatzgruppe* units forward again. The Army Group allowed this after about a week, particularly since up until then we had not received a single report about criminal actions against the Russian population. During these first weeks we also received no reports of the shooting of Soviet commissars, which allowed us to hope that the senior commanders' efforts to sabotage the infamous Commissar Order had succeeded.

In July 1941, Army Group Center's headquarters (which had already been moved forward again, to Baranovizhi), was transferred to the small city of Borissov, on the Beresina River.[22] It was here that I had a most remarkable encounter. A high-ranking Nazi functionary called on me, introducing himself as the head of a *Vorkommando Moskau* (Moscow Forward Command) that had been provisionally established in Warsaw.[23] He explained that for the moment he only wanted to open up a line of communication with me. After Moscow had been surrounded by our troops, his command was supposed to flow through the front lines, in order to force its way into the city and carry out "security missions" there. According to him, Hitler had ordered that not a single member of the Wehrmacht would be allowed to enter Moscow. Since we on the military side had never heard of such a unit as this, I immediately had inquiries made about my visitor's identity; these inquiries confirmed his statements.

Since he showed himself to be very happy to talk, I attempted to drag out of him everything that I possibly could. In the process he informed me that Hitler intended to push the eastern boundary of the Reich all the way to the Baku-Stalingrad-Moscow-Leningrad line. East of this line there would be a *Brandstreife* (fire strip) extending to the Ural Mountains, within which all human life would be extinguished. The approximately thirty million Russians living within this tract of land would be decimated by hunger, as all food supplies would be removed from the gigantic region. The German personnel taking part in this action would be forbidden under penalty of death to give a Russian so much as a piece of bread. The big cities, from Leningrad to Moscow, were to be razed to the ground; and the SS commander Erich von dem Bach-Zelewski would be responsible for carrying out all these measures.[24]

Speaking in a most cheerful and casual tone, my visitor informed me that within the new eastern zone of the Reich, "SS fortresses" would be built up in the vicinity of important transportation hubs; here, large SS forces were to be stationed along with air force troops, special forces units, and transportation units. The countryside would be governed from these fortresses. The Russians would be slave-laborers pure and simple, used for the optimal exploitation of the conquered region's industrial and agricultural capacities. After the Russians had been defeated, a three-year military service term would be introduced in Germany, during which every conscript would be trained for one year in the homeland and then assigned for two years to the eastern military frontier.

In the circle forming ever more closely around Tresckow, my report on my unpleasant visitor's remarks strengthened the conviction that it was not enough simply to prevent the worst things from happening: rather, something had to be done. Day by day, Tresckow's intimates coalesced into a conspiracy that demanded with increasing force the act that would bring liberation. But initially Tresckow still remained cautious around most of us. For him the main thing was to have colleagues around him upon whom he could utterly rely. At this point, nobody other than Schlabrendorff and Berndt von Kleist knew anything certain about his long-standing plans, connections, and activities in the active resistance. But within our circle it was already being said that Hitler's elimination represented the sole possibility of saving the German Reich and people from downfall.

During those autumn weeks of 1941—at a time when we still had more military successes than failures—Tresckow described with amazing foresight the end of Germany, just the way it finally happened in 1945. His towering personality and his unswerving steadfastness made a deep impression on my comrades and on me. In the course of my lifetime I have come to know many important or notable people, but to this day, I have never met anyone whose mental caliber and strength of character were even comparable to those of Henning von Tresckow.

During the following months, I was affected by other military, political, and personal experiences. These drove me more and more decisively from passive opposition to a determination to commit high treason. In the course of these months, I overcame the many inhibitions that stemmed from my whole training in military obedience; from the prejudices of class and religion; and, not least, from the oath I had sworn.

From the military point of view, questions about the continuing strategic prosecution of the war dominated my thoughts during this period. Before the start of the Russian campaign, practically all our plans extended only as far as the line we anticipated reaching after the initial frontier engagements. Obviously Hitler had wished to put off making any further decisions. Completely misjudging Soviet capacities, he had reckoned on the Soviet Union's swift collapse. Army Group Center's high command had submitted a plan for a Moscow operation on a grand scale, in which the city and its surrounding area would be encircled in a far-ranging pincer movement using the majority of all available Panzer forces. Within the Army Group we were convinced that in the course of such an operation the mass of the Red Army could be drawn in, trapped, and annihilated. OKH put forward the same strategic concept, and supported the Army Group's proposal—a proposal that was also in keeping with the old axiom that an attack should be pursued at the point where it had already been most successful.

Hitler, however, wanted a huge operation in an easterly and southeasterly direction, to be conducted by Army Group South, in order to get our hands on agriculturally rich Ukraine, the ore deposits of the Donets Basin, and the oil of Baku. His plans were in fundamental accordance with the economic considerations that he regarded as compelling. However, he overlooked the fact that in every war, the very first order of business is to strike and annihilate the opposing armed forces. His military objection against the Moscow operation rested on his fear of the wide southern flank that it would necessarily create.

His ingrained sensitivity about flanks showed itself here, just as it had done during the campaign in France.

On 4 August 1941, Hitler, escorted by the chief of the operations section of OKH, Colonel in the General Staff Heusinger, visited the Army Group head-quarters in Borissov in order to announce his decision in the presence of the army commanders.[25] (In contrast to the constantly repeated rumors among the troops, this was Hitler's first, and for a long time his only, "front-line visit" in Russia.) After arguments that at times became heated, he announced his final decision to the commanding generals. It meant practically bringing to a complete stop the successful offensive in Army Group Center's operational area. Of even more consequence was the operation's extensive use, at Hitler's direction, of the available armored forces. The 2nd Panzer Army, on Army Group Center's right wing, would be transferred to Army Group South for the battle of Kiev; Panzer Group 3, operating on our left wing, would be moved into the Valdai Hills to support Army Group North, which was attacking in the direction of Leningrad.

Despite this decision, OKH and Army Group Center did not yet give up on their own solution to the future strategic conduct of the campaign in the East. As a last resort Bock and Halder decided to send Colonel General Guderian, the commander of 2nd Panzer Army and a man who was particularly well regarded by Hitler, to the Führer's headquarters. He was to make a last-ditch attempt to convince Hitler of the correctness of the Moscow solution. First, however, on 23 August, Guderian came to the Army Group headquarters at Borissov, where Halder was also staying, in order to talk through the whole "plan of attack" for the Hitler mission with Bock and Halder.

Guderian was convinced of the rightness of the Moscow solution not only because he was the creator of the Panzer forces and of a new, armor-based, military strategy. He also regarded Hitler's order to march away toward the right as being technically impracticable because of the current condition of his troops and the state of the roads that were available for such an operation. As a result he appeared to be firmly determined to resist what was, from his own point of view, Hitler's fatal decision.

On the same day, 23 August, Hitler received him at the *Führer-Haupt-quartier*. According to his representation of the events that took place, Guderian also presented his own doubts about the decision, but he was obviously unsuccessful in changing Hitler's mind. In the end, Guderian not only assured Hitler that he would carry out his orders, but even offered him the XXIV Panzer Corps as well, a unit he had just previously depicted as being not yet mission-capable.

When Halder informed Field Marshal von Bock by telephone about the total failure of Guderian's mission, Bock is supposed to have only said of

Guderian, in his native Berlin-Brandenburg dialect, *Ooch so'n Jummilöwe!—* "Oh, what a rubber lion!" But Hitler had won again.

My personal conviction is that this was Hitler's most momentous wrong decision, for in the final analysis, it both initiated and laid the foundation for the loss of the entire war. Tresckow had perceived Hitler's catastrophic weaknesses as a commander from the very start, and was now more convinced than ever of the necessity of his timely elimination, if Germany were to be spared its certain path into the abyss.

Events of a political nature, however, had an even stronger and more lasting effect on us—removing our last doubts about Hitler's criminal nature.

The staff of Army Group Center had transferred its headquarters to Krassny Bor, a few kilometers north of the city of Smolensk.[26] One day a good friend from Silesia, Manfred von Heydebrand, walked into my office there.[27] His face was chalk-white; so white, in fact, that the first thing I did was offer him some cognac, on the assumption that he was airsick. But he explained with a trembling voice that the Junkers-52 cargo plane on which he had been flying to the front from a home leave had stopped along the way in Borissov. Even from the airfield he had heard continuous pistol and machine-gun fire. When the flight resumed he had observed—shortly after the takeoff, from a low altitude—a hideous orgy of executions. It was plain to see that SS members had bestially murdered thousands of people.[28]

We knew that in Borissov, which lay on both banks of the Beresina River, there was a Jewish ghetto with a population of several thousand. While our headquarters had still been at Borissov, many of the Jews had even worked for us as skilled craftsmen or as auxiliary laborers. Field Marshal von Bock had personally received their leader, and expressly assured him of his protection and aid.

The Beresina formed the boundary between the Army Group's operational area and that of *Zivilkommissariat Weiss-Ruthenien,* the Civil Commissariat for White Russia or Belarus. Since the ghetto was on the river's eastern side it still belonged, just as before, within the Army Group's area of responsibility. With feverish haste I notified Tresckow, the army group's chief of staff, and the field marshal; but above all I notified Nebe, who was visibly completely surprised by the news. In a short time Nebe flew the approximately 125 miles to Borissov in a light plane that we had placed at his disposal, to put a stop to these events. Needless to say, we also sent corresponding orders to the local military authorities through the various radio networks.

But everything came too late. When Nebe reached Borissov, the *Aktion* had already been over for a long time; all the Jews in the ghetto—men, women, children, and suckling infants—had fallen victim to it. Nebe reported to us the results of the investigation he had immediately set in motion. The leader of a

small detachment of his *Einsatzgruppe,* which he had stationed in Borissov
to protect the ghetto, had gone home on leave and had stopped off in Minsk
to visit with an SS comrade. He had asked this individual to keep an eye on
the Borissov detachment during his absence, and make sure everything was
all right with it. Several days later, this other SS man had gone to Borissov
and found the untouched Jewish ghetto there. Although he reported to the
Zivilkommissar (Civil Commissioner) of White Russia and had no authority
whatsoever in East Borissov—that is, on the far side of the Beresina—he had
alerted an SS detachment made up of Lithuanians, and pronounced the "liqui-
dation" of the Jews.[29]

The whole affair had been played out in the most hideous possible manner.
First the Jews had to excavate vast, deep trenches. Then they were driven into
these ditches stark naked, in groups of one hundred, and machine-gunned en
masse by Lithuanian SS men. Without any attempts being made to determine
who might still be alive, the next group of Jews was forced to trample on
those who just had been shot, and they were then gunned down in their turn.
An SS man was observed holding an infant up high by its legs, shooting it in
the head with his pistol, and tossing it into the trench. A few Luftwaffe troops
who had come over from the nearby airfield out of curiosity were seized
by bloodlust and also fired at the Jews who had been driven down into the
ditches. Dreadful scenes took place at the edge of the fatal trenches. Desperate escape attempts by some people, and the offering of their own bodies by
young Jewesses who only wished to save themselves and their children, all
ended the same way—in a hail of SS bullets.

Without delay, the field marshal forcefully demanded that the *Zivilkommissar* in Minsk, whose name was Kube, report to him in Smolensk immediately
and take responsibility for this overreaching on the Army Group's territory.
He simultaneously demanded the handover of the SS commander, so that he
could be condemned by a court-martial. (Tresckow had urged Bock to have
the man shot immediately, without a trial.) Kube—who was one of the most
brutal SS viceroys in the East next to his colleague in Ukraine, Koch—arro-
gantly replied that the field marshal might just as well come to him in Minsk.
He had no intention of seeking out the Army Group's headquarters, and the
surrender of the guilty SS man was roundly rejected.[30] It was never even possible for the Army Group to find out his name; but the military commandant
of East Borissov, who was going to be held responsible for the deficient performance of his oversight duties, took his own life out of guilt over not having
prevented the massacre.

The support that the *Reichssicherheitshauptamt* (RSHA, or Reich Security
Central Office) offered Kube and the SS and SD (*Sicherheitsdienst* or "Security Service," the intelligence arm of the Nazi Party and the SS) men under

his authority left the Army Group practically defenseless. It goes without saying that this event was reported upward to OKH by the swiftest means and with full details. In 1946, I found this selfsame document—which I had personally drafted and signed—once again: this time while I was looking through the prosecution's files in the "witness wing" of the Palace of Justice at Nuremberg. The upper right-hand corner of the document was now marked, "C-in-C Army is aware of this—Sievers [?], Lt. Col. in GS." That meant that this report had been placed before the commander-in-chief of the army, Field Marshal von Brauchitsch. We were not in a position to know what he did about it. In 1945 he could no longer recollect anything about the matter.

Within Tresckow's circle the Borissov incident probably left the most lasting impression of all, and eliminated the final inhibitions in the struggle against Hitler and his regime. Shortly afterward we also learned about mass murders of Jews in the rear areas of our neighboring army groups, as well as in the various *Zivilkommissariaten* behind the entire Eastern Front.

As a witness and expert consultant in Nuremberg after the war, I was forced to accept the fact that Nebe had also sent reports up to the RSHA about the mass executions that he had denied in his dealings with us.

During my frequent front-line visits, junior and senior officers alike spoke to me over and over again about these shocking occurrences, word of which had swiftly traveled around our entire front. I myself saw to it that the Borissov incident was recorded in the Army Group's war diary. In addition, I inserted in the diary an excerpt from a report of a visit to the front, in which I had written the following:

> In every long discussion with officers I was asked about the shooting of Jews. I have gained the impression that the shooting of Jews, of prisoners, and also of commissars, is disapproved of by almost the entire officer corps; the foremost objection with regard to the shooting of commissars is that, as a result, enemy resistance is markedly strengthened. *These shootings are regarded as an injury to the honor of the German Army, and in particular to that of the German officer corps.*

At that time, a war diary entry of this sort bordered on high treason.

On the evening of the day we learned of the Borissov massacre, Tresckow yet again urged Bock to fly to the Führer and to confront him. But Bock rejected this, just as in Posen he had avoided intervening personally against the Commissar Order.

Other than the Jewish question, the problem of Russian prisoners of war and the effects of the Commissar Order were our biggest concerns. I had mentioned both points in my war diary entry. The number of Russian prisoners in Army Group Center's operational area was, to be sure, smaller than the quantities stated in the official "Wehrmacht Reports." But it was still so enormous that it resulted in apparently almost insoluble problems in sheltering and feeding them all. On top of that, Hitler had prohibited feeding prisoners with supplies meant for the German troops. They had to be fed from their own soil—which had been laid waste.

Providing for war prisoners was the business of the Chief Quartermaster's department. But in addition to my feelings as a human being, I was also involved in this matter in my capacity as Ic/AO, inasmuch as large quantities of deserters to our side could only be expected if we adhered to the assurances of good treatment given in our propaganda leaflets. After the battle of Roslavl-Smolensk, and above all after the *Kesselschlacht,* or encirclement battle, of Vyazma-Bryansk, frightful conditions prevailed inside the so-called "Dulags" (*Durchgangslagern,* or transit camps). Thousands died of exhaustion merely during the long march to a temporary Dulag.

When Field Marshal von Bock learned for himself that German escort detachments had shot down straggling and sick prisoners of war, he addressed the problem energetically and without delay. In a sharply worded order, he forbade the shooting of prisoners on pain of severe punishment. But in view of the ever-worsening conditions in the Dulags, the Army Group could do nothing else but see to the swift removal of the war prisoners to Germany. Standing in the way of this project were the lack of railcar space for their transport and the constantly repeated dynamiting of the few railroad lines by Russian partisans. Therefore, bleak and frightful conditions were the rule even where the military authorities on the scene did everything they could to look after the hundreds of thousands of prisoners.

By contrast, the Commissar Order was put into effect only a few times. I was personally able to rescue a whole string of senior political commissars who were brought to the Army Group headquarters for interrogation because of their importance. We compelled them to remove their distinguishing insignia, so that after their interrogations they could be treated as ordinary prisoners of war. (In many cases, however, they were subsequently betrayed by their own comrades in the rear-area prison camps.)

On the other hand, at the front commissars were probably shot most often whenever German troops had just learned of the mutilation of wounded Germans who had been left on the battlefield. However, even in such cases line commanders attempted to prevent these retaliatory measures, as comprehensible as they were in human terms. In the campaign history of the 28th Infantry Division, for example, it says:

The members of the 28th Inf. Div. were shocked that the atrocities inflicted on wounded men that have been set forth here took place in the division's sector. The division commander, General Sinnhuber, resolutely rejected any orders that did not correspond to the international regulations regarding nations at war.[31] Therefore the Commissar Order was also not applied in the division.

When the Soviets had found out about the Commissar Order, the effect was to stiffen substantially the Red Army's resistance and its will to fight. The commissars in the troop units—who for the most part were thoroughly beloved by the Soviet soldiers, and to a certain extent played the role of "the mother of the company"—had every reason to fight literally to the last bullet with their units, and preferably to fall in battle rather than be shot in captivity.

Since Hitler was never going to be convinced by humanitarian arguments, the evidence that the Commissar Order was costing the German side endless bloodshed became the main theme in the struggle by OKH and all the front-line commanders for its repeal. Even so-called "Old Fighters"—Nazi comrades from the party's earliest days—who had been assigned to the front, joined in this campaign. A genuine flood of memoranda was directed at OKW and Hitler. It was said, however, that Keitel and Bormann did not allow a single one of these memoranda to reach Hitler, and also warded away from him all oral suggestions on this topic.[32] An OKH document dated 23 September 1941, which once again requested the order's repeal, bears this marginal note: "The Führer has rejected any alteration to the currently existing order for the handling of political commissars." Hitler only abandoned his resistance on 6 May 1942. The repeal of the Commissar Order for all practical purposes was based on the following proposition:

> In order to encourage desertion to our lines, and the surrender of encircled Soviet troops, the Führer orders on a trial basis that in such cases all Soviet commanders, commissars, and *politruks* (political leaders) can be assured that their lives will be preserved.[33]

Another problem that not only burdened us morally but also angered us because of our responsibility for the troops under our command, was the treatment of the Russian population, something else which went back to Hitler's personal decrees. The deeper that Army Group Center drove into White Russia, and the more the partly criminal orders made themselves felt, the more clearly we could see what tremendous opportunities were being thrown away. After the initial push through the formerly Polish region, the German troops entered into a country in which they were often greeted as liberators. The military leadership attempted to make use of this situation whenever possible.

Above all, the churches that the Soviets had shut down, and to a certain extent had desecrated, were reopened. All of us were witnesses to unforgettable scenes. The Russian peasants came from far and near to be able to attend a religious service again at last. Sometimes they brought along with them the exhumed corpses of long-dead family members, in order to have them blessed by a priest and then buried in holy ground. Many people tried to kiss our hands or the hems of our tunics in gratitude. Of particular beauty were the services in the magnificent, reopened Smolensk Cathedral. Here the Soviets had installed a Museum of Atheism, which was intended to make the Russian priests and the Orthodox faith seem ridiculous.[34]

Like the reopening of the churches, our measures to restore private property also had an unimaginable effect. The grant of a bit of private land, a cow, or some goats caused the rural folk to come streaming in from all sides. We all saw just how easy it would have been to defeat communism in Russia. If this type of occupation policy had been pursued, and the population had retained a certain amount of national autonomy, it would have been a bigger danger to the Soviet system than all the oppressive measures of the SS.

Very soon, however, we heard from headquarters that Hitler had foamed at the mouth with rage when he learned about the measures being taken in the front zone. The church reopenings had to be reversed to a considerable extent, while the land and cattle transferred to the peasants were taken away from them again. A short time later all the "subhuman" propaganda started up. The euphoria of liberation from the Soviet yoke melted away after a few months.

Our letters from home did all else that was needed to increase the pressure upon us. In almost every letter that she sent me, my wife told me about the persecution of the Jews in Berlin. Tremendously distressed, she shared with me many individual incidents that her women friends had told her about, or that she had witnessed herself. One day she wrote that in our own immediate neighborhood—we lived on Brückenallee in the Hansa Quarter—it was said that an elderly Jewish lady whom we had particularly treasured had been picked up by the Gestapo and transported to some unknown destination in the East. My wife kept on asking me the same things in all her letters: "What's happening with these unfortunate people? Where are they being taken? Are the rumors true that they're being sent to Poland and the Baltic region?" (Since our mail went through the Army Group's courier office in Berlin, she was to some extent protected from the postal censors.)

At the same time, the number of reports from our subordinate commands, in which accounts from the homeland about criminal and capricious acts on the part of the Party were depicted as a growing danger for troop morale, multiplied. Such reports, with the Army Group's pointed comments attached, were passed along to OKH. News of the mass deportations of German Jews to concentration camps—whose names, other than Dachau and Oranienburg, were not yet known, however—contributed measurably to the decisions made in the conspiratorial group within the staff of Army Group Center, which led to actions that would be carried out during 1942–1943.

An additional experience that left a deep mark on me was a meeting in the early autumn of 1941 with my friend Count Paul Yorck von Wartenburg.[35] He came directly from Warsaw, where he had been assigned for a time to the "Führer Reserve" while awaiting further orders, and now he was on his way up to the front.

Paul Yorck was a direct descendant of Field Marshal Count Ludwig Yorck von Wartenburg, who in 1812 had signed the Convention of Tauroggen against the will of his sovereign, and with that act had ignited the movement for the German "War of Liberation" against Napoleon. The majority of the field marshal's descendants were top-flight scholars and magnificent soldiers, sometimes combined in the same person. Paul Yorck's father and grandfather were well-known and respected scholars and philosophers who had created an intellectual atmosphere in their Silesian castle of Klein-Öls; the philosopher Wilhelm Dilthey also belonged to the Klein-Öls circle.[36]

When Paul Yorck inherited the estate (which had been presented to the field marshal as a royal gift after Napoleon's fall), he continued with his siblings to carry on the dutiful traditions of his noble house. At the same time, he was one of the most progressive landowners in Silesia: he instituted social arrangements on the Klein-Öls lands that went far beyond what the Nazi Party had promised by way of social reforms. But for all that, he was and remained a conservative revolutionary. It was always something special to be a guest at Klein-Öls, and to this day I am happy and grateful to have experienced the spirit of that place and to have been Paul Yorck's friend.

It was almost inevitable that he and his brother would be passionate opponents of a regime that had simultaneously declared war on Christianity, the intellect, and humanity. It was above all else his Christian faith, which was part of him to the depths of his soul, that compelled Paul Yorck to his uncompromising hostility. For him, Hitler was the Antichrist, or "the epitome of evil" as Claus Stauffenberg put it once, later on. It therefore was only natural that he refused to take any oath to Hitler. Yorck had done his military reserve training in my squadron at Brieg. When, prior to his promotion to reserve officer rank, I placed in front of him the written declaration by which he would oblige himself to serve Hitler as a loyal follower, he refused to sign it—and so did his younger brother Hans. Even the urgings of the commanding general of Military District VIII, General von Kleist, could not wrench him away from his decision.

The two brothers went to the Polish campaign as sergeants in the army reserve. Hans was one of the first men to be killed in action; while Paul received a battlefield commission for bravery in the face of the enemy, without ever having taken an oath or signed a loyalty declaration. Only someone who lived through those times can truly appreciate just how much courage such an attitude required. At the time, thousands of reserve officers signed the same declaration willingly or even against their own consciences.

During his visit to Army Group Center's headquarters, Yorck gave me a comprehensive report about the horrible crimes committed by the SS and SD against Poles, Jews, and gypsies, which were the order of the day in the formerly Polish areas. He peremptorily demanded a massive intervention by the military high command that would put an end to the criminal behavior of the National Socialists. At the time, I still knew too little to be able to inform him about the plans and intentions of an organized resistance: I thus could only tell him that most of our staff was in favor of the army taking such a step, but they had not yet been successful in winning over the high commanders in the East for such a liberating deed. Yorck's impatience burst forth in a passion; from no other man did I ever hear such fierce words about the failure on the part of the senior generals. He denounced the guilt they would share—and the guilt all of us would share, too—if decisive resistance against the dictatorship's unimaginable crimes was not soon forthcoming.

I arranged a meeting between Yorck and Tresckow, which proved to be a disappointment because the latter gentleman was, in the first place, very busy, and in the second place, was far too cautious ever to open up on first acquaintance. Yorck, who had never practiced such caution in his own life, couldn't understand Tresckow at that time.

In the fall of 1941, German strategic planning in the East was affected by a grotesque "zigzag strategy" of Hitler's own creation. In mid-September the battle of Kiev, fought against the wishes of OKH and Army Group Center, had turned into a great success. Hitler was triumphant about this, and despite the approaching *Schlammperiode* [autumn weeks when the Russian roads turned into slimy mud] and the impending approach of winter, he ordered us to go on the attack again, heading eastward from Smolensk.

This offensive was under enormous time pressure. The combat forces required for such a grand offensive had to be regrouped. Guderian's 2nd Panzer Army had already been pulled out of the fighting on 26 September 1941, before the battle of Kiev had really ended. But it could only reach its jumping-off point for the new operation (on Army Group Center's right wing) by the mandatory date of 30 September by means of a relentless forced march. As a result, thousands of Soviet troops were overrun, only to fall back into the forests and later reconstitute themselves as a regular partisan army behind the German lines.

The 4th Army and the 9th Army, with their respective armored units, Panzer Groups 4 and 3, were to commence their attacks on 2 October. Therefore, only two or three weeks remained until the probable beginning of the *Schlammperiode* to wrap up the operation successfully. For this reason, the vast enveloping maneuver with the encirclement of the Soviet capital became impossible from the start. Instead, the two forward pincers, consisting of the right and left wings of the Army Group, were to meet east of Vyazma—that is, far to the west of Moscow. Since Hitler simultaneously ordered Army Group South to continue attacking toward the southeast in the general direction of Stalingrad, and Army Group North to carry on with its own offensive in a northeasterly direction, he stuck fast to the "eccentric" [as opposed to concentric] strategy: this did indeed bring great partial successes to all three army groups, at first; but in the final analysis, it was the decisive error with which the loss of the entire Russian campaign began.

As the battle of Vyazma-Bryansk drew to a close on 19 October, there was no question that a great victory had been won. Powerful enemy forces had been enveloped and annihilated. The high numbers of war prisoners as well as of captured and destroyed war materiel, however, led Hitler into the mistaken assumption that the Soviet armed forces had been so decisively defeated that they were no longer capable of a major offensive operation. This misjudgment (which on the German side even led to partial demobilization measures and a slowdown in munitions production) took into account neither the Soviet Union's virtually inexhaustible human and material resources, nor the strong forces which were waiting in readiness in the Soviet far east and which were, moreover, especially well-equipped for winter warfare.

A subsequent experience revealed to me just how resolutely, and with how much foresight, Stalin had reacted to the severe defeats during the border battles. During the battle of Vyazma-Bryansk, a Soviet general became our prisoner; he had removed his emblems of rank and volunteered as an auxiliary worker in the supply column of one of our infantry divisions as a "Hiwi" (*Hilfswilliger,* or voluntary laborer). Russian prisoners of war recognized him, however, and gave him away as a high-ranking Communist Party official and an army commander. And so in November 1941, I got to know him in the course of an interrogation.

During the process he told me the following story: As an armaments industry executive in Moscow, he had been ordered to attend a conference in the Kremlin in mid-July, a month after the German army had invaded the Soviet Union. A thoroughly anxious mood prevailed among the Party functionaries and the generals. Everyone was talking over everyone else, chain-smoking cigarettes, and visibly frightened about how the situation would progress. Only Stalin had remained completely calm, gazing around the agitated circle with a smile. Then, as cold as ice, he made his decisions known. They concerned the evacuation of Moscow-based industries and the formation of a number of "people's armies" for the defense of Moscow, which to my recollection were numbered 32 through 34. Later on in the same meeting, Stalin named my conversation partner to be the commander of one of these armies. At the same time, Stalin led this man (who as an industrial manager had no military experience and no understanding of military command) to an open window—the room was on an upper floor of the Kremlin—and said, "If you're beaten, I'll personally throw you out of this window!" This announcement was the reason the newly-minted general had preferred to surrender to the Germans after his army's total destruction.

But the battle of Vyazma-Bryansk had also cost the German side heavy losses that could only be insufficiently replaced. Unit strengths tumbled sharply. Moreover the *Schlammperiode,* which had started in the meantime, brought all large-scale movements to a standstill and prevented a strategic exploitation of the victory. Only a few weeks later the winter began, catching the German troops completely unprepared. Although the Army Group had sent the word up over and over again about the lack of winter clothing, the low combat-strength of the line units, and the ever-worsening supply situation (the result of partisan activity), the supreme command had done little or nothing. Concerning winter clothing, the supreme headquarters contented itself with explaining that the war was practically over: the troops would spend the winter in warm quarters, and therefore each company needed only two or three fur coats and a like number of pairs of felt over-boots for sentries at outdoor posts.

But first, with total incomprehension of the real situation at the front, OKH ordered the attack on Moscow to continue.

Despite the onset of winter frost, Army Group Center returned to the attack on 18 and 20 November from the previously reached Mtsensk-Kaluga-Kalinin front line. The objective that the 2nd Panzer Army had been ordered to reach—the city of Gorky on the Volga River, far to the east of the capital—was a mere fantasy, and the objective was finally switched to Kolomna, southeast of Moscow. The initial general objective was stipulated to be the course of the Moskva River and the Volga Canal.

The attack by the German units, much weakened in quantities of fighting men, tanks, and artillery pieces, ran into an enemy that was once again prepared to defend its positions—but above all, it ran into "General Winter." Vehicle motors ceased to function; locomotives froze up, so that at times only a few of the thirty-two trains per day required to supply the Army Group reached the front at all. Given the lack of winter clothing, the number of frostbite and exposure casualties climbed to the tens of thousands. To tell the truth, initially the offensive made good forward progress on both wings; but the combat strength of the line units grew less and less due to battle casualties, frostbite, illnesses, and the winter-related failure of weapons and vehicles.

During these days I was personally at the most advanced front lines as often as I could be in order to learn as early as possible, from the unfiltered statements of war prisoners, about the arrival of new Soviet units. At the end of November, I stood at a road sign northwest of Moscow indicating that the distance to the center of the Soviet capital was thirty-five kilometers [about twenty-two miles].[37] But I saw during these visits to the front how the German ability to mount attacks was steadily decreasing at the same time that the Soviet resistance was growing ever stronger.

The decisive factor in the end was the deployment of elite Soviet divisions from eastern Siberia that had been moved from Vladivostok to Moscow along the single great railroad line, without our detecting it. They had been pulled from the far eastern end of the USSR after Moscow's spy Richard Sorge had reported that the Soviet Union would not have to reckon with Japan's entry into the war against it in the immediate future. Given this situation, it was almost a miracle that the retreat of the German forces, which began on 6 December, went generally according to plan, even if it also cost us significant losses in men and materiel.

Then in mid-December the "commander carousel" started up; it would continue to operate until the end of the war. On 19 December, Field Marshal von Bock was replaced by Field Marshal von Kluge.[38] On the same day, Hitler fired Field Marshal von Brauchitsch and personally assumed the supreme command of the army. One of his first interventions was the strict order to defend every position to the utmost or "to the last bullet."

Nowadays many old soldiers and postwar publications regard this order as having been Army Group Center's salvation from total destruction. Based on my own experience, I am of a different mind. Preserving the *Auftragstaktik* [the German army's standard principle of leaving the method of carrying out a mission mostly up to the commander on the scene] that had been the making of German command superiority in the conduct of the war up until then would have been the right thing to do. Only the army, corps, and division commanders, as well as the line-unit commanders on the spot, were in the position to reach the correct decisions concerning their responsibilities in the existing conditions. The defense against the Soviet counteroffensive would probably have succeeded with fewer casualties than it did with Hitler's unimaginative stand-fast orders from his distant headquarters in East Prussia.

Hitler's personal command, in which he was far too concerned with personal details, also led, quite rapidly, to severe crises of confidence. I can still recall the disgraceful dismissal of the commander of Panzer Group 4, Colonel General Hoepner.[39] A few days earlier, the commander of 2nd Panzer Army, Colonel General Guderian, had also been relieved of his post. Field Marshal von Kluge, the commander of the Army Group, had resisted these decisions in vain; Keitel, for his part, was all too ready to reprimand the alleged guilty parties and to find scapegoats for Hitler.

Now on an almost daily basis we all witnessed the absurdity of the new management style. Hitler got on the phone many times each day with Field Marshal von Kluge. We General Staff officers invariably needed to listen in on these discussions, so that if necessary we could chase down the information for questions from Hitler that the field marshal could not answer immediately. It was in this fashion that I personally experienced the following conversation:

Hitler: "*Herr Feldmarschall,* how many machine guns are currently in action at the cemetery in Maloyaroslavets?"

Kluge: "I'll have someone find out right away."

After some time, the answer was obtained by an inquiry going through the responsible army and then by way of the corps, division, regiment, and battalion.

Kluge: "*Mein Führer,* there are four machine guns in action at the Maloyaroslavets cemetery."

Hitler: "*Herr Feldmarschall,* see to it that at least six machine guns are assigned there."

Along with Hitler's grotesque interference in low-level command, the following conversation also shows his remorselessness where the ordinary soldier was concerned.

Kluge: "*Mein Führer,* 4th Army has requested the pullback of the such-and-such Infantry Division, which is in a salient jutting way out to the east, to a preferable position. By this means a reserve force could finally be created, which just isn't possible with the current situation at the front."

Hitler: "Has the new position in the rear been constructed?"

Kluge: "No, not yet."

Hitler: "Then I forbid the withdrawal."

Kluge: "*Mein Führer,* you really need to come here sometime. It's fifty degrees below zero. It's completely impossible to dig in, because the soil is frozen as hard as rock. The troops are lying in snow caverns up front, and they'll be lying in the same kind of snow caverns to the rear."

Hitler: "Why haven't any holes been blasted in the ground?"

Kluge: "Because there isn't any blasting material to be had."

Hitler: "I don't believe any of this. I am denying the army's request. You are responsible for keeping the troops in their forward position."

In those weeks and months the troops at the front learned to "get around" militarily senseless decisions. "Attacks by numerically superior enemy forces and the effect of extraordinarily heavy artillery fire" would be blamed for limited withdrawals of the front line.

The new Army Group commander, Field Marshal Günther von Kluge, was initially depicted to me as being hostile to intelligence officers. But after Tresckow had prevailed upon him to have me summoned once or twice a day to the briefing on the enemy situation, Kluge increasingly developed into a friend of the hostile-forces intelligence service. Whenever I walked into his office, he would call out as soon as I was in the door, "What intelligence do you have from this-or-that source?" or "Has the presence of the Soviet armored corps at such-and-such a position been confirmed?" He even made wagers as to whether a particular enemy assessment would be confirmed or not. In this way an especially trusting relationship soon grew up between Kluge and me, which led in the end to an almost paternal friendship.

Kluge, who had been nicknamed *der kluge Hans* ("Clever Hans") in the Wehrmacht, had a glittering General Staff career behind him. Although he could never free himself from certain vanities, such as emphasizing his physical resemblance to Frederick the Great, and from a marked class-consciousness, he was basically a simple man with personally noble qualities. Once he said to me, "I'm a *märkisch* peasant, not a great lord like your big Silesian landowners." [He was referring to his little estate near Rathenow, in that part of Prussia called "Mark Brandenburg."] His manner of thinking and behaving was decent and straightforward. As a strategist his abilities were unquestionably limited, and not to be compared with those of Field Marshals von Bock, von Rundstedt, and von Manstein. But he always led with a lot of personal presence, which earned him the devotion of his subordinates and of the ordinary soldier.[40] However, the most fateful role of his life was more than Kluge was able to manage, and in the end he took the consequences for that fact.

A few days after Kluge had taken over the command of the Army Group, I got a telephone call from my friend Paul Yorck von Wartenburg, who had been posted in the region of Maloyaroslavets, south of Moscow, at the extreme forward edge of the battle line. He asked me to come to him as quickly as possible, because his unit was supposed to carry out orders that were both dishonorable and criminal. By airplane, automobile, and horse-drawn sledge, I succeeded in reaching the reconnaissance battalion of the 34th Infantry Division. There Yorck and his superior officer, Count Friedrich von Oberndorff, explained to me that the commanding general of XII Army Corps (to which the division belonged) had given an order to shoot every Russian in his corps operational area who wasn't from that vicinity in order to curb partisan activity, which had become unbearable.[41] Owing to the chaos in the combat zone, it was nearly impossible to distinguish between the Russians who were local residents and those who were strangers to the area, so this order meant (practically speaking) that every Russian male civilian could be shot on sight.

I immediately took myself over to XII Army Corps and exhorted the commander, whom I knew from when I was on the corps staff at the West Wall, to withdraw his order, contrary to international law as it was. He refused, and told me that a very short time earlier his corps veterinarian had been shot to death by partisans; we of the Army Group HQ had no idea of how things really looked at the front. From his own desk I telephoned the commander of the Army Group. I described the situation and asked for his decision. And just like that, Field Marshal von Kluge immediately relieved the general of his command and countermanded his order. The general was to report to Kluge the very next day. He was sent back home, and never got another promotion or another front-line assignment. Reserve Lieutenant Count Yorck had prevailed against his commanding general.[42]

All the same, the partisans really had become an ever-increasing danger to the fighting troops. Initially the German supreme command had assigned far too little significance to the hundreds of thousands of Soviet soldiers who had been overrun during the border battles, and above all during the battle of Kiev. People forgot that guerrilla warfare was a Russian tradition. Even before the outbreak of war, there had been partisan bands in certain areas of Russia such as the Pripet Marshes. During the war there were also said to have been partisans fighting against Soviet oppression behind the Russian lines.

But meanwhile an increasingly dense network of partisan units in varying strengths had sprung into being behind German lines. They established communications with each other, got support from the civil population—either willingly or by compulsion—and increasingly threatened the Wehrmacht's rear-area lines of communication and its supply facilities. Germans could only travel in convoys along most roads, including the *Rollbahnen*.[43] The few railroad lines were so constantly dynamited that the German railroad troops could scarcely keep up. As a result, only a fraction of our supply trains made it to the front, and steadily worsening supply problems began. In the wake of the rapid German advance, vast stocks of weapons in secret caches and forest hiding places were ready for the partisans' use.

Initially the partisan units consisted almost entirely of Soviet soldiers. From the beginning of 1942 onward, however, they also received an influx of civilian inhabitants who sought to evade being swept up to be sent as laborers to Germany. Soon there were literally entire Soviet armies behind the German front lines! Soviet generals and commissars parachuted over the German rear areas to organize and command these units. Far behind the German lines, the partisans even conducted actual training maneuvers and artillery target practice. In this manner, the best-equipped partisan units could steadily improve their fighting prowess. Whoever is familiar with Russia's stupendous distances will be able to understand the conditions I have depicted.

At that time the big situation map in my office was always kept hidden behind a curtain. What was supposed to remain hidden from my visitors was the enemy situation *behind* our front lines. Because the enemy's positions were marked in red, the map often looked redder to the rear of our lines than it did in front of them.

During the winter war of 1941–42, a general transformation came over the German soldier. True, he was and remained the best soldier in the world, just as he had been before; but his previous feeling of superiority was lost and gone. One reason for this was the fact that in many categories, Soviet arms and equipment were suddenly superior to our own. This began with quilted winter uniforms and went all the way up to tanks. The new Soviet T-34 tank proved itself superior to all German tanks and anti-tank weapons. I repeatedly saw how shells from our tanks and tank destroyers ricocheted off the sloping sides of the T-34. The introduction of the Soviet Katyusha multiple rocket-launcher—a very simple weapon, but extremely effective against morale—also made quite an impression on the German front-line troops. On two occasions I have lain down in the middle of a Katyusha barrage, and I could understand the feelings of the *Landser,* the German common soldier. Our request to have the Katyusha copied was indignantly rejected by the experts in the Ordnance Department, to whom this primitive weapon with such low accuracy seemed like a waste of materials. The German soldier on the Eastern Front may also have instinctively sensed the loss of superiority at the command level. More and more, the initiative now passed from us to the Soviets.

Remarkably, in the front lines Hitler himself was not blamed for any of this. The troops preferred to believe in treachery and betrayal on the part of others rather than in any defective leadership on Hitler's part. Worthy of note in this connection were the ineradicable rumors about Hitler's visits to the front. Although Hitler never came any closer to the front than an army headquarters, it was constantly being said that he had appeared somewhere or other in the most forward line of battle. Anyone who contradicted this usually ran into a wall of disbelief.

Beginning in December 1941, an opposite process of development could be observed on the Soviet side. The Red Army, which had suffered from poor leadership and low combat morale during the engagements along the frontier, made itself over into a Russian national army. Even at the time, we said within Tresckow's circle that Stalin needed to erect a monument to Hitler in Moscow's Red Square: for no other man had rendered so much service in the defense of the Soviet Union. The earliest commanders of the Soviet "fronts" [a "front" being their equivalent of an army group] had by and large failed at the command level. As soon as younger and more capable generals replaced the old command, the top-level leadership of the Soviet armed forces improved rapidly and noticeably. At the troop level, the development into a true national army still needed some time. During the first half of 1942, many deserters still crossed over to the German lines. In our Army Group's area of operations, the numbers were so great that they amounted to the strength of one or two battalions every day.

At the beginning of March 1942, two Russian emigrants, Colonel Konstantin Kromyadi and Lieutenant Igor Sakharov, reported to me.[44] Admiral Canaris had sent them to the front because they had gained experience in guerrilla warfare during the Spanish Civil War, and so they could advise us. They put forward a plan that sounded like a fantasy. The Army Group would enable them to create a brigade-size unit consisting of Russian prisoners of war. The unit would be equipped exclusively with Soviet-issue weapons, uniforms, and other gear. After a short training period, the Army Group would let the unit filter through the German lines to conduct an offensive operation of limited scope. The two men wanted to "march to Moscow and drag Stalin out of the Kremlin!" Despite this highly utopian announcement, I introduced them both to Tresckow, who was willing to give it a try.

We all drove together to a nearby prisoner-of-war camp in which several thousand freshly captured Soviet soldiers of all ranks were to be found. The *emigrés* stood up at a podium, and then Kromyadi gave a fiery speech: Stalin and the Party had betrayed them all, and they had to set Holy Mother Russia free from her oppressors and corruptors. Kromyadi received thunderous applause. After that, the two former World War I officers urged the prisoners to decide whether they were for Stalin or against him. Every man who wanted to fight for a free Russia should step forward. After taking barely a moment to think it over, the entire crowd rushed forward. Only a few sick or wounded men remained where they had been standing. The whole affair was so impressive that Tresckow decided to propose the creation of a Russian volunteer force to the field marshal. When Kluge agreed after some hesitation, the AG Center Experimental Unit was born.

To begin with, a force of some seven thousand men, divided into four infantry battalions and a field artillery component, was mustered in the vicinity of Orsha. When difficulties arose between the old exiles and the new officers, we asked OKH, which had silently tolerated our activities, for some suitable senior Soviet commanders who were willing to work with us. We were sent

General Georgi Nikolaiivich Zhilenkov as well as a certain Colonel Boyarski, who made a terrific impression.[45] Our plan was to first create a brigade, and then an entire division.

The first missions of the Experimental Unit demonstrated the competence of the Russian volunteers. However, during anti-partisan fighting they went after their own countrymen with so much atrocity that we could only restore order with the threat of courts-martial. Difficulties also cropped up when the Soviet commanders raised demands of a political nature, which we were not able to satisfy.

For a long time Field Marshal von Kluge warded off ever increasing pressure to employ the unit in a front-line mission. The first chance arose in the summer of 1942. A Soviet cavalry corps under the command of General Belov had broken out of a salient, left over from the fighting during our great retreat, that projected deep into our territory near Sukhinitzhi; the Soviet corps had crossed the Roslavl-Maloyaroslavets *Rollbahn* and now posed a significant threat to one of the most important German supply lines.[46] Kluge thus approved sending a task force from the Experimental Unit to attack General Belov's headquarters. Their passage through our lines went perfectly smoothly, but shortly before reaching its objective, the commando operation was discovered by the Soviets. Despite all the detailed preparations, a discarded German cigarette carton and the tracks made by several German hobnailed boots were enough to put the task force into an almost inescapable situation. Only after severe fighting and suffering many casualties could at least a portion of the task force fight its way back to the German lines.

But the good impression that the unit had made with this dubious mission contributed significantly to the activities that finally led to the creation of the army of General Vlasov.[47] The AG Center Experimental Unit later became part of Vlasov's army as well. Their patriotic idealism and their burning anti-communism are overshadowed today by the Volunteer Army's tragic end in 1945.

In creating the AG Center Experimental Unit, we had worked harmoniously with all the pertinent departments of OKH, but above all with the Foreign Armies East section. This OKH department was my immediate superior authority in the General Staff sense. It was magnificently directed by Reinhard Gehlen, a General Staff colonel at the time.[48] Since he had become the section chief, the quality of the military intelligence had improved by leaps and bounds. In the course of many visits to OKH and daily long-distance telephone calls with Foreign Armies East, a fine working partnership had grown up between the leaders and staffers of the OKH enemy-intelligence service and that of Army Group Center. In addition, Tresckow and Gehlen always had a relationship of mutual trust. They kept each other constantly informed about their respective activities. More than once Tresckow assigned me to deliver these updates, and in doing so I was able to learn that he and Gehlen were united by the same political opinions.

Our completely trusting relationship with the *Ausland/Abwehr* department in OKW was based, above all, on the friendship between the chief of its main section, General Hans Oster, and Tresckow himself. But the department head, Admiral Canaris, was also in complete understanding with Tresckow and his circle. Canaris and Oster once visited us together. Otherwise the Admiral usually came with his three faithful followers: Colonel in the General Staff Piekenbrock (*Abwehr I*), Colonel in the General Staff von Lahousen (*Abwehr II*), and Colonel in the General Staff von Bentivegni.[49] When he was with us at the Army Group, Canaris set aside his habitual caution. He and his section chiefs hated Hitler just as much as Tresckow and his circle did.

The conspiratorial nucleus within the command section of the Army Group (Ia and Ic/AO) was coalescing into something ever more solid, and by now things were being discussed almost completely in the open. We met each day in the "Fireplace Room." All visitors to the Fireplace Room were carefully checked out beforehand. The only man from the "other side" who was a guest in the Fireplace Room—on numerous occasions in the course of his frequent visits to the front—was General Rudolf Schmundt, Hitler's adjutant and the chief of the army officer personnel department. He had a distinct soft spot where Tresckow was concerned. After World War I they had been lieutenants together in the Reichswehr 9th Infantry Regiment at Potsdam. Working as a team in 1919, they had saved the regimental flags of the imperial Guards Corps from the grasp of the Inter-Allied Control Commission. Schmundt told me once that he had the impression that Tresckow disapproved of the Führer, but that he (Schmundt) knew Tresckow so well that he could trust him completely. Tresckow made use of this incredible naiveté to put through personnel changes in the interests of the conspiracy; to learn about the plans and schemes emanating from the *Führer-Hauptquartier*; and to influence them for the furtherance of his own plans.

Generally speaking, during his visits to the front Schmundt was deeply affected by the ever-worsening conditions that the troops faced. He often said that he would report the situation to Hitler. Once I flew along with him to East Prussia. As we sat in Hitler's elegantly appointed Condor airplane and the familiar atmosphere wrapped itself around him again, he said, "I simply cannot tell the Führer about all the negative impressions that I've received. If you only knew how much he tortures himself and how hard he works, then you'd understand that you just cannot tell him all these things so harshly." Well, I did not understand this in the least; but all my attempts to change Schmundt's mind were failures.

V

Soldier and Traitor

We can do nothing else but this, if we wish to keep our self-respect.
It *must* happen.

—Henning von Tresckow

One day in the summer of 1942, Tresckow came to me and said something along these lines, "Please don't ask me any questions, but I need a particularly effective explosive substance that doesn't take up much space and an absolutely reliable time-fuse, one that doesn't make any noise. Can you get hold of them for me?" I knew immediately what this was all about. But without raising any questions, I promised him that I would do everything in my power to find suitable materials. Since within my area of responsibility, explosive substances were most likely to be found in *Abwehr II* (Sabotage), I directed myself to the section chief Lieutenant Colonel Hotzel.[1] I told him that due to lack of time, I had until now devoted far too little attention to his line of work, but now I wanted to learn about everything from the ground up.

Pleased by my sudden interest, Hotzel presented me with a plan for inspecting his section—a plan that included a long visit to his very well-stocked storage room. There I had myself shown every type of explosive, fuse, and other device that was intended for the use of saboteurs behind Soviet lines. The German materials impressed me as being solid; however, they were for the most part inappropriate. Above all, German fuses had a ticking clockwork mechanism.

Next they showed me blasting materials that the British had airdropped over occupied countries to supply French and Dutch resistance fighters. By means of captured and "turned" enemy radio operators, German counterintelligence had been able to establish seamless connections with the transmitting stations in Great Britain. The blasting materials were requested during "radio games." Afterwards, the items only needed to be gathered up from the ground. Vast quantities of British blasting materials were also captured after failed British commando operations along the Channel coast.

The English explosive consisted of a plastic mass that could be molded by hand into any shape one chose. The fuses that went with it were of the chemical type, and therefore made no noise at all. They were constructed in the shape of a thick pencil. At the upper end, underneath the metal jacket, there was a capsule full of acid above a cord. The cord was surrounded by cotton. If you crushed the acid capsule, the acid drained into the wadding and after a certain time ate through the cord, which caused the fuse to ignite the bomb. There were fuses with durations of ten, thirty, sixty minutes or longer, all according to the strength of the cord. The duration was shown by means of colored rings on the fuses. For example, the ten-minute fuse bore a black ring.

I asked for a demonstration. The effect of the English explosive was astonishing. A few grams of it tore railroad rails to shreds. Then I had a charge of about 250 grams [a little over half a pound] placed on a captured Soviet tank; it blew off the tank turret and hurled it several meters through the air. This material had to ideally satisfy Tresckow's wishes. I asked Lieutenant Colonel Hotzel to put an assortment of different devices at my disposal, because I wanted to show the field marshal the latest equipment for sabotage missions. Hotzel let me pack up every possible device, including the British explosives. The master sergeant in charge of the storeroom quite properly asked me to confirm my receipt of the materials by signing my name in a ledger wherein they were listed in detail. As I wrote my signature, I asked myself whether I was signing my own death warrant.

When I showed Tresckow the British explosive, he was extremely pleased that I had been able to answer his wish so rapidly. After only one experiment, he was convinced that he held in his hands the right material for his purposes. In the course of a long series of tests, however, it was established that the duration of the chemical fuses depended on the ambient temperature. The durations indicated by the colored rings had been calculated at normal room temperature. During his experiments, Tresckow prepared charts on which he wrote the true durations at various temperatures. I had to keep coming up with fresh excuses for taking more explosives from the *Abwehr II* storage room. I most often tried to explain my requests by saying that during my visits to the front I wanted to bring these effective foreign explosive devices to the troops as presents. I had no idea whether this somewhat incredible-sounding explanation was accepted or not. At any rate, my name appeared more and more often in *Abwehr II*'s ledger.

When Tresckow visited the explosives storage facility himself once, he came across a British magnetic mine called a "clam." Like similar German devices, it was primarily intended for use against tanks. With its standard charge of fifty-five percent tetryl and forty-five percent TNT, the mine could blast through a twenty-five-millimeter [one-inch] steel plate, and thereby proved itself to be more effective than German magnetic mines. It could also be filled up with the plastic explosive. Because of the clam's curved shape, by placing one on top of another you could create a rounded object that felt like a bottle when the whole thing was concealed in wrapping paper. In the following weeks, Tresckow and Schlabrendorff carried out further blasting experiments with all of these materials. The tests confirmed the suitability of the British clams and fuses for a bombing-style assassination. In fact, it was with these devices that all the assassination attempts of 1943–44, including that of 20 July 1944, were carried out.

Tresckow now opened up to me completely about the necessity of doing away with Hitler. In doing so, he used the following expression: that mankind had to be liberated from its greatest criminal. He explained that after long consideration, he had decided on using explosives for the assassination, because this method offered the greatest assurance of actually killing Hitler. The fulfillment of that condition was the prerequisite for the remainder of the coup d'état plans to proceed successfully. One had to be absolutely certain that Hitler could not survive the attempt, even as a wounded man. It was for this reason that the most obvious idea, that of using a pistol, had been discarded. Schmundt had told Tresckow that all of Hitler's vital areas were armored against pistol bullets. During a visit by Hitler to Army Group Center, we had been able to ascertain that even his service cap had steel inserts. A would-be assassin, therefore, would have to be able to shoot him in the small target area consisting of the middle of the face, in order to kill him with any degree of certainty.

Tresckow's decision in favor of a bombing attempt was strengthened by an expert opinion from the experienced modern pentathlon competitor, Cavalry Captain Baron Georg von Boeselager.[2] When Tresckow asked him whether, while in a state of (understandable) nervous agitation and from a distance of several meters away, he could trust himself to hit such a small target with absolute certainty, this superb pistol marksman said no. On top of that, even drawing a small handgun created the danger that the attack could miscarry. Hitler and his immediate surroundings were under the sharp eyes of his SS guardians. After the war, my cousin Count Hyazinth von Strachwitz, well-known as *der Panzergraf* (Panzer Count), told me that once while standing in front of Hitler in the *Führerbunker* to receive a high decoration, he had reached into a trouser pocket to pull out his handkerchief.[3] At that very same moment an SS man standing behind him had seized his wrist, and only let go of it when he saw that Strachwitz held nothing in his hand but a square of white cloth.

In the meantime, the unstable style of leadership that had come into being with Hitler's takeover of OKH got even worse. We at Army Group Center experienced this state of affairs to a particularly high degree. After giving up a Panzer army to Army Group South, we were no longer in the position to conduct large-scale strategic operations on what had up until then been the most critical front. Army Group Center's entire front ossified into positional warfare, in which, moreover, due to Hitler's strict orders to "hold at all costs," an extremely unfavorable front line had been created. Requests to straighten out the front were refused over and over again, but replacements of men and materials remained utterly insufficient. The initiative now lay completely with our foe. If we were still able to withstand the Soviet counteroffensives until April 1942, the credit was due solely to the local commanders and to the unbroken, the incomparable, fighting spirit of the German troops. In July 1942 it was even possible to smooth out the critical position that our left wing (9th Army) had held since the winter retreat.

The area around Rzhev remained the sore point for the whole Army Group front during all of 1942. In my frequent trips to the front, which often lasted for several days, I personally experienced, sometimes from the most advanced line, the heavy and costly combat in this sector. Again and again the Rzhev sector needed to be reinforced with units pulled out of other sectors of the Army Group's front. Many times, freshly arrived divisions were hurled straight from their troop trains into the fighting, regiment after regiment. As a result, there gradually came to be such a muddle of units that it was scarcely possible to sort them all out. The bleeding-white of the German defenders in the Rzhev sector—as insisted upon by Hitler—proved to be a serious military error.[4]

Another example of Hitler's weaknesses as a commander arose in 1942 and concerned the seam where 4th Army and 2nd Panzer Army's zones met, in the Sukhinitzhi sector. Here in the course of their counteroffensive, the Soviets had succeeded in making a deep penetration in the direction of Bryansk. Securing this breach cost us heavily. A pincer movement conducted by parts of 2nd Panzer Army, coming from the area southwest of Tula, and parts of 4th Army, coming from the vicinity of Yukhnov, was intended to "iron out" this strength-sapping salient. But the forces that had been prepared to form the northern pincer around Yukhnov had needed to be pulled away to restore the situation in the Rzhev sector; and 2nd Panzer Army had established the fact that their own area of attack was completely unsuitable for tanks. Since the enemy situation in the Sukhinitzhi sector had also developed to the German side's disadvantage, the Army Group sought to have the planned operation abandoned for the time being. It all came down to a weeks-long tug of war between Hitler and Field Marshal von Kluge, in which each man tried to convince the other one of the correctness of his arguments. I can still hear the last telephone conversation in this dispute. This was the exchange, almost word for word:

Kluge: "*Mein Führer,* for the reasons I've already stated, the now single-handed offensive by 2nd Panzer Army has absolutely no prospect of success. It will only cost us a great deal of blood and bring us nothing. *I implore you to call off this attack.*"

Hitler: "*Herr Feldmarschall,* you'll see; the attack will go through like a knife goes through butter. I order it to be carried out, and that's final."

It all came about as Kluge had predicted. After some slight initial successes, the German attack stalled amidst rough terrain and powerful Soviet counterattacks. The operation had to be halted, with heavy losses of men and materiel. Hitler never again returned to this affair. From a desk in East Prussia, acting against the urgent counsel of every commander on the scene, he had brought about the senseless deaths of thousands of German soldiers.

In light of such experiences, the Stalingrad catastrophe came as no surprise to us. We had already heard several months earlier that there was a "Forward Command Tiflis" in Breslau.[5] Obviously Hitler wished to press onward over the Caucasus Mountains and Persia to India, to strike the British Empire at its Achilles' heel. The prerequisite for such a far-reaching goal was this halting-point on the Volga front, on both sides of Stalingrad. In the final analysis, that was the reason for the shocking tragedy of the 6th Army. Neither the army commander, Field Marshal Paulus, nor the commander of Army Group South, Field Marshal von Manstein, showed themselves to be capable of preventing the catastrophe that had been foreseeable for so long.[6]

I learned from the following experience how Hitler sought to put his field marshals under personal obligation to him: On 30 October 1942, Field Marshal von Kluge celebrated his sixtieth birthday. In the late morning we staff officers, led by General Krebs (the new chief of staff of the Army Group), walked to the field marshal's blockhouse to congratulate him together.[7] During this reception Kluge's aide-de-camp, First Lieutenant Baron Phillip von Boeselager, announced a surprise visit by Hitler's adjutant, General Schmundt.

Schmundt bowed to the field marshal in his suave manner and expressed his best wishes for the future. Then, visibly embarrassed, he drew from the pocket of his tunic a large envelope, which he passed to Kluge with some words that were almost too inaudible to understand. I was standing close by, and I could see that the envelope was marked "top secret." Kluge tore it open with his fingers and pulled out a Reichsbank check for a six-figure sum—it was probably 200,000 or 250,000 Reichsmarks—bearing Hitler's spidery signature. Kluge wordlessly stuck the check back into the envelope and, with a display of nonchalance, tossed it onto the desk. He asked Schmundt whether he would be able to stay for lunch; but Schmundt explained that he had to keep flying to 2nd Panzer Army and then be back in East Prussia by evening, and so unfortunately he could not accept the invitation.

After Schmundt's departure, we sat down to the meal that had been laid out in the dining room. When we had seated ourselves around a table, the following conversation took place:

Kluge: "Gentlemen, what does one actually do upon receiving a tip?"

Krebs: "But *Herr Feldmarschall,* you really can't look at it that way. Field Marshals Blücher, Yorck, and Moltke all got and accepted gifts."[8]

Kluge: "My dear Krebs, that was quite a different matter. In those instances, field commanders, after victorious campaigns, received presents in the form of land from the hand of their sovereign. But nobody ever sent them a check halfway through a war whose outcome is still very much in doubt."

Tresckow: "*Herr Feldmarschall,* you know how much we respect you, and how much respect you enjoy throughout the Army Group. If you wish to preserve that respect, then I can only beg you to separate yourself from this money as quickly as possible."

Kluge: "But how?"

Boeselager: "*Ach, Herr Feldmarschall*—we'll send it to the Red Cross."

Kluge: "Close your snout, you fresh puppy! Yes, gentlemen, I'll have to give this matter some thought."

Tresckow: "*Herr Feldmarschall,* I would like to make a point of stressing to you, one more time, that you have to find a way to get rid of this money. You ought not to use a penny of it for yourself."

Then the conversation turned to other things. I was never able to find out for sure to what use the check was put. But we all knew that Hitler had also distributed large sums of money to other field marshals.

Meanwhile the conspiratorial group around Tresckow had been strengthened by the addition of several young officers. Above all, besides Phillip von Boeselager, who had been the field marshal's aide-de-camp since earlier in 1942, his older brother Baron Georg von Boeselager had entered our circle. Georg von Boeselager was a superb human being from every angle. He was a product of the 15th Cavalry Regiment in Paderborn. Before the war, I had competed against him in numerous hunter-jumper events at western German racetracks. During a visit to his brother at Army Group Center's headquarters, he had made a suggestion to Tresckow to collect all the divisional reconnaissance-battalion cavalry squadrons—whose men had been doing practically nothing but playing cards ever since maneuver warfare had come to a halt—and form them into a battle-ready cavalry force for special missions. Tresckow had swiftly agreed to this suggestion, and he overcame all opposition to turn it into a reality.

Because Tresckow and Boeselager were completely as one in their political and military views, it was soon clear to us all what they had in mind. A combat unit was to be formed that would be reliable—in the conspiratorial sense!

I myself made several visits during the formation and training of Regiment "Boeselager"; within a relatively short time Georg von Boeselager was so successful in welding together the officers, NCOs, and men that this cavalry troop was ready for any mission, be it ever so "special." But later it was never possible to use this unit politically, for ever-shifting reasons. After March 1943, Hitler never again came to Army Group Center; and on that single occasion Kluge refused to allow a surprise attack within his own headquarters area. The cavalry unit, much reinforced over time, was then assigned over and over again to wherever combat had flared up, proving itself as an elite force. Georg von Boeselager himself fell in one of these battles while giving a shining example of personal valor and devotion to duty.

In the meantime Tresckow had finished his preparations for a bombing assassination attempt. Now he was only waiting for an opportunity to arise that offered absolute assurance of success. But the waiting period was also necessary because the timing of the attempt was dependent on the preparations going on in Berlin for a political coup d'état. I myself knew little about these preparations at the time, and knew nothing about the projected utilization of the "VALKYRIE" plan. Tresckow believed that no member of the conspiracy ought to know any more than was absolutely necessary. It was very clear to him that once a conspirator had by any chance been arrested, he would be forced to talk by the Gestapo, which would employ the severest possible tortures. He didn't even trust himself to withstand that kind of torture. Therefore he did not want to burden anyone with knowledge that could lead to the endangerment of the entire conspiracy.

At this time in the Army Group Center resistance group, apart from Tresckow, only Fabian von Schlabrendorff was aware of all the details of the preparation for the coup d'état. I didn't know until March 1943 that the work on Operation VALKYRIE had been provisionally concluded in February of the same year. When Hitler's second—and last—visit to our headquarters was announced for the date of 13 March 1943, it was nonetheless apparent to me that Tresckow would not allow this opportunity to get at Hitler to go by unused.

Hitler came with a grand entourage (which also included his personal physician, Dr. Theo Morell, and his private chef) in two Condor airplanes, which could not be visually distinguished from each other.[9] A squadron of fighter planes escorted the flight from East Prussia to Smolensk, although Soviet aircraft almost never appeared in that airspace. All the other security arrangements were the same as during his first visit to Army Group Center in Borissov in the summer of 1941. For days before the visit, our headquarters was crawling with SD and SS men. Hitler's special cars had arrived from faraway East Prussia, just in time to make the short drive from the Smolensk airfield to the headquarters. There was absolutely no prospect of getting at the Führer's Mercedes-Benz to attach a time bomb without being observed.

The conferences took place during the morning in the field marshal's quarters; only the army commanders, and from our staff only the chief of staff and the Ia, took part in them. Lunch was served in the wooden lodge that served as our officers' club. Hitler sat with the generals at the central table. I sat at a round table nearby with a number of General Staff officers, among them Tresckow and Colonel in the General Staff Brandt from OKH.[10] When an SS orderly wanted to serve Hitler the meal prepared by the cooks he had brought along, Dr. Morell tasted the food before it was put on the table. It was not clear whether this was done for reasons of security or of health. At any rate this prelude made a macabre impression.

Then I overheard Tresckow asking Brandt whether he would be flying back to East Prussia on the same airplane as Hitler. Brandt answered yes. During the flight he was supposed to present a briefing about the situation on other fronts. After a pause, Tresckow asked Brandt to do him the favor of taking along two bottles of cognac that he, Tresckow, had lost in a wager with the chief of the Administrative Department of OKH, Colonel Stieff.[11] Brandt declared himself ready to do so. I first learned several days later that this packet contained four clam magnetic mines shaped like a pair of bottles, and equipped with a thirty-minute fuse, which Schlabrendorff had set off just before handing it over to Brandt. If the fuse had worked, Hitler's plane would have been blown to bits high in the sky, somewhere over the vastness of Russia. This type of fuse had never once failed during our series of tests. On that day of all days, though, the fuse (which, as Schlabrendorff later investigated and established, had been put into action quite correctly) did fail. And just like that, the most promising assassination attempt of the entire war ran aground.

The way Tresckow regained his energy and enterprise after this truly unforeseeable failure was incredible. Scarcely had Schlabrendorff succeeded in recovering the bomb, which if discovered would have put the entire conspiracy into the gravest danger, than Tresckow was already planning new opportunities for an assassination. A few days after 13 March, Schmundt told him over the telephone that as part of the Heroes' Memorial Ceremony, Hitler wished to visit an exhibit of captured Soviet weapons that Army Group Center had installed in the Berlin Arsenal.[12] Before the exhibit was opened to the public, he wanted to walk around it for about half an hour, accompanied by a small escort party. Hitler desired Field Marshal von Kluge, as the Army Group's commander, to take part in this walk-around along with his wife. My Ic/AO section had organized the exhibit. Of all the General Staff officers in the Army Group, I had the greatest justification for being present when Hitler viewed it.

Tresckow asked me whether I would be prepared to make an assassination attempt on this occasion, when, besides Hitler, it might also be possible to liquidate Goering, Himmler, and Goebbels, too. He could give me no instructions as far as carrying out the task, for this would depend on the conditions on the spot. But it would probably be necessary for me to blow myself up along with Hitler. At that time we were so caught up in the mission we had set for ourselves, that of eliminating Hitler, that I did not need much time to answer "yes" to the most momentous question that anybody ever asked me.

Then Tresckow shared with me the full details of the unlucky assassination attempt of a few days before, and initiated me for the first time into the preparations for the intended coup d'état. The assassination would be the spark that would ignite Operation VALKYRIE, which, with the prerequisite condition of Hitler's death, would guarantee the certain success of the coup.

Tresckow very deftly managed to convince Kluge not to fly to Berlin, but to have himself represented by the commander of 9th Army, Colonel General Model.[13] Tresckow believed at the time that after a successful assassination, he would still need Kluge around to be the *Reichspräsident* or the supreme commander of the army. By contrast, Model was known as one of Hitler's willing followers, so he didn't need to be saved. The toughest thing was talking Kluge out of having his wife participate in the event.

Before my flight to Berlin, Tresckow invited me to go on a long walk in the meadows along the Dnieper. We discussed all the possibilities that awaited me in Berlin. Suddenly Tresckow stood still and said, "Isn't it a monstrous thing, that here are two German General Staff officers, conferring together about the best way to kill their commander-in-chief? But it has to be done. It is now the only possible way to save Germany from her downfall. The world has to be set free from the biggest criminal of all time. *He must be struck down dead like a mad dog who threatens all mankind!*"

On 20 March 1943, I flew to Berlin with Colonel General Model. After our arrival we drove immediately to Schmundt's office to get the details about the ceremonial program. Schmundt initially declared that I could not take part in the viewing, because Hitler had personally decided who would be part of his escort. Only after Model had insisted on my participation in the walk-through because he could give no explanations at all about the items on display was Schmundt prepared to agree to my presence, on his own head.

Then Model wanted to know the exact time when the event would begin, because he still wanted to fly to visit his wife in Dresden that day, and then return to Berlin on the morning of the 21st. Schmundt explained that it was forbidden under penalty of death to give away the time of Hitler's arrival at the Arsenal, something that was known only to Hitler and himself. But in this special case he would make an exception. The time differed from the official opening time by about ninety minutes. Next, Schmundt reconfirmed that Hitler's visit to the exhibition was expected to last for about half an hour. This was of decisive importance for my plan, because in the unheated Arsenal building, I would have to reckon on the ten-minute fuses taking twelve to fifteen minutes to work.

I used the rest of the day on 20 March to investigate all the possibilities for an assassination attempt in the Arsenal. There was still work going on everywhere: both inside the *Lichthof* (the Sunlight Court); the metal-and-glass-roofed central courtyard of the Arsenal, where the actual Heroes' Memorial Ceremony would take place; and in the exhibition area. In the *Lichthof,* the platforms for the Berlin Philharmonic Orchestra and the guests of honor were being constructed, the speaker's podium was being erected, and the whole space was being decorated with laurel wreaths and flowers. In addition to the workers, the whole place swarmed with SS and SD personnel. It was utterly impossible to install an explosive device anywhere without being seen. In any case, it would really only have made sense to do this at the podium in the center of the *Lichthof,* but no large object could be hidden within or near it. It was just as useless to plant a bomb anywhere in the large exhibit hall, because one could not anticipate where Hitler would pause.

During these hours, it finally became clear to me that the assassination could only succeed if I carried the explosive devices on my person, and kept myself in Hitler's immediate vicinity, so as to blow us both up. I was so involved with all this reconnoitering that I scarcely had time for reflection until late in the evening. Only when I was in my room in the Hotel Eden did the enormous significance and responsibility of my plans bore in on me again.[14]

In accordance with our prior arrangements, Fabian von Schlabrendorff brought me the clam mines sometime around midnight. Since I had only brought two quite old ten-minute fuses with me from Smolensk, I asked Schlabrendorff whether he could get me any others. But he had already made every effort to do so, and could not help me. I never shut my eyes that night; my feelings were similar to those of a condemned man in the death cell on the eve of his execution.

When I entered the Arsenal on the morning of 21 March, everything was just as it had been the day before. Work was still going on everywhere, and the police observation and surveillance of the preparations were even tighter than they had had been previously. From 11 A.M. onward, the first military officers and party functionaries began to arrive, having no idea that the ceremony would not commence until one o'clock in the afternoon. Several acquaintances spoke to me; I probably gave them the impression of being completely distracted. During the ceremony, I sat wedged in on the dais opposite the speaker's podium. After we had listened to the first movement of the *7th Symphony* by Anton Bruckner, Hitler began his speech, which I only vaguely absorbed. I do recall that despite all the optimistic assertions about the military situation, it had a peculiar mysticism about it, with overtones of the *Götterdämmerung,* the "Twilight of the Gods."[15]

Since I could have no idea how long he would speak and how long afterwards the orchestra would play, it was out of the question to arm the fuses while the ceremony continued. I swallowed a Pervitin amphetamine tablet that Tresckow had given me for safety's sake, and then, during the closing notes of music, I walked to the entrance of the exhibition hall. There I linked up with Colonel General Model and the museum curator. The three of us took our positions at the entrance, with me standing between Model and the uniformed curator. It took some time, however, before Hitler appeared. At his side walked Goering, who in his white uniform, heavily laden with badges and medals, and his red, morocco-leather boots, gave the impression of a prince in a comic opera. In addition his face was painted with cosmetics: the effect was grotesque. Himmler, Keitel, Dönitz, and Schmundt also accompanied Hitler, as well as two or three of his military aides-de-camp.[16]

While he was still in the doorway, Hitler suddenly turned and said, "*Herr Feldmarschall* von Bock, I pray that you will join me, as Army Group Center's former commander." Bock complied with a rather over-affected bow, and entered the hall along with his escort officer, Reserve Major Count Carl-Hans von Hardenberg. I used this moment, while all attention was focused on Hitler, Bock, and Hardenberg, to arm the fuse of the clam explosive in my left coat-pocket. I had the other one in my right pocket, but like both of my neighbors I already had my right arm raised in the Hitler salute. Model was the only one whom Hitler greeted with a handshake.

Then the tour of the exhibition began, with me staying very close to Hitler's left side. Hitler was obviously not listening while I attempted to provide explanations of the various items on display. I received no response even when I called his attention to a Napoleonic eagle-standard which German combat engineers had found in the bed of the Beresina River during bridge-building operations. Instead Hitler walked—or rather ran—along the shortest route to the side entrance. Not even Goering, who in the meantime had taken a look into a glass case filled with documents and wanted to show Hitler a patriotic appeal to the Russian people from the Metropolitan of Moscow, was deemed worthy of a reply.[17] At the exit door to that side of the Arsenal where the great memorial statue of Frederick the Great stands, Hitler took his leave of Model and me with the usual right-angled raising of his right forearm. Hitler had never spoken a word, and had hardly glanced at a thing, during his entire walk through the exhibition.

After the war one heard that the BBC had recorded the entire ceremony from the German radio broadcast, and that the time that elapsed from Hitler's entrance into the exhibit hall until he left the Arsenal building was only two minutes. In my memory it seemed to have lasted several minutes longer. In any case, the time had been too brief even for a normal fuse-duration of ten minutes. While I was inside the nearest lavatory yanking the fuse out of the bomb, Hitler was outside of the building, clambering on top of one of the captured Soviet tanks that had been put on display between the Arsenal and the statue. It seemed to be the only thing that interested him.

Without waiting for the honor battalion to pass in review, I walked over to the Union Club in Schadowstrasse, hoping to be alone there at that time of day.[18] But instead I met another member, Baron Waldemar von Oppenheim, the Cologne banker who also owned Schlenderhan, Germany's oldest and best thoroughbred stud farm.[19] Shortly after we had exchanged greetings, he stunned me by saying, "I could have murdered Adolf today. He came riding slowly along Unter den Linden in his open car, right in front of my first-floor room in the Hotel Bristol. It would have been the easiest thing in the world to toss a hand grenade across the sidewalk and into his auto." But he had neither known when and where Hitler would come by, nor had he had a suitable weapon with him. Although Oppenheim knew me and could guess my political views, his statement showed a lot of spirit. I said nothing to him about what I had just been through, so as not to burden him with such knowledge.

When I got back to Smolensk, Tresckow told me that he had listened to the radio broadcast of the Arsenal ceremony, and had known, on the basis of the elapsed time between Hitler's entry into the exhibition and his exit from the building, that due to the ten- to fifteen-minute duration of the chemical fuses, it had not been possible to carry out the assassination. But even after this new failure, Tresckow was by no means discouraged. With remarkable energy he drove ahead with his plans.

Above all, he now exerted himself to win over Field Marshal von Kluge. Kluge was a sharp critic of Hitler's, decidedly an opponent of the Nazi Party, and apart from that was clever enough to see which way things were going. But he lacked the personal and political greatness to be able to bring himself to commit high treason.

One evening Tresckow and I went out for a walk with him. Once again Tresckow tried to convince him of the necessity for action. Kluge responded with weak counterarguments, even if he also agreed in principal with Tresckow's line of thinking. All at once Tresckow said, "*Herr Feldmarschall,* someone is walking by your side who, a very short time ago, made an assassination attempt against Hitler." Kluge stopped with a jolt, grabbed my arm, and said, "For God's sake, Gersdorff, what have you done?" I answered, "The only thing that's left to do in the current situation." Then Kluge walked ahead several steps further, spread his arms out somewhat theatrically, and said, *Kinder, ihr habt mich!* ("Children, you have me!")[20]

Afterwards, Kluge really did do everything that Tresckow asked of him; he got in contact with Beck, Goerdeler, and other leaders of the resistance, and even sought to win over other high-ranking military commanders for action.[21] Nonetheless, we soon got the impression that he could never completely set himself free from Hitler's influence; and that he regarded the planning for a coup d'état and, above all, the preparations for an assassination, not only with great skepticism, but also with an inner repugnance.

At any rate, Tresckow succeeded in getting Kluge to send Lieutenant Colonel in the General Staff von Voss (Army Group Center's Ia/op) to Field Marshal von Rundstedt at Paris, and me to the commanding general of Army Group South, Field Marshal von Manstein, as his representatives.[22] At a much earlier date Tresckow had been able, using Schmundt as his middleman, to get our previous Ia/op, Colonel in the General Staff Schulze-Büttger, assigned to Manstein's staff, so he would be able to influence the field marshal in the direction of our plans and also use any opportunities that came up at Army Group South for an assassination attempt.[23] But Schulze-Büttger had let us know again and again that he couldn't get any farther ahead with Manstein.

Before I flew to Army Group South's headquarters at Zaporozhie, in Ukraine, Kluge said to me, "Let Field Marshal von Manstein know that I implore him, following a coup d'état, to take the position of chief of the General Staff of the Wehrmacht—that is, of the combined General Staffs of the army, the air force, and the navy." He expressly added that in such a situation he, Kluge, would be willing to be subordinate to the younger man. Tresckow gave me letters from Goerdeler and Popitz to bring along with me, letters in which both men beseeched the army generals to take action.[24] However, Tresckow directed me not to show these letters unless I was certain that Manstein would make no "use" of them. Tresckow also ordered me not to say a word in the presence of General Busse, the chief of staff of Army Group South.[25]

After my arrival in Zaporozhie, I first spoke with Schulze-Büttger and with yet another of Tresckow's confidants, Manstein's personal aide-de-camp, First Lieutenant Alexander Stahlberg.[26] Both men held out little hope for my being able to influence the field marshal in our direction. They then arranged for me to have a one-to-one conversation with Manstein. Its beginning and its important passages went like this:

Manstein: "You're coming from Army Group Center. I'll have my chief of staff sent for."

Me: "In General Busse's presence I would only be able to present the Field Marshal with a briefing about the military situation in Army Group Center. But I wouldn't be able to say a single word about my real mission."

Manstein looked at me, rather nonplussed, and said, "Well, then, fire away."

I led off with a topic that I expected would amount to pushing on an open door with Manstein: namely, the organization of the top-level military command, which was an oft-discussed issue in all of the staffs. I stated to him that Field Marshal von Kluge was highly concerned about this problem, and about the future conduct of the war in general. In view of the rivalry between OKW and OKH, and Hitler's ever-more clearly dilettantish leadership style, the collapse of the Eastern Front would be only a question of time. It had to be made clear to Hitler that he was steering towards a catastrophe.

Manstein: "I am of the same opinion entirely. But I'm the wrong man to tell it to Hitler. Without my being able to do anything about it, the enemy propaganda has turned me into the man who allegedly wants to compete with Hitler for power. Now he regards me with nothing but suspicion. Only Rundstedt and Kluge can take on a task like this one."

Me: "Perhaps all the field marshals should go to Hitler together and hold a pistol to his chest."

Manstein: "Prussian field marshals do not mutiny."

Me: "There are enough examples in Prussian history of high-ranking generals acting against the will and command of their sovereign. I will mention only Seydlitz and Yorck.[27] And beyond all that, Prussian field marshals were never before in a situation that could even be compared to the current one. Such a unique situation demands the use of methods that were never used before. But we also don't believe any longer that some kind of joint action by the field marshals would have any prospect of success. We've been convinced for a long time in Army Group Center that every means must now be seized upon to save Germany from catastrophe."

Manstein: "You people really want to kill him?"

Me: "Yes, *Herr Feldmarschall*: to kill him like a rabid dog."

Manstein jumped up, paced excitedly about the room, and cried out: "I won't have any part of it. That would cause the army to collapse."

Me: "The Field Marshal has already conceded that if nothing else happens, Germany will have to collapse. The army isn't the main consideration here: it is Germany and the German people."

Manstein: "I'm a soldier, first and foremost. You don't know the front the way I do. I talk with young and old soldiers every day, and most of all I talk with the junior officers. I see the enthusiasm in their eyes whenever they talk about 'the Führer.' They would never understand an 'action' being taken against him. Something of that kind would surely lead to a civil war within the army."

Me: "I'm often at the front, too, and I talk with junior officers. I admit that the majority are as enthusiastic about Hitler as ever. I also know many, however, who have a wholly different view. But above all else, I'm convinced that the officer corps and the troops would stand behind their military leaders with absolute obedience, and would carry out every order that was given to them. Most likely, a short time after Hitler disappeared nobody would even mention him any more."

With the last claim, which I threw out heatedly, I certainly went too far. In any case, Manstein energetically contradicted me. He stuck to his own opinion and declared that he would never involve himself in an undertaking that was bound to lead to the army's collapse. Long before this point in the conversation, Manstein could have had me arrested; I had spoken very openly about the necessity of Hitler's elimination. And so I left the letters from Goerdeler and Popitz in my pocket. In view of Manstein's inflexible attitude, it seemed to me too risky to put these men's lives in his hands.

When, after some further discussion, I had to acknowledge to myself the uselessness of my efforts, I carried out the "selfless" assignment I had received from Field Marshal von Kluge.

Me: "Field Marshal von Kluge authorized me to ask you whether you would be prepared, following a successful coup d'état, to serve as chief of the General Staff of the Wehrmacht."

Manstein bowed slightly and said: "Please inform Field Marshal von Kluge that I thank him for the trust he reposes in me. Field Marshal von Manstein will always be faithfully at the service of the legitimate national government."

With that, the conversation was at an end. Until my plane took off, I had to keep reckoning on being arrested. According to the laws of war, the field marshal would have been perfectly justified in having me sentenced to death by a summary court-martial and shot then and there. His continued silence after 20 July 1944, is one of the reasons for my survival. Despite all my disappointment, I will never forget that. On the other hand, his attitude was representative of the majority of the senior generals. Manstein's behavior typified the grave sins of omission that they all committed. Long before this time, Tresckow had felt nothing but contempt for these men.

My own opinion is that the commanders of the German armies and army groups in World War I could not match such strategists of genius as (for example) Field Marshals von Bock, von Manstein, and von Rundstedt; but that in their personal characters, they were superior to the German commanders in World War II.

In stating this opinion I do not overlook that it was easier for generals in high places to preserve their characters under the monarchical system, because they could rely on the fact that their political and military leadership would not give them orders that were in direct contradiction to their soldierly honor. But thinking back on my father, and on the many ex-officers of the old army whom I got to know in my younger days, I am convinced that if such a thing had happened, the imperial officer corps would have reacted more sharply, more decisively, and with far more unity than did the officer corps of the Wehrmacht. In contrast to the opinions of many other people, I do believe that the spirit of the resistance—that is, the obligation to place conscience above obedience—was more firmly anchored in earlier times, and even during the imperial era between 1871 and 1918, than it was later on in the Third Reich. Prussian history alone is full of examples of such resistance in action. Perhaps the many and varied oaths that they had taken—to "Kaiser and King," to Ebert, to Hindenburg, and finally to Hitler—negatively affected the personal values of the top Wehrmacht generals.

While in captivity after World War II, Field Marshal von Rundstedt is supposed to have asserted on some occasion that throughout his long military career—Rundstedt was the senior serving general in the Wehrmacht—he was never instructed about questions of international law or about the Hague Convention on Land Warfare, not even once. This may be true, and in that case it would demonstrate a monumental failure in the military educational system. All the same, one might well have expected that an officer who was a top-ranking commander and a court-martial convening authority would, on his own initiative, undertake to do everything needful to make himself adequately informed both about his own national military-justice system and about the rules and standards of international law. As a court-martial convening authority he ought not to have relied solely on the advice of his subordinate military-justice officers.

In the spring of 1943, Army Group Center's front underwent a certain consolidation, since after Stalingrad Hitler needed troops to prop up the southern front; therefore, he ordered the evacuation of the great projecting salient around Rzhev. During the entire month of March, in "Operation BUFFALO," the left wing of the Army Group was withdrawn to prepared positions in the rear. Once again German troops showed their tremendous soldierly capabilities. The new front corresponded somewhat to the line the Army Group had reached during the battle of Vyazma-Bryansk. Operation BUFFALO caused the main battle line to be shortened by about 330 kilometers (205 miles), and allowed for the withdrawal of fifteen infantry divisions, two mechanized infantry divisions, and three armored divisions.

Hitler, however, was already thinking of new offensive operations. On 13 March 1943, the Army Group received the first instructions to prepare for "Operation CITADEL."[28] A Soviet advance in the region on either side of Kursk was to be headed off by means of a northward attack from the Kharkov area by Army Group South, and a simultaneous southward attack by elements of Army Group Center, coming from the Orel-Bryansk sector.

As always, Hitler was convinced of the superiority of German leadership and of the German armed forces. But in contrast to his wishful thinking, the Soviet Union's capacities had proved quite sufficient to replace the heavy losses in the first years of the war. Hitler denied all the information that the intelligence service had garnered, and proceeded mainly on the basis of false judgments about the enemy.

In early 1943 our signals intelligence section, which had proved itself to be by far our best source of intelligence during the Russian campaign, reported an ongoing series of radio transmissions between Soviet artillery commanders, which at first could not be interpreted. The radio traffic produced the unit numbers of over sixty artillery regiments, which had plainly been established at widely separated points behind the entire Soviet front. In contrast to the German army, in which the 6th Division had the 6th Artillery Regiment, the 6th Signals Company, the 6th Reconnaissance Battalion, and so forth, the numerical designations of Soviet troop units permitted no conclusions to be drawn as to the division number.

One of my aides, First Lieutenant Conrad, whose job it was to evaluate intelligence data, was convinced that the Soviets wouldn't be numbering their troop units willy-nilly. There had to be a system behind it all. After intensive thought and calculation, he discovered a mathematical formula with which one could derive the division number from the number of the artillery regiment. With this logarithm we had the key that allowed us to conclude, with a high degree of probability, that the Soviets had created a large quantity of brand-new divisions. After reviewing our theory, the Foreign Armies East section at OKH and Canaris's department at OKW were both convinced of its correctness. Hitler, on the other hand, rejected our final conclusions as completely impossible and defeatist. But in fact, a few months later every one of the new Soviet divisions we had suspected showed up on our front lines.

During Operation CITADEL's preparatory period, the enemy situation had completely altered without our being able to convince Hitler of the new facts on the ground. On 5 July 1943, the assault forces from Army Group Center—9th Army, with twenty-one divisions; and Army Group South, 4th Panzer Army—went on the offensive. The German forces ran into superior enemy forces, which soon opened up a counterattack by powerful armored reserves. The operation had to be called off by 11 July to forestall the demolition of the entire German front.

In 1943, an event occurred in our zone that would acquire worldwide significance.[29] There was a small *Feldpolizei* detachment assigned to my Ic/AO section; its primary mission was to act as a personal security detail for the field marshal.[30] Since we had been living in the same headquarters near Smolensk for almost two years, we had to reckon with the possibility of Soviet commando-style operations against the Army Group staff. I therefore gave the leader of these field-police troops, *Feldpolizeisekretär* Voss, the assignment of routinely monitoring the inhabitants of the neighboring villages, so we could learn immediately about the arrival of strangers.[31]

One day in the spring of 1943, Voss reported to me that Russian peasants with whom his people had established a good relationship had given him the following information: Polish soldiers who had been quartered in their homes—these Poles were working as volunteers in the supply units of a German division that was marching toward the front—had sought to find out whether Polish prisoners of war taken by Soviet forces had ever been seen in the Smolensk area. It had then occurred to the Russians that three years earlier, in April 1940, numerous transport trains carrying Polish war prisoners had unloaded at the Nyezdova railway station and that the men had been led into a small nearby forest, after which gunshots were heard from that direction for days. After hearing this news, the Polish volunteers had made excavations in the little forest, swiftly located mass graves containing the remains of Polish officers, and erected a tall birch-wood cross at the site of the discovery.

I reported this initially mysterious-sounding story, and gave orders to have the matter investigated. The woods lay in the immediate vicinity of the so-called "Little Castle on the Dnieper," a former NKVD (*Narodnii Komisariat Vnutrennikh Del,* or People's Commissariat of Internal Affairs) vacation resort in which the commander of our signals regiment was now billeted. By dint of trial excavations, my people located numerous mass graves in which there quite obviously lay thousands of Polish officers. They had all been murdered by a shot to the back of the neck. In response to our report, OKH ordered us to open the graves, establish the number and the identity of the victims, and investigate the circumstances of their murder. The forensic surgeon Professor Dr. Buhtz, who happened to be on the staff of our Chief Quartermaster's section, directed the exhumation of the bodies.[32]

The Propaganda Ministry had directed that the discovery of the mass graves should be employed for propaganda purposes. Therefore I sought a suitable label for the matter. During the preparation of the initial statement, we had noticed that quite close to Nyezdova (the nearest village to the mass burials) there were mound graves from ancient Russian history that the Soviets could use as an explanation for the discovery. (And not long afterwards, the Soviets actually did so.) I thus looked on the map for a larger place nearby with a memorable name, located the little city of Katyn about five kilometers away, and decided to designate this affair by that title.

Thus, and in no other manner, did the story of the discovery of the "Katyn Massacre" play itself out. All other descriptions are either false or completely made up, including the tale about the wolf that was supposed to have dug up the graves.

Later we established beyond dispute that the murder of the Polish officers had taken place in April 1940, and therefore could only have been carried out by the Soviets. The evidence for this: the clear and unanimous statements of the Russian inhabitants; the three-year-old tree growth over the graves; numerous and still well-preserved documents (such as diaries, letters, newspapers) that were found on almost all the corpses; the results of forensic medical investigations of the time and manner of death; and the type of murder weapons and projectiles in question.

We also established that in many large, deep graves, thousands of corpses were found which could be identified as Polish officers—including two generals—from their well-preserved uniforms. After the Polish campaign in 1939, they were held by the Soviets in the prisoner of war camp at Kozielsk near Orel, and transported to Smolensk in the spring of 1940, one and a quarter years before the start of the Russian campaign. All the diary entries ended during this railroad journey or upon arrival at the Nyezdova station.

Thirdly, all the victims were murdered by being shot in the back of the neck. Some had their hands bound with wire or typical Russian cordage.

Up until the summer of 1943, about 4,500 corpses were exhumed, identified and reburied. The precise number of bodies was never established, because for hygienic reasons we had to call a halt to the exhumations by midsummer, and we were compelled to evacuate Smolensk in the early autumn. Estimates varied from 8,000 to 12,000 bodies.

During the exhumations, numerous commissions and delegations from Poland, Germany, and many neutral countries came to view the graves. I recall the following visitors in particular: the Polish Archbishop of Krakow, Dr. Jasinski; a delegation from the Polish Red Cross, which was actively involved in the work of exhumation and identification; a commission of medical examiners from twelve neutral and occupied countries, who had total freedom to conduct their own examinations of bodies they had chosen themselves, as well as to make all other inquiries; a commission of journalists from neutral and occupied countries; and delegations of Polish, American, British and French prisoners of war.

I spoke with almost all of the visitors at the time, and I never met a single one who was not convinced of the Soviet Union's guilt for this crime. The evidence at the site was so indisputable that even the discovery of bullet shells bearing the name of a German munitions factory did not cause doubts, since it could be shown that that very factory had shipped pistol ammunition to the Soviet Union in 1939.

The Bulgarian medical examiner Professor Markov stated in a conversation with me in 1943 that there was not the slightest doubt that the murder of the Polish officers had been the work of the Soviets. Later, during the trial of the major war criminals at Nuremberg, he said the exact opposite—this time as a witness called by the Soviet prosecutor.[33] Nonetheless the Katyn allegations against the German army were dropped as soon as the western prosecutors saw how the Soviet charges looked. Significantly, I was never deposed as a witness about Katyn while I was at Nuremberg. The witnesses who were called to testify were all members of the Army Group's signals regiment or the staff of the chief signals officer, men who had been involved only as spectators and who were hardly in a position to give solid testimony.

In 1952, a United States congressional committee re-investigated the Katyn case. On the basis of all the witness statements, it reached the undisputed conclusion that this had been a Soviet crime. This committee's investigative files rest in the archives in Washington, D.C.

Katyn, however, could not take away from the crimes of National Socialism. The persecution of the Jews and the measures taken against Russians and Poles remained the driving force in our struggle against Hitler and his regime. But at the same time we were thinking about the survival of the German Reich, which was drifting towards its final downfall. What did it mean to be the murderer of a tyrant?

After the failure of Operation CITADEL, the steady Soviet counteroffensive along the entire front necessitated Army Group Center's withdrawal. The headquarters was pulled back from Krassny Bor, near Smolensk, to Orsha. With their combat strength in steady decline, German units were forced onto the defensive at all points. For a long time already, most divisions had been equivalent only to reinforced regiments. Nonetheless, Hitler sent them into action as if they were at their full, authorized strength. It was during this summer that the "flag game" started on General Staff maps, a game that finally got to the point where the supreme command was conducting operations with divisions that scarcely even existed any longer.

In mid-September 1943, I was transferred to the Führer Reserve because I needed to undergo a stomach operation in Breslau.[34] I took along with me the explosives that were still in my possession and several of the chemical fuses. At first I hid them all in my brother's apartment. About a fortnight after my operation, I was already able to take part in a big rabbit hunt at Klein-Öls with my friend Yorck. In the evenings we sat by the fire with several like-minded friends, including my older brother and Count Hans von Sierstorpff (who was later murdered by the SD), and talked about the possibilities of a political coup.[35] I drew a picture of the refined security measures that had been put in place for Hitler's protection, and all the difficulties involved in even getting near him at all. When I spoke about how Hitler was said to be armored at all the vital areas of his body, Yorck sprang to his feet and shouted, in the presence of his elderly servant, "Even this swine still has a face to be shot in!"

I took part in a training course for commanding generals and corps chiefs of staff held at Döberitz, near Berlin, in January 1944; General Brennecke was the director.[36] It gave me the opportunity to reestablish my connections with significant resistance figures in Berlin. I was particularly impressed during my one and only meeting with Count Claus von Stauffenberg, the future would-be assassin on 20 July 1944.[37] He had taken over the management of all the preparations for a coup d'état. I met him at a conference in Schlabrendorff's apartment, at which Tresckow and my old friend and regimental comrade, Baron Wessel von Freytag-Loringhoven, were also present.[38] For some time Freytag-Loringhoven had been the chief of *Abwehr II* in Canaris's department. He had already declared himself willing to procure more explosives and fuses for Stauffenberg and Tresckow (of the type I had obtained a year and a half earlier) from his section's supplies.

Stauffenberg, whom I had previously only heard about from his classmate at the *Kriegsakademie,* my friend Count Adrian von Pückler, impressed me from the very first moment. His extraordinary personality, and above all his boundless willpower, could be observed at once. With great seriousness and firm determination, he spoke of the absolute necessity of eliminating Hitler as quickly as possible. I immediately had the feeling that in Stauffenberg, Oster and Tresckow had found a partner who would give the German resistance movement a powerful boost. Tresckow—whom I saw for the very last time on this occasion—told me that I should hold myself in readiness while serving in my probable future position as a corps chief of staff on the Western Front, and come to Berlin immediately in the event of a coup d'état, so as to be available for a new mission.

Freytag-Loringhoven had for some time wanted to persuade me to take over the post of chief of *Abwehr III,* which had been left vacant when Colonel in the General Staff Heinrich had suffered an auto accident. Although I had little desire for this position, I went with him a few days later to see Admiral Canaris, who made me the same offer. The admiral wanted to have reliable colleagues (in the conspiratorial sense) around him, with Colonel in the General Staff Hansen at *Abwehr I,* Freytag-Loringhoven at *Abwehr II,* and me at *Abwehr III.* When he noted my hesitancy, he grasped me by the swordknot and said that I had to make this sacrifice. On that basis, I declared myself willing. At that very moment, someone brought Canaris the news that Colonel in the General Staff Heinrich, who had taken over *Abwehr III* from his predecessor Bentivegni a short time before, would be able to return to duty within a few weeks, contrary to previous expectations. Canaris said immediately that under the circumstances, he would have to do without me, since he could not remove the well-tried Heinrich from his post due to such a brief interruption.

I have no doubt at all that without this surprising turn of events, I would have been one of the sacrificial victims of 20 July, just like Hansen and Freytag-Loringhoven were.

During our time in Döberitz, Goebbels invited the course participants to a luncheon at the Ministry of Propaganda. When ration tickets for twenty grams of bread and ten grams of fat were collected from us at the door, I expected to dine on a thin stew. Instead a five-course dinner was served, a dinner such as I knew only from the years of deepest peace. A ministry official sitting at my side explained to me that most of the dishes—fresh strawberries in January, for example—had been flown in from occupied countries. Goebbels appeared not to notice how generals and staff officers fresh from the front lines reacted to this meal.

After the meal there followed a long conversation with Goebbels, during which he basically talked about the power of propaganda. When he remarked ironically that it would be possible within a short while, with the help of propaganda, to turn even the Führer himself into the most hated man in Germany, the head of the Ministry's radio department, Hans Fritzsche, interjected, "*Herr Minister,* why don't you just do that sometime?"[39] The remark was treated as a joke and loud laughter ensued. Feeling sick, I left the building where, half a year, later the German resistance would meet its fate.

At the end of January, the Döberitz class went to Posen to take part in a conference called together by the Wehrmacht's top-ranking "National Socialist Leadership Officer," General Reinecke.[40] There were about three hundred generals, admirals, and General Staff officers in attendance; they heard presentations from officials of the Reich ministries and the Nazi Party about their different lines of work. At the end of the three-day conference, there was a briefing from Heinrich Himmler on issues of internal and external security [at Posen on 26 January 1944]. During the speech he talked in an almost maudlin way about the difficulty of the mission that Hitler had given his SS, that of carrying out "the total solution to the Jewish question."

His voice trembling, he explained that despite "emotional trauma" the SS had executed its orders and had completely fulfilled the task. There was no more Jewish question. Truly remarkably, the majority of the audience absolutely did not seem to grasp what Himmler had been saying. Otherwise it cannot be explained why he received such lively applause and was finally pressed to stay and dine.

It was only for a small minority that this experience in Posen was the most shocking of their entire lives. There were only six or seven officers who did not join in the applause and who refrained from attending the dinner. We met together in a nearby restaurant. I remember my cousin Baron Smilo von Lüttwitz; Generals von Rothkirch, Krüger, and von Choltitz; and Count von Schwerin-Schwanenfeld as well.[41] We, at any rate, clearly understood the monstrous significance of Himmler's words.

At the end of the Posen conference, we were commanded to the *Führer-Hauptquartier* in East Prussia. Hitler wished to make a speech to the generals. Before entering the assembly room, we had to hand over all our weapons. Inside the chamber, we were discreetly monitored. Hitler's speech was gloomy: the "Twilight of the Gods" mood was very much evident. When he said that he had always expected that in his hour of need, the generals and senior officers in particular would rally around him, an incident occurred involving Field Marshal von Manstein (who was seated right in front of the Führer) that has been variously depicted and interpreted in the post-war literature. According to my recollection, Manstein interjected, "But, *mein Führer*, that is the case!" Hitler appeared irritated by the interruption, and said only, "I will make note of it, *Herr* von Manstein." Later on, there was said to have been a quarrel between Hitler and Manstein.

On 1 February 1944, I entered into my new duty position as chief of staff of the LXXXII Army Corps. The Corps was in charge of the Dunkirk-Calais-Boulogne section of the Atlantic Wall, and its headquarters was in the town of Aire-sur-la-Lys. It consisted of six infantry divisions, three of which had been positioned directly along the coast. The initial Allied invasion was expected here. As a result, the Atlantic Wall's construction was farther along here than in other comparable corps operational areas. The armored divisions being kept on standby in the French hinterland were prepared, above all else, for rapid movement to the Pas de Calais area.

My initial impressions were dispiriting. The long period of tranquility had plainly had a bad effect on the "Western Army," whose forces had to some extent been almost on peacetime duty in France ever since 1940. A certain bureaucratic spirit had instilled itself in the troops, along with a devotion to routine; this didn't seem too promising for their combat prowess. Even with most of the infantry divisions, one was dealing with so-called "fortress divisions" whose artillery was only partly mobile; "Luftwaffe field divisions" that had been formed from unemployed air force troops; and "convalescent units" (stomach ailments, concussions, and so on). I ran into grotesque situations over and over again. For example, in one of the seaside resorts on the Channel coast, I found a master sergeant who had been assigned to guard a villa in 1940 and was then forgotten about. In the intervening period he had married a Frenchwoman, and for three years he really had lived *wie Gott im Frankreich,* "like God in France," as Germans say of the sweetest possible existence.

With the invasion expected, the army and division commanders and General Staff officers had begun to be replaced by officers with Eastern Front experience. But this was only possible to a limited extent. Everything improved after Field Marshal Rommel was named commander of Army Group B on 1 April 1944, and took on the special assignment of putting the entire Western Front, from Denmark to where the Alps meet the Mediterranean, into the best possible defensive condition, and to unify all defense-related activities as well.[42] With great energy, and a ruthlessness that was often refreshing, he soon succeeded in eliminating the worst deficiencies.

I got to know Rommel in the course of the field marshal's numerous visits to my corps operational area. I knew that he had connections to the German resistance, and I felt that he knew all about me, too, perhaps through his Chief of Staff, General Dr. Speidel, a resistance member. With Rommel I always had the sense of a secret accord, although it never came to our speaking out openly. He always spoke critically to me about the ever-pressing issues of the military supreme command. Once, during a conversation, he cast doubt on the correctness of Hitler's notion that the main threat of invasion lay in the Pas de Calais. This particular judgment could be traced back principally to the navy, which held an Allied landing on the Normandy coast to be impossible because of the reefs there. Rommel was skeptical about that, and appeared to regard a landing operation on the section of the Channel coast between Le Havre and Cherbourg as thoroughly possible.

In view of German air inferiority, he placed special emphasis on defense against the anticipated operations of airborne troops. Every large, empty, open space along the coast and in the rear areas was secured with long, slanting, partly metal stakes—the so-called "Rommel's asparagus"—as well as barbed wire. He had beach obstacles put in place right at the waterline at all points that were suitable for a landing. These obstacles, which would be invisible below the water at high tide, were fitted with explosives. By this means enemy landing craft would be destroyed, or at least halted, just before reaching the shore.

With the exception of increased Allied air raids, the beginning of the invasion of Normandy on 6 June 1944, left us undisturbed at first in the Pas de Calais. Since Hitler was as convinced as ever that the main invasion—on both sides of Calais—still lay ahead of us, for the first few weeks of the invasion we hung on to all six of our divisions. Not until July was the first division pulled away from us to the invasion front. Given the Allied command of the skies, the division's crossing of the Seine at Elbeuf cost it serious casualties.

The bombardment of London with V-1 rockets began on 16 June 1944. There were a number of launching sites in my corps operational area, so I was able to get a close-up look at the wonder weapon. Frequently they went into a spiral and landed somewhere in the hinterland of France. We were also able to see the way several V-1s were shot down by British fighter planes. I got the impression that this new weapon would not have a deciding effect on the war.

Field Marshal Rommel's severe wounding in an attack on his car by a low-flying Allied plane on 17 July 1944 was not only a heavy blow to the leadership of the defense of the invasion front: it also, at a decisive hour, robbed the German resistance of one of its most capable and determined personalities.

Mother, Baroness Christine von Gersdorff (*née* von Dohna-Schlodien). *(Au.)*

Father, Baron Ernst von Gersdorff, during World War I. *(Au.)*

Gerdorff's wedding at Schloss Matzdorf, Silesia, 1934. *(Au.)*

Lüben, early twentieth
century. *(Tr.)*

Gersdorff's school in
Lüben. *(Tr.)*

Gersdorff at a horse race
in the 1930s. *(Au.)*

Ruins of Schloss Matzdorf. *(Tr.)*

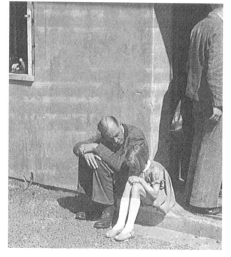

Baroness Renata von Gersdorff with Lory
(above), circa 1940. *(Au.)*

Daughter Lory visits Gersdorff (above right
and right) in 1947 while he is a POW at
Allendorf. *(Au.)*

Gersdorff (left) with Henning von Tresckow, Smolensk, 1943, probably taken during T's farewell party from the staff when he finished his assignment as Ia of Army Group Center. *(Au.)*

Claus von Stauffenberg (above) *(Tr.)*

Henning von Tresckow, circa 1944. *(Tr.)*

Hans Oster. *(Tr.)*

Fedor von Bock

Günther von Kluge

Gerd von Rundstedt

Erich von Manstein

Heinrich von Lehndorff-Steinort (far left) *(Tr.)*

Arthur Nebe (left) *(Tr.)*

Erich Brandenberger (below far left)

Wilhelm Canaris (below) *(Tr.)*

Walther von Brauchitsch (far left) *(Tr.)*

Hyazinth von Strachwitz (left) *(Tr.)*

Heinz Guderian (above)

Josef "Sepp" Dietrich (left)

Wilhelm Keitel (above)

Paul Hausser (right)

Karl Dönitz (left)

Walter Model (above)

Ewald von Kleist (above)

Franz Halder (right)

Hans Krebs (right)
(Tr.)

Rudolf Schmundt
(far right) *(Tr.)*

Phillip von Boeselager
(right) *(Tr.)*

Georg von Boeselager (far
right) *(Tr.)*

Wessel von Freytag-
Loringhoven (below) *(Tr.)*

Lothar Rendulic (below
right) *(Tr.)*

Claus von Stauffenberg (left) at the Führer's headquarters, 1944.

Wilhelm Keitel (left) with Adolf Hitler at the Führer's head-quarters.

Heinrich Himmler

Hermann Goering, Adolf Hitler, and Albert Speer

Dr. Gerhard Buhtz and an assistant (in smock) present the corpse of a murdered Polish officer to visitors investigating the Katyn Massacre.

Hans Speidel (at left) and Erwin Rommel, April 1944.

Albert Kesselring

Günther von Kluge

Gersdorff in the 1950s (left) and in later
years (above). *(Au.)*

VI

Soldier in the Downfall

Everything is lost, except for honor.
> —*Francis I, King of France,*
> *after the battle of Pavia (1525)*

Translator's Note: On the morning of 20 July 1944—an oppressively sultry day across northern Germany—Colonel Claus von Stauffenberg traveled by air from Berlin to Wolfsschanze, *the "Wolf's Lair," for a strategy conference. Hitler's semi-secret compound near Rastenburg in East Prussia was probably the most high-security zone in the Reich whenever the dictator was in residence, but as a trusted General Staff officer, Stauffenberg was able to smuggle in two small bombs, hidden inside his leather briefcase. Prior to the beginning of the conference, Stauffenberg went into a restroom and armed the time fuse on one bomb. Presumably because of his mutilated hands (the result of combat in North Africa), he only armed one bomb before being urgently summoned into the meeting. During the conference he was able to place the briefcase beneath the conference table, close to where Hitler stood looking at maps. He then excused himself from the room and was outside the small building when the bomb exploded at about 12:40 P.M. Assuming that Hitler had been killed, he hastened to the airfield and back to Berlin, departing at about 1:00 P.M.*

Hitler was, of course, not dead. After Stauffenberg's little-noticed departure from the room, another officer had shoved the inconvenient briefcase behind a solid leg of the heavy oak conference table. This table leg absorbed enough of the blast to prevent Hitler from receiving any serious injuries, although several other men in the room were killed or maimed.

Stauffenberg's plane did not land in Berlin until about 4:00 P.M. To his surprise he then learned that the coup d'état in the capital city had not yet been instigated. He soon discovered that during his flight, a co-conspirator had telephoned Berlin from the Wolf's Lair to report that Hitler had survived the assassination attempt after all. Insisting that this could not be so,

Stauffenberg urged that the "Operation VALKYRIE" plan for a military take-over be launched. For the next several hours, working from his desk in the army's Berlin headquarters, the valiant colonel did everything in his power to make the conspiracy succeed, both on the spot and over the telephone.

By later that night, however, Himmler and Goebbels had reversed the coup's initial successes, Hitler's survival was no longer disputable, and loy-alist officers overcame the Berlin plotters in a brief gun battle. Stauffenberg and three other leading conspirators were executed by firing squad the same night. At about the same time, Hitler had gone on national radio to assure the people that he still lived, and to call for the fiercest revenge against the trai-tors. During the approximately eight remaining months of the war, hundreds of conspirators were arrested and put to death.

The assassination attempt on 20 July 1944, which in the final hour manifested the will of the German resistance to free the world from Hitler and his crimi-nal regime, was the beginning of the end not only for the opposition, but also for the German soldier.

Count Stauffenberg's deed was no longer only about the success or failure of the coup d'état. More significant was that Germans, and German soldiers in particular, had shown the entire world their resolution to restore the honor of the German people. The events of 20 July thus represented the only positive point that the German nation could show for itself before having to surrender to the mercies of the victorious Allied powers.

Everything that I lived through as a soldier after 20 July took place in the full awareness of our approaching destruction. Now that our struggle against the unjust state had become hopeless, there remained nothing left for us but that soldierly conduct which was capable of sparing the German people, and the soldiers entrusted to our command, from the worst—as far as possible.

I first learned of Stauffenberg's attempt on the afternoon of 20 July; and a few hours later I heard about the failure of the coup d'état. After several tele-phone calls to sound out the situation, I decided not to go to Berlin, contrary to Tresckow's instructions. One thing was completely clear to me: I had to reckon with being arrested on very short notice. During the night of 20/21 July, I made up my mind to do whatever it took not to be taken alive by the Gestapo; I was afraid that I would not be able to withstand the tortures that could be anticipated, quite apart from the fact that I could only expect certain death on the gallows.

To gain distance and time, on 21 July I set off, accompanied by my faithful orderly, Paul Kühn, on a multi-day inspection tour of all of our component divisions.[1] Before departing I told my Ia, Major in the General Staff Sven von Mitzlaff, that I would phone him daily and tell him where I could be reached.[2]

In case anyone wanted to talk to me, he should let me know by telephone. By this means, I would gain the time I required to make my next decision. I had three choices: suicide, an attempt to cross the Channel to England, or a less promising attempt to hide myself in France.

If I remember correctly, Mitzlaff's message reached me on 23 July. Field Marshal von Kluge, the new Commander-in-chief West (OB-West) and simultaneously the commander of Army Group B, was coming to our corps command post and wanted to speak to me. Although I was suspicious, I perceived no immediate danger in the request. When I got back to Aire-sur-la-Lys I met up with Kluge, who was already there. He told the corps commander, General of Artillery Sinnhuber, that we were two old acquaintances. Would he kindly be so understanding as to let us speak together privately?

The first thing Kluge said to me when we were by ourselves was, "I've done everything in my power to protect you. I've sent up a report about you which will hopefully preserve you from any investigation." Then suddenly he said, "What do you have to say about this tragedy?" I replied, "*Herr Feldmarschall,* I don't understand how you could have sent your declaration of loyalty to the Führer." Pensively, and as if asking for my understanding, Kluge said, "I had to choose between my pistol and the pen that Blumentritt (his chief of staff at OB-West) held out to me to sign the telegram to Hitler. I would have chosen the pistol, but I wasn't ready to shoot myself in the presence of my son, whom the army personnel office had just sent to me in Paris. But you can be certain that I will still take the required step."

I urged Kluge not to make any hasty decisions. Germany had no use for a dead field marshal; because of his status as OB-West, he was now the only man who was still in the position to turn aside the catastrophe that threatened us all. It was time to make an audacious decision. Kluge tersely replied that he needed me, and that I should be ready to come to him on short notice. I had the feeling that he was thinking about Tresckow, and wanted to have one man near him upon whom he could rely.

Only four days later, I received the order to come immediately to Army Group B's headquarters at La Roche Guyon, without even waiting for my replacement's arrival at LXXXII Corps. When I arrived at the magnificent palace of the Duke de la Rochefoucauld on 28 July, the field marshal was strolling with the duke in the palace garden.[3] It was an unforgettable sight: two superb-looking gentlemen in incomparable medieval surroundings. After I had reported to the field marshal, the duke took leave of us. Kluge and I picked up our conversation where we had left it four days earlier.

Kluge: "You recently spoke of a decision. What are you thinking about?"

Me: "I am convinced that there is only one possibility open. As OB-West, you must immediately commence negotiations with the western Allies. I consider it to be technically possible to get into radio communication with the commander of the U.S. 12th Army Group, General Omar Bradley, and by this means to begin oral negotiations with him and eventually with Field Marshal Montgomery, too. The negotiating terms should be a ceasefire, a systematic withdrawal of all German forces on the Western Front to behind the 1939 borders—that means the evacuation of France, Belgium, Holland, and Luxembourg—and a guarantee of the elimination of the Nazi regime.

"During the evacuation process, reliable combat units should be quickly pulled off the front lines so they can be used to seize power in Germany. The majority of the troops who will become available must be used for the defense in the East, with the goal of also gaining a cease-fire there."

Kluge: "Gersdorff, if this went wrong, then Field Marshal von Kluge would be the biggest swine in the history of the world."

Me: "*Herr Feldmarschall,* the decision to either be condemned by history or to enter it as the savior in the hour of need, is a decision that all the world's great men have faced."

Kluge put a hand on my shoulder and said: "Gersdorff, Field Marshal von Kluge is not a great man."

We saw each other again at the evening meal. Taking part were Field Marshal von Kluge; his chief of staff at Army Group B, General Dr. Hans Speidel; the general in charge of signals troops, Major General Gehrke; and Major General Elfeldt, who was supposed to replace General von Choltitz as the commander of LXXXIV Corps.[4] During the meal, the Ia of Army Group B, Colonel in the General Staff von Tempelhoff, reported to the field marshal that 7th Army had just communicated its decision to break out to the southeast.[5] That meant the loss of the connection with the Channel coast at the Cotentin Peninsula, and an opportunity for the Americans to push ahead into undefended French territory. Kluge was beside himself. He demanded an immediate telephone connection to the 7th Army's commander, *SS-Oberstgruppenführer* (SS-General) Hausser.[6] The connection was made, but it was so bad that understanding and communication were scarcely possible. Kluge just roared into the handset over and over, "I forbid the withdrawal to the southeast. You must preserve the connection to the coast."

Finally, although still angry, he told me in a calm tone of voice, "Please get yourself over to 7th Army immediately and relieve the chief of staff there, General Pemsel, of his duties.[7] Do everything you can to reverse the army's unfortunate decision. A breach at Avranches means the loss of the entire war." He wanted General Elfeldt and me to rush forth immediately, but General Speidel asked him not to send us until early the next morning, since during a night journey we might possibly fall into the hands of the *maquis,* the French resistance fighters.

At the crack of dawn on 29 July, Elfeldt and I first drove to Le Mans, where 7th Army's main headquarters was to be found. To my supreme astonishment, we encountered an almost peacetime-like situation. But I had no time to get the army's rear-echelon staff moving. After a difficult trip, during which we had to take cover again and again from low-flying enemy planes, we reached the army's forward command post at Chavoy (about four miles northeast of Avranches) in the late afternoon. General Elfeldt immediately drove onward to the headquarters of LXXXIV Corps.

General Pemsel was flabbergasted when I informed him that he had been relieved. Communications with the Army Group were so poor that the advance warning I had asked for had not come through. The corps commander, *SS-Oberstgruppenführer* Hausser, made an excellent impression on me. He radiated the calm of an experienced front-line soldier. As a former Reichswehr general, he had come from the *Stahlhelm* association into the SS, where he had proved himself to be a good and upstanding troop leader.[8] He accepted my addressing him as *Herr Generaloberst* [the army equivalent of his SS rank] and appeared to place no importance on the "Hitler salute" which had become mandatory after 20 July.[9]

Other than Hausser and a few aides, only the Ia and the Ic/AO were present at the forward headquarters. Its equipment, particularly communications gear, was also completely inadequate. I immediately attempted to use every possible means that could stop an American breakthrough at Avranches. But I saw very rapidly that it was all too late. By this point, American tanks had already forced their way into Avranches—which lay to our rear! Our own position was between two main roads that led to Avranches, along which mechanized forces from the U.S. 3rd Army were already rolling. All we could do was just patchwork, and could no longer reverse the already accomplished American breakthrough.

If we did not wish to fall into captivity, we had to try to break out to the east across the St. Lô—Avranches road. After darkness had fallen, I had the radio equipment and motor vehicles blown up. Then we set off on an adventurous foot march. We got across the highway one by one, taking advantage of breaks in the endless stream of American vehicles. For the first time I witnessed the overwhelming superiority of the U.S. Army. Only after some hours did we once again run into German units; they were able to put some motor vehicles at our disposal, in which we reached our new command post at Mortain, sixteen miles east of Avranches.

Because we had vanished for many hours and the Army Group had had to assume that we had been taken prisoners, Field Marshal von Kluge had personally assumed command of 7th Army at its main headquarters in Le Mans. As soon as we had reported again from Mortain, he came to us to discuss the decisions that had to be made next. Because Hitler had rejected the most rational course of action under the existing circumstances—the withdrawal of the entire Western Front behind the Seine Line—there remained only one strategic possibility: to restore the coastal connection and cut off the part of the U.S. 3rd Army that had broken through, by counterattacking as rapidly as possible from the vicinity of Mortain toward Avranches with all available armored forces. But to do this, the various tank units had to be pulled out of the front held by 7th Army and 5th Panzer Army, and assembled in the Mortain area.

We could have attacked very swiftly with XLVI Panzer Corps (2nd and 116th Panzer Divisions). However, in obedience to our superiors, we had to wait until 1st SS-Panzer Division *"Leibstandarte"* and II SS-Panzer Corps had been brought up. Therefore, it was not possible to begin the attack until 6 August. The day before, I had a visit from the chief of all fighter-plane squadrons in the West, *General der Flieger* (General of Aviators) Bülowius.[10] In a discussion of the risks that a German armored attack faced, given the Allied command of the air, he said, word for word, "Tomorrow morning early there will be two hundred fighters over the attack area, and they'll sweep the skies clean."

Despite this assurance, we cautiously decided to go on the attack while it was still dark, in order to avoid the expected onslaught of Allied fighter planes. Due to a gross error on the part of the *Leibstandarte,* things went otherwise. The poorly reconnoitered route to its pre-attack assembly area led through a narrow ravine. The *Leibstandarte*'s tank regiment, newly equipped with Panther and Tiger tanks, found itself stretched out along this ravine like a string of pearls when an enemy plane shot down by our anti-aircraft fire landed precisely on top of the leading tank. This had the effect of corking a bottle. It took hours before the regiment could tediously travel backwards and emerge from the ravine. The 1st SS-Panzer Division could not attack until it was already broad daylight.

In the meanwhile, the army's 2nd Panzer Division, under the command of my former regimental comrade Baron Heinrich von Lüttwitz, had come far ahead under cover of darkness. At the outset, the American flank only seemed to be covered by an armored reconnaissance section.

At first light, however, massive aerial attacks by powerful Allied air force units began. The promised support from the German fighter units did not turn up. I myself saw only a single German flight (consisting of two airplanes). For the first time in the history of warfare, a land battle spearheaded by strong armored forces was decided by a counterattack from the sky. After two days, our losses of tanks and other armored vehicles were so great that the offensive had to be brought to a halt. The only successful unit, 2nd Panzer Division, had to pull back practically to its jumping-off point.

On 7 August, we received the Führer Order to go back on the attack in the direction of Avranches on 8 August, under the direction of General of Panzer Troops Eberbach, and after reaching Avranches to turn northeast "and roll up the entire Allied invasion front from east to west."[11] Really, all you could do was laugh—if these unrealistic ideas didn't cost thousands of lives. Apart from the fact that we had neither enough fuel nor enough ammunition for such a wide-ranging operation, the designated objective was a total fantasy.

From that day until the end of the war, I never saw another order from the supreme command that wasn't completely unrealistic and utopian. Hitler's leadership, which was plainly not being influenced by either OB-West or OKW [responsible for the armed forces in the West], very swiftly made the threat of encirclement to 7th Army and 5th Panzer Army (its neighbor on the right) more and more obvious. The U.S. 3rd Army under General Patton, who led it according to the methods of Rommel and Guderian, proceeded after the breakout at Avranches in a wide southward movement toward the Alençon-Argentan area, so that the final envelopment was only a question of time.

The army commander, SS-General Hausser, shared my opinion completely in all these affairs. He also appeared to have a notion about my attitude toward the regime. He asked me one day, point-blank, "You're not one of the Führer's supporters?" I answered just as openly, "No, *Herr Generaloberst,* I regard him as the ruination of Germany." Hausser remained very calm and said only that he understood me; but I would be so good as to understand in turn that as an SS commander, he still had a sense of loyalty toward Hitler.

During these days, Field Marshal von Kluge came to our command post a number of times. He always sought to have a conversation between just the two of us. He called me by my first name now, and spoke of personal matters. On each such occasion, I urged him all over again to start up negotiations with the Allies on his own initiative. As a technical matter, this would have been possible without any difficulty.

On 12 August, I received a phone call from the chief of staff of the Army Group, General Speidel. When he asked whether the field marshal was with us and I answered no, he ordered me to immediately send out as many officers as possible to search for the commander. My first thought was: now Kluge has actually followed my suggestions. Obviously people in the higher head-quarters believed that he wanted to make contact with the enemy. Telephone inquiries concerning his whereabouts never ceased.

Kluge did not arrive at our position until late in the evening. He had been stuck more than once in stalled traffic, and halted again and again by low-flying enemy aircraft. The radio set that accompanied him had been shot up and destroyed. I can still recall the ironic way he remarked, "Just imag-ine—Field Marshal von Kluge had to play traffic policeman all day long."

Unquestionably he had made no attempt to get into radio contact with the western Allies.

On 15 August, Kluge appeared for the last time at 7th Army's combat headquarters, which in the meantime had been relocated to the neighborhood of Flers. When we were alone, he told me that he had been relieved of command and replaced by Field Marshal Model, and that he was supposed to report to the *Führer-Hauptquartier.* It was clear what that meant, he said. Now, therefore, he would take the final step that he had already meant to take for a long while. At the same time he handed me farewell letters addressed to his wife and son. All my attempts to steer him away from this decision and get him to dare a political action instead, failed. He took his leave of me with an unnerving courtesy. Three days later, while riding between Verdun and Metz on the way back to Germany, he took his own life.

Meanwhile the "pocket" forming around 7th Army and part of 5th Panzer Army got closer and closer to being sealed off. During the night of 17/18 August, an order reached me to come to 5th Panzer Army's command post, where Army Group B's new commander, Field Marshal Model, wanted to speak with me. General Eberbach received the same order. Through a narrow but still-open "hole," we succeeded in exiting the slowly closing pocket. At the headquarters of the commander of 5th Panzer Army, SS-General Sepp Dietrich, located far to the rear, Eberbach and I urgently depicted the untenable nature of our position, and asked for immediate permission to break out.[12] Model turned this down, and declared that the newly refreshed II SS-Panzer Corps would lead a counterattack against the enemy's "fangs," and clear up the situation.

While we were eating at noon, the Ia of 5th Panzer Army reported that the pocket had finally closed. Eberbach and I immediately declared that we would attempt to re-enter the pocket and reach our staffs. Sepp Dietrich emphatically counseled us against this, but Model was in agreement. However, he asked Eberbach to go first to II SS Panzer Corps, in order to coordinate the attack preparations. The detour Eberbach was compelled to make made it impossible for him then to re-enter the pocket. As for me, I left my automobile, my driver, and my aide-de-camp with the forward-most units of the Panzer Lehr Division (which was cordoning off the pocket from outside), and walked alone into no-man's-land. Avoiding roads and inhabited places, I pushed my way through woods and brush until I came into the vicinity of a village that was under heavy artillery fire. I had no idea whether it was our own artillery fire or the enemy's, but I suspected the latter, since we had little ammunition inside the pocket.

I took cover in the cellar of a house that stood alone. Suddenly I heard voices, but was unable to discern whether they were speaking in German,

English, or French. With my pistol drawn and the safety off, I walked into the room from whence the voices came. There I found my former 7th Cavalry regimental comrade, Count von Brühl, now the commander of the tank regiment in the 116th Panzer Division, drinking *cidre,* the typical apple-wine of Normandy, with several sergeants and enlisted men.[13] I told him the route he could take to get his tanks out of the pocket with no danger, and asked him to put a motorcycle with a driver at my disposal, which I wanted to use to travel onward in the suspected direction of 7th Army's command post.

During this journey I saw horrible sights. Thousands of German soldiers came toward me in total disarray, without their weapons. Badly wounded men lay by the roadside covered in their own blood without anyone caring for them. When the motorcycle broke down I continued on foot, the only person heading in the opposite direction through the ever-larger groups of fleeing men. At around nine o'clock that night, in a stone quarry, I found the commander and what was left of my staff. Hausser embraced me. He had never expected my return.

The conditions inside the pocket were indescribable. The 7th Army staff, the staff of Panzer Group Eberbach, four corps staffs, and all that was left of twelve divisions had been encircled within an area the size of Berlin. The artillery of the surrounding American, British, French, Canadian, and Polish forces fired ceaselessly into the constantly shrinking space. By day hundreds, or maybe thousands, of American and British warplanes hung in the skies above the pocket; they attacked every moving or uncamouflaged vehicle, and even went hunting for individual men.

Inside the quarry, there was also a field hospital with badly wounded men, doctors, and female nurses. During the night, direct hits landed relentlessly in the quarry. On my staff alone, several of the officers were wounded. Nobody got any sleep, with a single exception: despite the hard stones and the artillery barrage, the old campaigner Hausser slept as though he was in a four-poster bed.

In the early morning of 19 August, I succeeded in convincing Hausser that only a breakout could prevent the army's total annihilation. We raced on foot from one command post to another, giving the appropriate orders by word of mouth. At the headquarters of the 116th Panzer Division, a shell splinter hit me in the knee. It wasn't a serious wound, but the knee swelled up so much that I could no longer run. Hausser commanded me to make the breakout along with Panzer Group Eberbach, riding in his own auto along with the other wounded staff officers. He and the unwounded members of the staff attached themselves on foot to the 3rd Parachute Division.

We broke out when darkness fell. I went into a deep sleep due to exhaustion and loss of blood. When the driver shook me awake in the early morning hours, we were sitting still at the head of a long column of vehicles, about a mile and a half from St. Lambert. The column wasn't moving forward: as soon as a vehicle got out in the open, it became the target of aimed anti-tank artillery fire.

I located two tanks from 2nd Panzer Division in our vicinity. They were damaged tanks en route to the division's maintenance company, but they could still be driven and they were capable of doing battle. With the two tanks, I scouted out the exact location of the enemy anti-tank guns. Hidden by some favorable cover, we were successful in putting them out of action with a few tank rounds. Then the two tanks drove ahead, and I put my *Kübelwagen* [the Wehrmacht version of a jeep] right between them.

Our start was the signal for tanks, armored personnel carriers, self-propelled artillery platforms, field artillery vehicles, automobiles and cargo trucks to emerge from cover and fall in around us like a bunch of grapes. There may have been more than a hundred vehicles, with clusters of men hanging on them. I directed this mob with hand and arm signals, and it felt to me like being on a foxhunt.

Without meeting any opposition, we crossed over a small river, the Dives, and passed through the village of St. Lambert. Then the enemy appeared to have recovered from his surprise. Heavy defensive fire suddenly commenced, but we were already in the middle of the forward lines of a Canadian infantry brigade. Hundreds of men surrendered to us with their hands up. Since there was absolutely nothing we could do with them, we disarmed them and left them standing there. When both of the 2nd Panzer Division tanks were knocked out in another push forward, I turned to the right in the direction of some cover. My vehicle got stuck while crossing a deep, wide gully. I climbed atop one of the *Leibstandarte*'s Tiger tanks.

We reached one of the apple orchards that are so characteristic of Normandy. Under this cover, and with the help of several energetic General Staff officers, it was possible to assemble and organize everyone and everything that had attached itself to us. There were some one hundred vehicles, and approximately 1,500 men, including members of almost every division in the pocket. I formed the combat vehicles into an armored group, and divided the randomly assorted soldiers—who included infantrymen, tank crewmen, artillerymen, and support troops—into companies of about a hundred men each. These companies were placed under the command of any officers who were present, including veterinarians and paymasters.

Meanwhile, the hostile fire had become much heavier. Even while the orders were being given out, several officers and men were wounded. Following a careful reconnaissance, our attack proceeded. Soon we ran into British armored forces. After about a dozen "Churchill" or Mk IV (A22) tanks had been knocked out, our assault moved rapidly forward. Finally we met up with the vanguard of 2nd SS-Panzer Division headed in our direction. We were through!

I immediately drove back from whence I had come: first, to organize a defense of the area where we had broken through; and second, to locate my commanding officer. Soon we were running into streams of German soldiers. No word gets around as fast as the word of a hole in a pocket. Inside the church at St. Lambert, I found the commander of the 2nd Panzer Division, General Baron Heinrich von Lüttwitz. He had been grazed by several bullets and was lying on the steps of the altar receiving medical treatment, painted all over with iodine. I begged him to use the forces at his disposal to keep the breakout point open for as long as it took until the last of the army was out of the pocket. Without any argument he accepted this mission, which any other man would probably have turned down, and carried it out until 21 August.

I did not locate the army commander, Hausser, but I heard that he had been badly wounded and had already passed through the hole in a cargo truck. Then I met him at our new command post in Vimoutiers. Hausser could still stand up, but a shell fragment had torn away his lower jaw. At the same time that he reported his wounded status to the supreme command before going into the field hospital, he transmitted his request for his chief of staff to be awarded the Knight's Cross.[14] A few days later Field Marshal Model presented me with the medal.

I wore this decoration, which after all could be traced back to an institution established by the Prussian king Friedrich Wilhelm III, because due to my initiative as a leader, holes had been knocked open through which tens of thousands of German soldiers were able to emerge from an inferno of death and annihilation in the encircling ring of the Falaise-Argentan pocket; and because in doing so, I had acted contrary to Hitler's express orders. He wanted another Stalingrad!

After the crossing of the Seine, 7th Army's staff was without a commander for several days. I used the time to thoroughly reorganize it. During the battles in Normandy, I had already relieved a number of staff officers (the Ic/AO, OQ, and Q-1) and section chiefs (the IIa and several others). Now out of all the leading positions in the staff, only our superb Surgeon-General remained in his old job. The army's new commander, General of Panzer Troops Eberbach, gave his full support to my "radical cure."

On 30 August, the 7th Army staff was supposed to replace the staff of 5th Panzer Army, because that team was supposed to take over a big armored unit in northeastern France, in order to "lead a decisive blow to the flank of the enemy units that had pushed across the Seine." This Führer Order was also total fantasy, because the Panzer units that were supposed to accomplish it existed practically only on paper, and the vast quantities of fuel necessary for such an operation were not available.

When Eberbach and I reached 5th Panzer Army's command post, its subordinate units had landed in another serious defensive crisis. The army's chief of staff, General Gause, was telephoning doubtfully and without a break to his corps chiefs and to the Army Group above, but without being able to provide any kind of help.[15] While all this was going on, the commander, Sepp Dietrich, rushed furiously about the room, saying only, "Just listen to me—there's no point in any of this!" He cursed Hitler and the supreme command with the harshest of expressions.

At Dietrich's request, we took over the command that very evening at midnight. During the handover, Gause informed me that a British armored unit of still uncertain strength had broken through one of our army corps; the corps was busy trying to find out where the tanks were now.

When I received the morning reports from the corps chiefs of staff by radio at 6:00 A.M. on 30 August, I was told that the enemy unit in question had apparently driven away in the direction of our army's command post. At that very moment, I heard an increasing amount of gunfire from outside, but I assumed that it was coming from our "friends"—the enemy's low-flying fighter planes. Just then Eberbach came into my office and cried out, "We have to get away immediately. There are British tanks all over the village!" I gathered up my maps and ran out of the house.

Already seated in his car, Eberbach told me that we could only leave the village in one direction, because SS-General Dietrich had been killed by tank fire at the other end. We went racing off. Besides the driver, I had my orderly Paul Kühn and an aide-de-camp in the car with me. As we came around a curve outside the village, we saw to our front about six British Churchill tanks, which opened up on us with every barrel from a distance of about 300 meters. Both autos were hit and put out of action. We rolled out to the right into a meadow; however, it offered scarcely any concealment. While I was unable to creep away due to my knee wound, all the others slid away on their bellies behind the next bend in the road, about fifty meters away, where they found some cover. I lay there, made myself as small as possible, and waited for the bullet meant to "put me out of my misery." Tracer rounds were hitting all around me.

Then Paul Kühn came running out of cover to me, bolt upright. I roared at him to get down, but with the words, "I have to get my colonel!" he came up, seized me under the arms, and pulled me under cover, all in a hail of bullets. Why we weren't both hit is a riddle to me still. Behind the road embankment, I took the Iron Cross 1st Class from my own tunic and pinned it on the senior corporal's chest. (Later I got a lot of aggravation about this, because certain people were unwilling to recognize this spontaneous award of a medal. Only after I had threatened to return all of my decorations was my independent act sanctioned.)

From the roadside we crept like hunters into the village we had just left. When I looked through an open barn door and saw my army commander standing on the village street in his black tanker uniform, apparently unmolested, we also walked into the street. In that instant we were taken prisoner by British armored troops. We were conducted into the village square and inside a circle of four or six tanks, on one side of which there stood a barn. Initially I tried to destroy the General Staff maps that I was still carrying on my person. They showed the locations of all the army's units, command posts and supply lines; not only that, they also showed adjoining units of the neighboring armies. While I attempted, unsuccessfully at first, to set the stiff map paper on fire, I saw that a superb-looking British lieutenant was observing me. As the flames flared up, he walked over to me at a dignified pace and said courteously, "That's forbidden to do, I believe." I "regretted" not having known this, but noted that it was now too late. Then I asked him when we would be transported from that place. He observed that one could simply not have an army commander riding on the back of a tank. Therefore some automobiles had been requested, but they would not arrive for several hours.

I whispered to Eberbach that I would attempt to escape at the first opportunity, and suggested that he join me; but he only shook his head in resignation. He was of course perfectly in the right. But I had been seized by a sportsman's ambition to get out of this somehow shameful captivity. In my personal situation, that was just as foolish as it was dangerous. I told only Paul Kühn to keep an eye on what I was doing.

While all this was going on, groups of German soldiers as well as individual vehicles tried again and again to break out. Soon it came to some serious shooting. Then a badly wounded German sergeant was brought to our location, screaming with pain. The Englishmen carried him over to us, and handed General Eberbach a morphine syringe. All of the Germans, and all of the British troops, too, turned their complete attention to the German general as he strained to inject the morphine. At this moment I disappeared unnoticed through a hole in the great barn door. Then I found a rear entrance and succeeded in reaching a garden. A patch of tall beanstalks afforded me some concealment.

After several minutes a French peasant appeared, who had probably heard some noise; he glanced around but didn't notice me. Then Paul Kühn turned up, having followed my escape route. I gave him a hand signal and we remained silently in our bean patch. After several hours had passed, Kühn dragged me through gardens and over fences to a country lane. There we established that British tanks had been stationed in a ring around the village, with about five hundred meters between each one. It was a matter of getting between two tanks to reach a forest that was about a kilometer away. We found a ditch, unfortunately not a very deep one, in which we could move forward at a tedious crawl. Finally, hours later, we reached the sheltering forest without the British having noticed us. Using every means of concealment, we plodded onward. In a lonely abandoned farmstead, Kühn found a little cart in which he could pull me along. After some hours we ran into my Ic/AO, Major in the General Staff Hirche, who had evaded captivity with a small group of staff members.[16] We set off together on the march toward the east, and reached the Somme in the vicinity of Amiens. As we got ready to swim across the river, which was about forty meters wide, a peasant told us about a nearby bridge that was still held by German soldiers. The escape had succeeded.

In the palace at Havrincourt, where Army Group B's headquarters was located, I found Sepp Dietrich, whom I had believed to be dead, sitting at a desk in Field Marshal Model's office. He had just reported to Model that Eberbach and I had been killed in action or taken prisoner. In his rough, common-soldierly way of addressing all of his peers and subordinates as *du* [the informal word for "you"], he greeted me with, "*Jetzt kannst du mich auch duzen!*"—"Now you can also call me *du*!"

This man's image has always remained ambiguous. I will not deny the guilt that he heaped up on himself as Hitler's personal bodyguard during the Nazi Party's so-called "time of struggle." But he was a capable front-line soldier, one who during the war had recognized the criminality of the dictatorship. When I told him one day that the SD had sent one of my wife's uncles to Auschwitz on the grounds of his friendship with a Jew, and had released him months later—after payment of a fine of over three million Reichsmarks—as a "dying parolee" with a severe case of spotted fever from which he perished only a few weeks later, Dietrich said only, "These swine!" Another time I heard him say, "I certainly think I can lead a company, or maybe even a battalion—but for Adolf to have turned me into an army commander, that was total idiocy!"

After the war it became known that, in answer to Rommel's question as to whether in a certain situation he would obey all of Rommel's orders, Dietrich was supposed to have answered, "You're my superior officer, so I'd carry out every single one of your orders." I remain convinced to this day that the same attitude could be ascribed to, at least, SS-General Hausser and SS-General Bittrich.[17] With this in mind, I believe that the advice I gave to Field Marshal von Kluge again and again after 20 July was not unrealistic.

At Havrincourt, General Speidel murmured to me that he had been ordered to report to Berlin, and strongly reckoned on being arrested. It was really not clear to me until that moment in what kind of a situation I had landed myself after escaping from English captivity.

Most of the 7th Army staff had returned without casualties, but the command section had to be reformed for the second time. General of Panzer Troops Brandenberger, newly arrived from the Eastern Front, was named to be Eberbach's successor. In this bitter opponent of the regime, I came to know one of the most upright men I have ever met.[18]

After a few more days, we were back up and running, from the leadership point of view. The retreat through Belgium turned into a race against enemy tanks. Our command section allowed itself to be "shot out" of every single command post. We reached German soil on about 10 September. Following an interim stop in Monschau, we took over the former headquarters of OKH, "Felsennest" near Münstereifel.

Our assessment of the situation was unanimous: if the western Allies succeeded in resolving their supply problems, and if they continued to attack rapidly, the war would have to end within a few more weeks. The German combat units, occupation forces, and support troops flooding back from France, Belgium, and Holland were in shocking condition. I recollect that I SS-Panzer Corps didn't even have ten battle-ready tanks left, and LXXIV Army Corps, with the remnants of several divisions, had a total of one artillery piece—and on top of that, the gun was damaged! The fortress troops positioned along the German border had an extremely low combat value, while the reserve units with which we had been supplied consisted of old men, sick men, and men fit only for limited duties.

The West Wall emplacements were to a considerable extent disarmed, since their weapons, armored shields, range-finding gear, communications equipment, and other appurtenances had been pulled out to equip the Atlantic Wall. The bridges across the Rhine at Düsseldorf and Cologne were no longer rigged to explode; because of bomber raids, the explosives had been taken far away again. At first there was not even enough blasting material at hand to refill the explosive chambers in the bridges. In order to reach Berlin, Dresden, Vienna, and Prague, practically all the enemy needed to do was keep on marching straight ahead.

Then came the astonishing "miracle on the West Wall." The Allies stood still and made us a gift of the decisive weeks to reconstruct a somewhat effective defense. In history books, this miracle is explained away primarily by the Allies' supply problems. But the deciding factor was something more like this: British Field Marshal Montgomery had the ambition of ending the campaign with a grand British victory because he felt, with justification, that the huge success of the battle for France was almost exclusively an American triumph. Therefore, he developed a strategic plan of crossing the northern

Rhine by way of Arnhem and through the Reichswald forest, so as to open up the German front from the rear.[19]

To carry out such an operation, Montgomery required the vast majority of available supplies; as well as having the U.S. 1st Army, then operating in the vicinity of the city of Aachen, subordinated to his needs. With Churchill's help he succeeded in putting his plan through, but the prerequisite for his plan was bringing the American offensive to a full stop. This grossly wrong decision on the part of the Allied supreme command had as its consequence the lengthening of the war by more than half a year.

The last deed of American arms for the time being was the capture of Aachen. Among the most grotesque sideshows of the fighting in these last months of the war was the Führer Order to replace one military commandant of Aachen with a different one. The incumbent was intolerable because he was a son-in-law of General Halder's. We reported that the exchange was no longer possible, since in the meantime the Aachen municipal area had been encircled. But then a rested and refitted Panzer unit was brought up; following a decoy attack, it broke through the American lines to bring the new commandant into Aachen and take away the old one. The operation was carried out with significant artillery support, and it actually succeeded, because the enemy was so completely surprised by it. The change of command with the old and new military commandants took place on Aachen's famed Turnierplatz.

Two or three days later, the new commandant very reasonably surrendered the city to the Americans. I no longer know how many casualties this operation cost us; it was an operation behind which there lay no strategic consideration, not even a tactical motive, but merely a caprice of Hitler's.

One night shortly afterward, I received a telephone call from supreme headquarters: the commander of the 116th Panzer Division, Major General Count von Schwerin, was a traitor and was to be arrested and shot immediately.[20] "The Führer expects a report by tomorrow morning on the performance of this order." I honestly didn't know if I was awake or dreaming. With a front-line soldier's reaction, I turned over on my side and went back to sleep.

While I was reporting the matter to my army commander the next morning, we received an order from Army Group B: General Brandenberger should present himself immediately at the command post of (I believe) LXXXV Army Corps, to meet there with Field Marshal Model. Several hours later, Brandenberger came back and informed us of the background to this Führer Order. Schwerin had driven into the city of Aachen before its final encirclement and had encountered unimaginable conditions there. The *Kreisleiter* [Nazi district leader] of Aachen City had ordered the population to evacuate, and had then fled to some unknown destination along with his colleague, the party district leader of Aachen Region. An elderly university professor was acting as the city's sole civil authority, and trying on his own initiative to put the necessary measures into effect. All that remained of the entire Nazi Party organization were some Hitler Youth boys at Aachen Cathedral, on the look-out for fires in the city.

Through a loudspeaker, Schwerin had the population informed that the evacuation that had been ordered was now cancelled, and they could go back to their air raid shelters. Next he went to the telephone exchange, an important switching station for the entire Rhineland. The officials there told him that they had the mission of damaging the station, but not completely destroying it, before the Americans came in. Then Count Schwerin wrote a message on a sheet of paper, the gist of which was: "I am the last German commander in Aachen. I have halted the idiotic evacuation of the city. I commend the population to your protection." He addressed the message to the commanding general of the American troops who were on their way into Aachen. The message was drawn up in English.

Count Schwerin gave the message to an official who had previously told him that he would remain in Aachen, and tasked him with handing it over to a senior American officer. On the assumption that the U.S. troops would occupy Aachen within only a few more hours, Count Schwerin returned to his division headquarters in Kohlscheid. When it became clear on the next day, however, that the Americans had halted their attack, he attempted to get the paper back. But the official had gone to Cologne and handed the letter to the local *Gauleiter* [regional party leader], who had transmitted its contents to the Führer's headquarters.

Brandenberger told me that Model had relieved Schwerin of his post as commander of the 116th Panzer Division, and ordered him to answer for himself at a court-martial to be conducted by 7th Army. Then he ordered me to put together the best court-martial board that I could—for the purpose of saving Schwerin! This was done: but Count Schwerin, who had made a final trip to his headquarters to bid farewell to his division, did not appear. Every hour we received questions from the *Führer-Hauptquartier* about the status of the situation. I reported that Count Schwerin couldn't be found; secretly, I hoped that he had broken through to the Americans in the meantime.

The next day a certain SS-Colonel Przybilski reported himself to me; his name indicated an Upper Silesian origin.[21] He had been given the mission of searching for the "traitor" with his *Standarte,* and bringing him in dead or alive. On the strength of our common Silesian heritage, I was able to convince the SS man to wait for twelve hours; I promised to get the general there by then. In the meantime, the responsible corps chief of staff, Colonel in the General Staff Wiese (who had likewise hoped that Schwerin would simply disappear), had found the general at his division.[22] Several hours later, Schwerin came into our headquarters and explained that he had been with his troops up until then. As soon as I had reported his arrival, the order came down that his pistol had to be taken from him immediately. I gave that mission to our IIa, a regular army infantry colonel. But he reported shortly afterward that his task could not be performed, because Schwerin was being guarded by heavily armed sergeants from his division, who had set up a position in front of his quarters complete with an armored car. I went over to see them immediately and made it clear to them that I only wanted to help their commanding officer. It was only reluctantly that they let me enter. Count Schwerin handed me his sidearm with a smile and told his people to go back to the division.

The court-martial board we had assembled acquitted General Count Schwerin after a short hearing. I believe that no court-martial verdict was ever signed, and thereby given the force of law, more quickly than my noble commander General Brandenberger signed that verdict. Now, of course, we had to report the outcome of the proceedings. Field Marshal Model was quaking with rage: he absolutely could not report this verdict to the Führer; it had to be reversed without delay. Cool and unmoved, Brandenberger declared that he was the court-martial convening authority, and the verdict would be changed only over his dead body.

Meanwhile, I had contacted the chief of staff of OB-West, General of Cavalry Siegfried Westphal.[23] He recommended placing the acquitted Count Schwerin under the protection of his own commander, Field Marshal von Rundstedt. We therefore sent Schwerin and a major to Headquarters OB-West at Ziegenhain. When the major returned, he reported that the armored car with the 116th Panzer Division sergeants had shown up at Ziegenhain at exactly the same time.

As for the rest of the story: Rundstedt had given Schwerin back his pistol, and let him know that the Führer had appointed him to command a Panzer corps in Italy! What had happened in the meantime? The Armaments Minister, Albert Speer, had visited some arms factories in the vicinity of Aachen, during which he had learned of the blatant dereliction on the part of the local party authorities. Speer had made a report to Hitler about this and had completely approved of Schwerin's conduct. Hitler had then made a surprising decision, ordaining that the district leaders of Aachen City and Aachen Region were to be assigned as ordinary riflemen to a combat unit in the 7th Army.

This arrangement had a sequel of its own. One day when I returned from a trip to the front, I found my headquarters surrounded by SS units. I immediately concealed myself and sent my orderly Kühn to reconnoiter my headquarters. He reported to me that Grohé, the *Gauleiter* of Cologne, was there and wanted to talk with me on behalf of his two district leaders, and so I went to Grohé.[24] The first thing I did was forbid this SS presence, and it was immediately withdrawn. When Grohé then asked me to transfer the district leaders to him, so that he could put them into a field training battalion in Cologne, I "regretted" being unable to grant him his wish. The district leaders had been assigned to the 12th Infantry Division under General Engel.[25] As Hitler's former military adjutant, he still spoke with the Führer frequently over the telephone, and would certainly tell him about any arrangements that ran contrary to his order.

Then I suggested to Grohé that he drive to Engel's location with me. When we came to the 12th Division's command post, which lay very close to the front, I at first spoke with Engel alone. He was just sitting down to some genuine coffee, complete with cookies and whipped cream, that the people he was quartered with had just put on the table for him, and he invited me to join him. Suddenly there was a powerful artillery barrage that landed quite near us, and led me to ask the location of the cellar of the house. Engel laughed and explained that the Americans kept on stubbornly firing at the same target, a nearby crossroads. If some American gunner didn't happen to make a mistake we would be completely safe where we were. We sat drinking coffee for a quite a while, and forgot all about the *Gauleiter.* When we remembered him, we learned that at the first shellfire he had headed back to Cologne with the greatest possible speed. I never heard anything more of Grohé again.

The Allied halt made possible a reorganization of 7th Army, so that by October 1944, it had attained a limited defensive capability. Above all, it was possible to reequip the combat units, to a certain extent, with arms and gear. This was due to the new Chief Quartermaster, Colonel in the General Staff Fussenegger, who proved himself to be a superb General Staff officer.[26] He had dispatched officers to the most important arms factories in the Ruhr District, who directed to us the weapons, vehicles, and equipment items we required without any intermediaries or instructions from above. The chief of staff of OB-West, General Westphal, took me to task about all this unauthorized activity, but then conceded that he wouldn't have done any differently himself.

In the meantime, 7th Army had handed over the Aachen sector to the adjoining army on our right. The front appeared to be in particular danger where our two zones connected, because the dams to the southeast of that point were obviously an intermediate objective of the U.S. 1st Army. The Americans must have been interested in the timely prevention of the possible flooding of this potential line of attack. As a result, Field Marshal Model had ordered a war game to be conducted concerning the situation at the "seam" between the two armies. The war game took place at Schloss Schlenderhan, the property of Baron Waldemar von Oppenheim, and was directed by General of Panzer Troops Hasso von Manteuffel.[27] A coincidence then occurred which was probably unique in the annals of warfare.

Before General Brandenberger and I departed for Schlenderhan, the chief of staff of our LXXIV Army Corps, situated on the right wing of our army, had reported a powerful American artillery barrage, which indicated possible attack preparations. Therefore we ordered that he and the commanding general of that corps, as well as all the commanders of the units on the right wing, not come to the war game.

Immediately after my arrival at Schlenderhan, I received a report that the Americans in the Hürtgen Forest had gone on the offensive along the entire front. Field Marshal Model decided, "The war game will proceed anyway. Now we're playing for real!" I remained on the telephone and continued to announce the current state of affairs. As the situation very soon became increasingly critical, Model assigned the 116th Panzer Division, which was standing by as the Army Group's reserve force, to 7th Army. The division commander, General von Waldenburg, and his Ia, Major in the General Staff the Prince of Holstein, were both present.[28] They received our mission orders right there on the spot, and were then able to send their own orders to the already alerted units of their division from the radio transmitter in the castle courtyard. By this means, the division was able to enter the battle within minutes. They put together an annihilating defeat for a U.S. division that had pushed out in the direction of Schmidt. The vast majority of the American tanks that had broken through were knocked out. Only after the war did the leaders of the U.S. 1st Army find out (from us) about the coincidence that had made possible the German command's lightning-fast reaction.

During this period, Albert Speer visited us a number of times on his way to the arms factories in the neighborhood of Eschweiler. Although extremely close to the combat zone, they were still operating. In our long and very frank conversations, it became clear that he had liberated himself from Hitler's influence. His main interest now lay in forestalling the "scorched earth" order—the destruction of nearly all German industry and infrastructure that Hitler had directed. Speer sought the support of the military authorities, of which he was fully assured.

I cannot recall the exact date in October 1944 when I, together with the chiefs of staff of 5th Panzer Army and 6th SS-Panzer Army, was let in on the plan for the Ardennes offensive by the chief of staff of Army Group B, General Krebs. The German high command had available to it a big package of rested and refitted armored divisions, and (to some extent) newly formed *Volksgrenadier* divisions; by means of their combat deployment on a massive scale, a decisive alteration in the course of the war was to be achieved.[29] This was possible only on the Western Front, where the plan was to push forward from the Ardennes to Antwerp in a repeat performance of the "Sickle Cut" [the massive Blitzkrieg-style flanking maneuver that had led so quickly to the defeat of the Allied forces and the surrender of France in 1940]. In response to our immediate question about the all-important air situation, we were told that the attack would commence during a period that was unfavorable for air force operations, and that all available German fighter-plane units would be pulled together to support this operation.

Despite all the optimistic forecasts, the insanity of this operation was immediately clear to me. Since for the purpose of deception, 7th Army's staff had been assigned to make the advance preparations for all three attacking armies, it was possible for me to see right through the unrealistic and unbelievably dilettantish design of the last German offensive in the war.

While the assault in quest of victory was to be conducted by 6th SS-Panzer Army on the right and 5th Panzer Army on the left, 7th Army was tasked to cover the southern flank of the German attack. For this purpose only, four divisions (three *Volksgrenadier* divisions and one parachute division) were initially put at our disposal. I let Krebs know that 7th Army would find it impossible to perform its mission with such a small force, considering that the flank would grow longer and longer and that we could expect attacks against it by powerful American forces. Even if the attack by the Panzer armies were a success, the threat to the southern flank would still prove fatal. Krebs saw my point, but had to limit himself to the uncertain prospect of supplying us with more units during the course of the offensive.

All the same, our objection was probably what led Army Group B to raise its own objection to the big plan, which was called "Grand Slam" in reference to an expression in the game of bridge, and suggest a significantly smaller operation ("Little Slam") in the vicinity of Aachen. Hitler insisted on his own plan and sharply rejected all countersuggestions. And so the Ardennes offensive became one of the last great mistakes of this war, following in the wake of Dunkirk, Moscow, Stalingrad, North Africa, and Normandy.

On the occasion of a quartermasters' conference in Münstereifel during the time leading up to the offensive, 7th Army's chief quartermaster (Colonel in the General Staff Fussenegger), its general quartermaster (Colonel in the General Staff Toppe), and finally the chief quartermaster of OB-West, were able to demonstrate that there had been fundamental errors in the calculation of fuel requirements.[30] To be precise: the fuel requirements for the armored units and the mechanized infantry units to move from their rest and refitting areas east of the Rhine, to their jumping-off points for the attack, had been left out of the equation. There was thus a serious deficiency. The result of the discussion—that the troops would have to collect their missing fuel from the enemy—was not too comforting.

At the same time, I learned by chance that 6th SS-Panzer Army was supposed to fire barrages from 600-millimeter [24-inch] guns, a type of cannon that had been nicknamed "Fat Karl." The target was the small but historically significant town of Monschau, which lay in no-man's land in their attack area. This would have meant the annihilation both of the German inhabitants who had stayed behind and of the town itself, which was especially precious for cultural and historical reasons. This fire plan, which could be traced back to Hitler's instructions, also made no sense from the military point of view. With Monschau's destruction, a narrow pass that the German tanks needed for their advance would be blocked. By making the latter argument I was finally successful in convincing the people responsible for the German artillery prep fire that the shelling of Monschau would hinder our own advance.

The Ardennes offensive could probably never have reached its planned objectives. It still could have been a much bigger success, however, if the flank protection provided by 7th Army had been more effective. Our divisions did, in fact, reach their initial objectives, but they were afterwards not capable of fending off the attacks led by General Patton's powerful American armored forces, even on a front that was only thirty miles wide (and it would have been 180 miles to Antwerp).

We spent Christmas Eve of 1944 at our forward command post at Wiltz in Luxemburg. We were under heavy artillery fire all night long. Both of the adjoining houses were destroyed by direct hits. In spite of everything, we sat beneath a Christmas tree. We recommended that our staff members seek out the cellar. Brandenberger and I remained upstairs on the ground floor. In our fatalistic mood, it had long since been clear to us that the offensive had failed.

During these days the Führer Escort Brigade, a well-equipped Panzer unit that had never seen any combat, was assigned to us.[31] Its commanding officer was the same Major Otto Remer who had become known for the role he played on 20 July 1944, and whom Hitler had promoted to general as a mark of gratitude.[32] Remer didn't turn up until two or three days after his troops, who had been sent into action immediately because of the threatening situation. Now, however, he found nothing but the remnants of his inexperienced soldiers, who without their leader had been devastated in the hard defensive fighting.

By the first days of January 1945, we were back to our original positions on the Sauer River, which the enemy, however, had already crossed at numerous points. The army headquarters was moved to Schloss Merkeshausen near Bitburg.[33] Here, on 20 February, Field Marshal Model relieved General

Brandenberger of command in an undignified manner. However his successor, General Felber, proved to be just as noble a man, with equal strength of character.[34]

During the early morning hours of the following day, four bombs from low-flying aircraft landed in the immediate vicinity of our house, without hurting anybody. Plainly, one of the numerous foreign laborers had given away our well-camouflaged main headquarters. Since we had to count on a repeat attack, all the civilians—the women and children above all—were sent out into the woods that surrounded the building. General Felber waited in front of the house in his auto, about to ride off and visit the front. We members of the staff had to get back to our workplaces. In my room on the ground floor, the Ia, Lieutenant Colonel in the General Staff Voigt-Ruscheweyh, briefed me on the morning reports from our subordinate corps.[35] Paul Kühn was in the same room, occupied with cleaning my gear.

At that moment came the second attack. Four fifty-kilogram bombs hit the mansion, which fell in on itself like a house of cards. I found myself down in the cellar, covered with soot and buried beneath the ruins. But I was still conscious, and General Felber, who had witnessed everything, heard my cries for help. I was freed after about thirty minutes. My uniform hung from me in tatters. Many years later, workers clearing the site found and returned to me my Knight's Cross and military paybook.

Except for me, every staff member inside the building was either dead or severely wounded. One of the bombs must have detonated right in my room; my faithful orderly, Paul Kühn, had his head torn from his shoulders, and Lieutenant Colonel Voigt-Ruscheweyh's back was ripped wide open by a bomb fragment. I had a serious head wound myself. After receiving first aid, I had a telephone apparatus mounted on a tree in order to carry on the work of command. I asked General Felber to go to the army's command post at Eisenschmidt near Wittlich, and from there to arrange for a new command section.

In the late evening I followed after him, riding in the truck that carried the dead. On top of their corpses sat the women and children of Schloss Merkeshausen, whom I dropped off at Himmerod Abbey.[36] Now a favor I had once been able to do for the abbot was repaid. Although Model ordered me to go into the hospital, I stayed with my staff. Here I still felt most secure.

On 25 February we buried our dead in the abbey garden. Voigt-Ruscheweyh had become a good friend to me, and so I was deeply shocked by his demise. But nothing hit me as hard as Paul Kühn's death. We both came from Lüben in Silesia; he had been with me through thick and thin since 1941, and a few months earlier he had saved my life. In January I had suggested that he return to Lüben to rescue his family from the Russians, but he did not want to leave me alone. Now I had to bid farewell to my best wartime comrade.

The emotional strain that stemmed from the developing situation on the Eastern Front increased from day to day. During that period, the loss of my Silesian homeland to the invading Russians, my ignorance of the fate of my daughter and my siblings, and my daily fears for my own front left me about as deeply depressed as I could be. For some weeks I had already observed a visible change in Model. Now he frequently had me come over to his head-quarters in the evenings in order to open up his heart. His faith in Hitler and National Socialism had given way to the recognition that he had served a false master and a false cause. Therefore his suicide on 17 April 1945, in the Ruhr pocket came as no real surprise to me.

On 4 March, our retreat began straight across Germany toward the east, finally to end on the Czechoslovakian border. The following highlights will represent the general situation in which we found ourselves.

We had long since crossed the Mosel River, heading south. During a com-mand post relocation on 16 March, we drove right into the middle of a group of American tanks that had broken through the adjacent army to our south. My army commander and I had to hide in a haystack for hours, until in the gathering darkness we succeeded in getting across the area and finding shelter from the enemy's incessant tank and artillery fire in a farmhouse on the other side of a river.

After things had calmed down, I once again located the remnants of my new staff—what number was this?—in Nieder-Olm near Mainz. I set up my command post inside a post office, since I could only reach our subordinate units over postal telephone lines. Around midnight, the latest Commander-in-Chief West, Field Marshal Kesselring, appeared. He interrupted me while I was reporting the army's catastrophic situation, and called my attention to the performance of his order "to hang all deserters from the nearest tree." He had come through the army's entire rear area, he said, and hadn't seen a single man hanging. He left me with an admonition to carry out his orders better in the future. This encounter was one of the most shocking that I ever had with a German field marshal. After the war, I couldn't get Kesselring to recall the incident.

On 22 March, we finally got permission to cross the Rhine at Ludwig-shafen. It was nonetheless clear from the start that the Rhine barrier could not be held either. Two days later, I drove from the command post to Wiesbaden to visit XII Army Corps, which had just been assigned to us. The chief of staff, General Fäckenstedt, invited me to share the noon meal in his house on the Neroberg.[37] We sat on the balcony in beautiful spring weather, and at each place at the table there was a telescope through which we could observe the tank battles over on the western shore of the Rhine. Fäckenstedt also had a telephone connection with the well-known competitive equestrienne Irmgard von Opel, who was at Westerhaus.[38] The Americans had already overrun her location, and now she was reporting to us the number and types of enemy tanks driving past her home. That visit was also not an everyday wartime experience.

On 25 March, American tanks that had meanwhile crossed the Rhine shot us out of our command post in Bensheim. On our way to the next command post, we came under heavy attack by dive-bombers. We succeeded in reaching a small forest, and threw ourselves under the cover of a heap of wood to watch the unceasing attack on the little forest. Loud detonations and bullets whistling all around made us suspicious. I investigated the woodpile more closely and discovered camouflaged stacks of munitions. We were lying in the middle of an ammunition dump!

On 26 March, we had set up our command post inside an inn at Heigenbrücken. Here the news reached us that General Felber had been relieved of his command, probably as a scapegoat for the unsuccessful defense of the Rhine. The new army commander General von Obstfelder—my fifth in less than half a year—appeared during the course of the day.[39] In the evening we sat down with Felber for a farewell drink. Suddenly we heard the sound of tanks, obviously approaching us. Since by that point we no longer had any tanks or any other tracked vehicles left in the entire army, we stepped cautiously to the doorway of the inn, which lay on the village high street. The first vehicles were already passing—tanks from the U.S. 4th Armored Division, a unit familiar to us from Normandy. Without paying us any attention, they drove right by at a distance of about twenty meters.

I sent all the staff members into the forest that began right behind the inn, and also asked General Felber to join them. I only forgot—and forgot completely!—about the new commander, who had gone to sleep on the upper floor of the building. Telephone calls with the units stationed to our front confirmed that a battle group from an American division had broken through, moving in an eastward direction. I knew that to our rear in Hammelburg there was a large prisoner of war camp for officers, and I suspected in turn that the Americans wanted to try to liberate their prisoners. The first thing I did was give the alarm to the camp. Then I called the responsible *Ortskommandant* [the soldier, frequently a senior NCO, who was the military "commandant" of a given small locality]. He put a major on the phone, who was coincidentally there on leave. I briefed this officer on the situation and ordered him to set up a defensive front with all available forces. He let me know that on that very afternoon, an obviously rested and refitted tank-destroyer unit had been unloaded from trains in Hammelburg. The major, who was an experienced Eastern Front veteran, executed his assignment so well that the American tank raid—carried out in Rommel style—ended up as a complete failure with heavy casualties.[40]

That was how this exciting event appeared to me at the time. The following facts were described in postwar American publications: On 26 March, the commander of the U.S. 3rd Army, General Patton, had a task force drawn from the U.S. 4th Armored Division. It consisted of 307 men, ten Sherman tanks, six light tanks, three 105-millimeter howitzers, twenty-seven half-tracks, seven jeeps, and an ambulance. He put Captain Abraham Baum in command, and gave him the mission of penetrating about sixty miles into the enemy's rear area and bringing nine hundred Americans out of the officer prisoner of war camp at Hammelburg (*Oflag XIII B*). American sources allege that Patton's primary reason for this operation was to liberate his own son-in-law, John Waters.

An entire American brigade (Combat Command B of the 4th Armored Division) was used to break through the thin German defensive line near Aschaffenburg, and the task force drove on towards Hammelburg in a night march. Initially it ran into no resistance worthy of the name, and in a number of villages it took several surprised German soldiers prisoner, even including one general. While still several kilometers away from Hammelburg, the Americans encountered three German tanks. But after some fierce combat, a few American armored vehicles succeeded in forcing their way into the camp, loading up and taking away some of the American prisoners of war. The other prisoners attempted to escape in small groups headed in various directions. In the meantime, Task Force Baum had suffered heavy losses in continued fighting with the German anti-tank forces. When Baum decided to turn back, he still had over a hundred soldiers capable of fighting; six light and three medium tanks; three tracked vehicles; and fourteen half-tracks. But the return march was soon halted by German forces who succeeded in surrounding and destroying the American task force. Baum was taken prisoner himself. Patton's son-in-law, John Waters, was gravely wounded. Not a single American soldier made it back to his own lines. Patton was said to have explained in a press conference, "We attempted to liberate the prison camp because we were afraid that the American prisoners might be murdered by the retreating Germans." The few American officers who knew Patton's true motive only broke their silence twenty years after the war had ended.

The 7th Army's retreat to the east went on without a break. We scarcely put up any serious resistance any more. Only the cautiousness of the American pursuit stretched out this final phase of the war. It was clear to us that our only real interest lay in letting the Americans push forward to the east as fast and as far as possible. During this period, the troops allowed themselves to be "shot out" of every single position. I knew very well what was going on whenever I received a report that a unit "had withdrawn to a secondary defensive line in the face of enemy superiority."

Nor did the orders we put out at the army level correspond to the facts any longer. Moreover, by the time the orders reached their intended recipients they had usually been outpaced by events. The commanders and the chiefs of staff of our subordinate units also understood that the execution of our orders was something that was being practically left up to them, in accordance with their capabilities and the rapidly changing situation. Many things still had to remain unspoken; even now, speaking openly was dangerous.

With few exceptions, the troop leaders were all making an effort to avoid casualties and to boycott senseless operations, even if they came in the form of an order. Such actions included, most of all, the orders to destroy bridges, power plants, and telephone installations—actions that in any case couldn't have halted the Americans, as highly equipped technologically as they were.

The relatively long duration of the retreat through Germany was due solely to the American military leadership, which brought its own forward movement to a complete stop at even the slightest resistance, and continued the planned attack only with guaranteed artillery and air support. Thus a few of our machine guns could halt entire divisions for hours, or even days.

It was astonishing that on the German side the organization kept on functioning right up until the end, including our command apparatus as well as the supply system and our long-range communications. The signs of disintegration were mostly in the personnel area. This was more than understandable, given the muddle of front-line troops with homeland troops. One could add the fact that, so close to the end, the wish to survive grasped men ever more strongly.

During this time, acting on my own initiative, I personally prevented many bridge demolitions and declared many small towns to be "hospital cities." I succeeded in doing this for Bad Kissingen, which as a result remained as good as unscathed. Over and over during these weeks, there were tragicomic experiences with high-ranking Party officials. For example, *Gauleiter* Sauckel was sent to us one day to get a military assignment.[41] We sent him to LXXXV Army Corps. He drove away from us with a large entourage and several vehicles to enter into his "front-line mission," but he never got there.

After 7th Army had reached the Czechoslovakian border in the course of its retreat, combat with the advancing Americans continued to push it backward. An increasingly critical situation consequently developed behind the army's right wing, because Soviet forces were advancing toward the Erzgebirge mountains and threatening the army's northern flank. The commander of the army group that was fighting the Soviets to the rear of 7th Army, Field

Marshal Ferdinand Schörner, now put in a bid to have 7th Army placed under his command and to set up a circular defense of the "Protectorate of Bohemia and Moravia Fortress."[42] Although we had lost contact with the neighboring armies on both of our wings, and Schörner's demand was therefore not without justification, we fought to stay under OB-West's command so as to not to be deemed "on the Eastern Front" in case of a surrender.

On 23 April, the partition of northern and southern Germany by enemy forces was finally complete. On 26 April, following a deep Soviet penetration west of Meissen, we ourselves were embroiled in a two-front situation. The U.S. 3rd Army had pushed past the army's southern wing by way of Passau, moving in the direction of Vienna. During these days, a high-ranking General Staff officer from OKW en route to the "Alpine Redoubt" paid me a visit. To my astonishment, he radiated as much confidence in victory as ever. He predicted that a breach between the western Allies and the Soviet Union was just around the corner; it was simply a matter of so successfully defending the areas that were still in Germany's possession that they could be used as bargaining chips in the subsequent negotiations. I explained to him that I not only didn't share in his views, but on behalf of the soldiers under our command, I regarded them as criminal. He stared at me in surprise and left my presence.

On 28 April, I was ordered to go to the *Ortskommandantur* of Teplitz-Schönau for a meeting with Field Marshal Schörner. Before my departure, I once again confirmed over the radio our status as a unit belonging to OB-West. When I arrived at Teplitz-Schönau, Schörner had not arrived. The *Ortskommandant* who received me saw a terrier inside my car, a dog whose former owner had given him to me at one of our many halting places during the retreat through Germany. The soldier asserted that as soon as Schörner saw the dog, he would immediately have me arrested and probably condemned to death; wringing his hands together, he begged me to make the dog disappear. But I was willing to wait and see what happened, and I parked the auto right in front of the *Ortskommandantur,* with the dog in the passenger seat. However, Schörner did not appear. Units of the "Vlasov Army" [Russian volunteers in German service] had halted his progress on the way from Reichenberg to Teplitz. Protracted negotiations with the Russian units had delayed him for so long that he called off the meeting with me.

I used the time to pay a visit to the palace of Princess Clary in Teplitz-Schönau, where I hoped to meet refugees from Silesia.[43] I actually met up with my younger brother, who had made it through the inferno of Dresden as if by some miracle; there was also a large number of relatives and acquaintances from my homeland. I counseled them all to continue their flight to the west that very night. When I recommended the same course of action to the lady of the house, Princess Clary, she referred to a conference over which she still needed to preside as the chairwoman of the local National Socialist women's organization! Such experiences indicate the amount of confusion that then prevailed among both soldiers and civilians.

Hitler's death, which we learned about on 1 May, gave most of us only a sense of relief. None of us believed even for an instant that he had "fallen in the battle."

The relative calm prevailing along the front lines at this time was only interrupted by persistent American advances in one particular sector. An envoy whom I sent across the lines to get an explanation came back with surprising news: General Patton had learned that all the horses from Austria's stud farms had been collected in Hostau, southwest of Pilsen.[44] It was said that he was highly interested in these horses. We immediately got word to Patton that he could drive or fly to Hostau at any time, and that we would establish a neutral corridor for this purpose. Afterwards, Patton really was in Hostau—far behind the German lines—on several occasions. We could not, however, satisfy his wish to have all the horses moved into his army's operational area, since the majority of them had just given birth to foals. Nonetheless, our obliging behavior in this situation helped us a great deal during the subsequent surrender negotiations.

Making use of the absence of the politically unteachable army commander General von Obstfelder, I sent my Ic/AO, Major in the General Staff von Mutius, over to the Americans on 7 May to start up the surrender talks.[45] He came back with the message that General Patton would expect the army commander the next day in his headquarters at Elbogen, southwest of Karlsbad.[46]

When I reported this to General von Obstfelder upon his return from a visit to our northern front, he fell into a rage. He threatened to have me arrested and subjected to a court-martial. I calmly replied that he wouldn't find a man on my staff who would arrest me—but on the other hand, I could have *him* taken into custody at any time. Obstfelder bowed to the inevitable; however, he refused to go to General Patton himself. Even the suggestion that he owed it to the troops under his command to take this last step was unsuccessful.

So it was that early on 8 May, I drove off toward Elbogen together with my headquarters commandant, Cavalry Captain von Deichmann, and a certain Cavalry Captain Gescher, who spoke English superbly.[47] An American general received us in no-man's land between the front lines; after a formal military greeting, he explained that he had the task of conveying me to Patton. In the Elbogen marketplace, we walked past an American honor guard that stood in formation in front of the hotel where Patton was quartered with his chief of staff, General Hobart Gay.[48] Then Patton stepped out of the hotel entrance with his officers and made a short speech in which he expressed his regret at having to greet me under circumstances that were so painful for me.

He said that, as a soldier, he had complete understanding for the emotions that afflicted me. I gathered from his words that he thought I was the commander of the army. When I therefore made myself known as the chief of staff, and excused my commanding general on the grounds of "illness," Patton briefly replied that, in that case, he would leave the negotiations to his own chief of staff.

The negotiations with General Gay proceeded in a dignified, even good-natured manner. For me, the most important thing was to persuade the Americans to take as many German soldiers as possible as prisoners of war, so as to preserve from Soviet captivity not only all the members of 7th Army, but also all the German troops who were now pulling back from the Eastern Front toward the west. Therefore, when Gay asked me a question about 7th Army's ration strength, I gave him the figure of a million men. He responded in an ironic tone, "So then, you're actually three times as strong as the 3rd Army." It was quite apparent that he had seen through me immediately. Nonetheless, he declared himself ready to take a million German soldiers as prisoners of war. Another concession I obtained was that the vast majority of all the German troops would be set free as rapidly as possible. It was agreed that, to begin with, our entire army staff would remain on the job for command and control purposes. To this end it was decided that the headquarters would migrate to the Hotel Pupp in nearby Karslbad.

When I returned to our headquarters in Welchau, Admiral Dönitz's offer of surrender had become known, so that now, even Obstfelder raised no more objections. Seventh Army's command section went into captivity on 8 May, while the quartermaster section remained temporarily responsible for provisioning German units. But within a short time, the Americans also terminated that arrangement.

The end of the war, as I experienced it, passed by without drama but also without disgrace. I was thankful that I had succeeded in saving many thousands of German troops from Soviet captivity. Unfortunately, other than rear-area troops, this only affected those mechanized units on the Eastern Front who were successful in getting across Czechoslovakia to the American lines. According to the report of his chief of staff, General von Natzmer, the commander of the Army Group, Field Marshal Schörner, fled to the "Alpine Redoubt" in a light plane, carrying a suitcase full of gold and wearing a Bavarian folk costume.[49] A short time afterwards he was taken prisoner there.

Soldiers in downfalls have very different fates, in which luck and chance play a great part. I felt duty-bound to take upon myself every kind of captivity for as long as the soldiers under our command had to go without their own freedom. For every man with the feelings of a soldier, the last year of the war had been very depressing. Things could not get too much worse.

Two things were certainly clear in my mind right from the start: first, my sense of relief that I was now finally free from worry about being hauled in front of a "People's Court" because of my involvement in the resistance; and second, that during the entire war—as during my entire life—I had never had to use a weapon against another person. Naturally that had to do with the fact that as a General Staff officer, I had much less occasion to do so than did a front-line soldier. On the other hand, I was in the front lines and in unpleasant situations often enough that I might have been forced to use my weapon; I have always regarded it as a happy fate not to be morally burdened by the necessary killing of a guiltless enemy soldier.

VII

Soldier in Captivity

The world will not forget this about us for hundreds of years.
—Henning von Tresckow

Mindful of the declaration of guilt that Henning von Tresckow had pronounced even before the Russian campaign started, and with no illusions, I became a prisoner of war on 9 May 1945. In contrast to other fronts, and also contrary to the original agreement in my surrender negotiations with the U.S. 3rd Army, my army staff did not remain in office for command purposes for the duration of the disbanding and release of our troop units. As a result the loss of freedom was felt more immediately for us than was the case elsewhere. My commander and I were immediately singled out and separated from the army staff. Our aides, as well as a car and driver, were only permitted to remain with us for the first few days.

At the outset we even feared being transferred to the Soviets, when we along with about thirty other generals and senior General Staff officers were driven eastward by way of Eger, under the command of an American staff officer and under strict guard. When we stopped for a long halt in the marketplace of Pilsen, we had no idea of what was being planned for us. Our open car was immediately surrounded by a large number of Czechs, who heckled us and spat on us. Since the American guards did not intervene, and apparently would indifferently allow it all to continue, there was nothing else for us to do but to sit there mutely and preserve our equanimity. My thoughts went back to 1939, when the Wehrmacht marched into Czechoslovakia and the Czechs were the objects of arbitrary German rule.

We were only released from this situation after a considerable amount of time, and then we were all put up in a relatively comfortable hotel. Here the uncertainty of all our future fates became clear. The commander of the American army corps in whose zone we had been taken prisoner had set up his headquarters in Pilsen. He was only curious to meet the German generals. During a sort of cocktail party we were treated with great kindness and interest. The next day we were transported back to a camp near Regensburg that had been established in the meantime.

With these initial impressions of captivity, I had a foretaste of everything that would come my way: hatred, contempt, curiosity, and arbitrariness. On the other hand, it was clear to me how thankful I had to be to my own fate not to have become a prisoner of the Soviets. Without a doubt they would have sentenced me, as the former Ic/AO of Army Group Center, to a minimum of twenty-five years in Siberian labor camps, no proof of guilt required. Being in American hands all seemed more like a big adventure—the length and variations of which, however, were unpredictable. I expected no privileges because of my involvement in the resistance. I also wanted to talk about that only if I were asked about it.

It was very soon apparent that all German General Staff officers were automatically under arrest, and not one could be set free. All the same, my attempt to get released quickly on the basis of my 1943 stomach operation foundered not so much because of the Americans, but because of the adverse decision of the German chief surgeon in the Regensburg hospital, where I had had myself admitted. From a medical standpoint he may have been correct; from the standpoint of humanity his conduct seemed incomprehensible to me. And so I prepared myself to spend a long duration as a prisoner of war. The main thing for me to do was to preserve my fundamental soldierly attitude in captivity as well. I attempted to maintain this resolution during the thirty-one months of eventful happenings and extremely varied treatment that lay ahead of me in fifteen different camps and prisons.

It was only after the earliest days, which were very hectic and during which I finally lost even the last items of personal property to American souvenir hunters, that I came to reflect on the monstrous changes brought about by the war's outcome, both for the fatherland and the German people as well as in my own personal circumstances.

The German Reich had collapsed in an inferno of blood, tears, and ruins. The partition into eastern and western halves was on the way. Regaining any national sovereignty, no matter how lessened, seemed to be an impossibility. But more than anything else, it was plain that the German East—that is, West Prussia, East Prussia, Pomerania, the Ostmark, and my own homeland of Silesia—had been lost to the Russian superpower, apparently forever. Like millions of my countrymen, I had to come to terms with losing everything that had made my prior life fulfilling: my homeland, my property, my profession, my circle of friends, and not least, my horses. I thought of the refugee situations I had witnessed—of the Baltic Germans who came to Silesia after 1918; of the French, Poles, and Russians during the war. Only now did I begin to grasp them in full measure. Perhaps I would also never again visit the graves of my parents and my wife; never again see the places where I had once been so happy; never again breathe the air of my Silesian homeland.

Only a considerable amount of curiosity about the very uncertain future kept thoughts of suicide from arising. The need to give a good account of myself, even in the most difficult situations of my life, was an additional incentive not to "desert the colors." The will to survive, which had understandably become predominant among the majority of German soldiers during the war's final months, was also stronger than my despair; on top of that, I had already prevailed not only over the dangers of war, but the much greater danger of the Gestapo. So, next to the loss of my homeland, my biggest concern was the fate of my family, with whom I had lost all contact. I did know that they were safe at a refugee camp in central Germany, where I had been able to visit them once for a short time during the retreat across the country. But as a result, I also knew that they would have to share in the full misery of the millions who had been driven from their homes.

In and of itself, the end of the war was not an unexpected or severe shock to me, because I had been prepared for this catastrophe for a long time. In 1941, Henning von Tresckow had already described for us just what would become of Germany if we did not succeed in liberating our state and nation from Hitler and his regime. Now it all happened just the way he had predicted it, almost down to the last detail.

After 20 July 1944, when all hope of eliminating Hitler by a German uprising had had to be abandoned, I had feared nothing so much as a victory for Hitler, however improbable this was. Only the total collapse of the National Socialist regime had preserved Germany and mankind from the worst calamity in their histories; so that even in the midst of my despair, I was grateful to the Lord God that at least that trial had been spared us. The men and women of the German resistance had dreaded nothing so much for the future as the victory of the Third Reich. Nonetheless, we officers had done our duty to the bitter end out of responsibility for the troops entrusted to us, and had attempted to save what could be saved, if only with slight success. I know of not a single case in which an officer in a high position committed sabotage.

Just as much as I had yearned for the end of the Third Reich, I was shattered by the fate of the Bismarck Reich and the apparently final end of Prussia. Both of these things were incomparably more painful for us eastern Germans than they were for the other citizens of our fatherland. At the same time I was aware, after all of my own previous experiences, that no matter how much helpfulness might be offered, true understanding of the fate of the expellees could scarcely be expected. It appears to be endlessly difficult for anyone to imagine that he might suddenly give up all the material and abstract things that he calls his own, and have to build a whole new life in an alien environment as a man with nothing. Thoughts of this kind haunted me day and night.

When I began my captivity, the Americans were truly an unknown people to me. Up until then I had only known them as enemies who, despite their very different command principles, and the almost excessive exploitation of their material superiority, had proved themselves as soldiers in the best sense. The now-constant contact with interrogation officers, guards, and curious visitors to the various prison camps very quickly provided me with surprising discoveries about the wide variety of types and characters within the U.S. armed forces. By this I do not mean so much the racial and other differences in the American mixture of peoples. What was much more astonishing to me, being accustomed to the thorough homogeneity within the German armed forces, was the striking contrast that existed between different groups in the American army, and above all within its officer corps.

Immediately after we were made prisoner, we first got to know the American common soldiers. The GIs behaved toward us more with a certain camaraderie than with hatred and contempt. In return, they took everything that caught their eye, from a wristwatch to the Iron Cross. They appeared to see nothing forbidden in this, but rather their legitimate claim to war booty and souvenirs.

The officers, including the generals, were overwhelmingly reservists, just as in the German army: however, these men had apparently enjoyed only a slight education in military matters. When I visited America twice for long periods after my release from captivity, I recognized this type of officer again in many middle-class civilian professionals. On the first day of our captivity, my commander and I were invited into a division commander's tent. This gentleman received the German army commander—who, after all, held the same rank as the American army commander General Patton—while leaning back in a folding chair with his legs up on the table. Aside from that, he was extremely kind to us, offered us drinks, and expressed his regrets for our fate. Nor did he alter his comfortable position when we were departing. I laughed about this experience at the time. Today, I know that the American general by no means wished to offend us; instead, he only behaved the way he was accustomed to doing in civilian life. (By contrast, during the war I had seen often enough how we received captured French or Soviet generals: with full military honors and in accordance with the rules of international courtesy.)

As in all the armies of the world, there also existed among the American troops the "bruiser" type who, due not only to propaganda, but above all to the German crimes that had been uncovered in the meantime, frequently enough lost all self-control.

Before the chief physician at the Regensburg hospital had informed the Americans of my medical fitness for imprisonment, I was almost released from captivity, unquestionably due to some oversight. On 26 June 1945, I was transported by truck to the pre-release camp located at the Hohenfels training facility, along with about twenty-five severely wounded German prisoners, mostly arm and leg amputees. When we reached the camp entrance, we were met by a lieutenant and several soldiers from the U.S. 4th Armored Division, a unit I had come to know during the Normandy fighting as being especially good in battle.

The lieutenant waved us off the truck with an automatic pistol, and then the Americans fell upon our meager packs. Suitcases, rucksacks, bags and bundles were torn open, and everything was taken that appeared worth taking to the GIs. Such conduct toward badly wounded men, who wished to preserve the miserable remnants of their property for their freedom, so enraged me that I roared at the American lieutenant the way I had never done to a subordinate in my entire career. At first the American was visibly taken aback; but then he brandished his automatic in my face in an ever-more menacing way. A Jewish interpreter in an American uniform urged me in German not to say another word; a short time earlier, he said, the young officer had gunned down some German officers who resisted his tyrannical behavior, right where they stood. So I resigned myself, and the friendly interpreter promised to do everything for us that was in his power.

Then the lieutenant led us to a tumbledown wooden barracks and ordered us into an empty room, in which we would only have enough space if we all squatted. Next he showed us two sentries with machine guns, who had orders to shoot immediately and without warning as soon as any of us attempted to leave the barracks. We got no food either on that day or the next. Only on the third day did someone toss a small box in to us; it contained completely rotten cheese teeming with thousands of white maggots. The only person who concerned himself about us was the Jewish interpreter. He exhorted us again and again to hang on, because within a few more days we would be set free. Then on the fifth day my badly wounded comrades were in fact allowed to go. But although the Jewish interpreter made a touching attempt to intercede on my behalf, I was transported back to the prisoner of war camp. The authorities in charge of releasing prisoners had realized, after making inquiries, that there had been an oversight in my case—one of the many errors that would so characterize my fate in captivity from then on.

In the interrogation and custody officers we met during our first year of captivity, we got to know another type of American soldier. The majority of these were former German Jews, who were amazingly well informed about all our individual details, and whose behavior toward each of us varied accordingly. They already knew about me quite well. This knowledge came from Allen Dulles who, as the resident officer of the Office of Strategic Services (OSS) in Bern during the war, had been in contact with representatives of the resistance such as Adam Trott zu Solz and Dr. Bernd Gisevius.[1]

But the interrogators weren't particularly interested either in military affairs or the German resistance. They were chiefly concerned with clarifying the historical background of the political developments in Germany. The question came up again and again about whether one was a Prussian, or even a Prussian *Junker* [landed proprietor of noble rank]. Obviously, in their eyes, Prussians and Prussian *Junkers* were even more dangerous than the Nazis themselves. Although my family really stemmed from Lusatia in Saxony and had spread itself out internationally, I always answered these questions with a "yes," and sought to make it clear to them that in the resistance to Hitler, the Prussian nobility had played an extraordinary role. Only the German Jews, and in particular the Jews from Berlin, were aware in general of how senseless this American prejudice was.

I got to know the best type of American officer through my collaboration with the U.S. Army Historical Division. After months of hunger and dishonorable treatment in different prison camps, I was transported, with a detour through the Freising city jail, to Oberursel near Frankfurt-am-Main, where I was put into the most scandalous prison that I had so far experienced (although since it was a camp that Goering had had built for captive Allied airmen, I could not even complain). After ten days, however, my admission to this camp turned out to be one more of many errors. I was conveyed to the so-called "Alaska House" in the same town.

About thirty prominent prisoners had been assembled in this former manufacturer's villa, including: the Hungarian regent, Admiral Horthy; the former Reich finance minister, Count Schwerin-Krosigk; Colonel General Lindemann, who had been my squadron commander in Breslau in 1924; General Heusinger and General Count Schwerin; my cousin, Colonel in the General Staff von Bonin; the retired General *Ritter* von Epp; the test pilot, Hanna Reitsch; and a whole string of ex-ambassadors and Foreign Ministry employees.[2] Here, the Americans approached me with the proposal that I might help them with writing their history of the war. After giving this proposal thorough consideration, I adopted General Heusinger's point of view: that this was our only chance to have an influence on the historiography of World War II, and by this means to have, in the end, our own German war historiography. It is primarily due to Heusinger that over the years a German historiography really was achieved, something that was only possible as long as the directly involved troop leaders and General Staff officers were still alive.

Groups of fifteen to thirty German officers were formed—first at St. Germain near Paris, and then once again in Oberursel. Their only duty, practically speaking, was to provide commentaries to the American texts. They thereby had the opportunity to put in the right light the performance of the German troops during the heavy fighting of 1944–45 against an enemy who was far superior in both numbers and technology.

But the smoothly running and almost friendly collaboration was possible most of all because the officers of the Historical Division consisted without exception of excellent soldiers and gentlemen, who distinguished themselves by their courtesy, extensive learning, and kindness. Many of them were career soldiers who had been trained at West Point, and who could also have stepped right out of the guards regiments of the British Army or the old Prussian Army.

Despite the gulf that lay between us, these men were always ready to help us and never insulting. While at St. Germain, we dined with each other and also celebrated the Christmas of 1945 together. The first speeches of reconciliation ever exchanged between the victors and the vanquished were probably heard at that celebration.

As the spokesman for the German officers, I very quickly came to have a good relationship with the Americans, which in certain individual cases has lasted to the present day. When we were moved to Oberursel because General de Gaulle had requested the departure from France of all American officers stationed there, our group leader, Major Howard P. Hudson, acted against regulations and allowed me a visit from my older brother, who brought me a few personal things that had been rescued from Silesia.[3]

The most interesting, but also most unpleasant, adventure of my captivity was my interrogation as a witness at the Nuremberg war crimes trial. I was transported to Nuremberg on 15 May 1946. I had no idea whether it was the prosecution or the defense that wanted me as a witness. Upon my arrival at the Nuremberg Palace of Justice, I was at first treated very kindly in the reception office. A group of white-helmeted military policemen received me behind an iron door; I shouldered my pack as they led me through wide squares and long corridors and more and more iron doors, until suddenly I was standing in the wing that housed the principal defendants. I knew it from the newspapers. In front of each cell stood a military policeman who watched his prisoner through a small window. I read the names of Goering, Ribbentrop, Keitel, and Speer.

Then I was led into a large cellblock area, where a number of officers and GIs took away my personal property and gave me a thorough search; I had to strip completely. Every object was confiscated, including my belt and shoelaces, and stowed away in a large envelope. Unfortunately the items included a heavy golden cigarette case, which apart from the value of the gold had a special value for me as a present from my wife, who had died in 1942. I believed that I had seen an American slipping the case into his pocket, and I loudly protested. Field Marshal von Manstein and General Siegfried Westphal, who were coincidentally also present, advised me to stay calm, because there was no use in making any protest or even in asking for a receipt. Then two military policemen brought me to a one-man cell and locked its door behind me.

For the next two weeks, some not very tasty prison food was shoved into my cell twice a day. The guards refused to accept the appeals I had written on the back of the list of prison regulations I had found in the cell and tried to hand them. The American guards were under the strictest orders not to exchange a single word with us. After about ten days an American Protestant military chaplain made an appearance. He counseled me strenuously against getting myself transferred to the so-called "witness wing." In my current cell, at least I had peace and quiet.

The witness wing, to which I was nevertheless moved several days later, was a section of the Nuremberg penitentiary. Several hundred prisoners of war had been lodged in its cells, among them Field Marshals von Brauchitsch, von Rundstedt, *Ritter* von Leeb, List, von Kleist, and von Manstein; numerous colonel generals; and even more lower-ranking generals and General Staff officers. But the majority of the prisoners were SS and SD members, party officials, and civil servants.

The prison commandant, Colonel Andrus of the U.S. Army, was said to be of Lithuanian origin.[4] He represented the very worst type of American officer. He was vain beyond all measure, arrogant, unrestrained, and cruel. With the helmet on his head gleaming as though it had been lacquered, and a club in his hand, he frequently spent time in the witness wing. As soon as he walked in, all the prisoners, who were free to move about the wing during the day, had to stop right where they were and turn to face him. He had ordered several of the field marshals to be lodged in the same cells with especially burdensome SD men or Nazi functionaries. Many a time he led American, English, or French visitors along with their female companions through the witness wing, loudly introducing them to Rundstedt "the criminal" or Manstein "the gangster."

I shared a cell in the witness wing with another general. The former chief of staff of OB-West, General Westphal, had asked me to help sort the documents that the prosecution had turned over to the defense. While doing so, I came upon the report from Army Group Center to OKW—written by me—about the horrific massacre of the Jews of Borissov that the SS had carried out in the autumn of 1941. That same day I reported to the former commander-in-chief of the army, Field Marshal von Brauchitsch, who was housed in a cell with his former chief of staff, Colonel General Halder. Brauchitsch asked me whether, as the former Ic/AO of Army Group Center, I knew anything about the persecution of Jews for which the prosecution had accused the German General Staff of being responsible.

Brauchitsch appeared to be astonished when I answered his question with a blunt "yes." Then I showed him the document, whose authenticity I could vouch for, and which was marked to show that Brauchitsch had taken cognizance of it. However, he declared that he could not recollect the incident. When I replied that it would be impossible to forget about a report with such monstrous contents, he furiously reminded me that he had had his head full of other things at the time. Halder, who in contrast to Brauchitsch probably never had seen the report, explained that he also knew nothing about the matter.

This experience led me to call General Westphal's attention to the "lack of memory" on the part of the top generals, which in my opinion had to endanger the General Staff's defense. I had also noticed this utter forgetfulness in conversations with some other generals. Westphal got Manstein, who played a leading role in the witness wing, to arrange a meeting of the most important men. In this conference I talked about my personal experiences at Army Group Center, and put forward my reservations about the defense tactics up to that point. I said that it would have a fatal effect if the witnesses in the main war-crimes trial denied all knowledge of the SS crimes behind German lines, and the prosecution then produced documents showing the opposite.

My arguments made an impression: Manstein directed the General Staff's defense counsel, a German attorney named Laternser, to alter his tactics and make the thrust of the defense the fact that nearly all the senior German generals had acted contrary to the criminal orders of Hitler and Himmler.[5] This change of course later led to the General Staff being acquitted as an organization. After my release from captivity, Laternser assured me that the success of his defense would scarcely have been possible without my initiative.

One night I was shaken awake in my cell. A number of American military policemen ordered me to get dressed as quickly as possible and to follow them. I was conducted through long passageways and up many flights of stairs, into the actual Palace of Justice. There I was brought into a large room. The light from several lamps was focused on me, so that at first I was completely blinded. Questions were immediately fired at me from the otherwise darkened room. I can no longer give the exact words now, but I remember that after my personal details had been established, I was interrogated about most of the points in the prosecution's case against the General Staff—the issue of offensive war, the Commissar Order, the measures taken against the Russian population, and the extermination of the Jews. My eyes gradually became accustomed to the blinding effect of the lamps. I could see a shadowy row of tables in front of me; uniformed female secretaries were seated at either end. Behind the tables I saw, but only indistinctly, a number of people whose faces I could not make out.

It was apparent that I was standing in front of members of the prosecution teams of the four victorious powers, who plainly wished to turn me into one of their chief witnesses. I forced myself into total concentration, and answered them as briefly and as slowly as possible. Without saying one false word, I also tried to say not one word too many. And so I did not deny having knowledge of war crimes, insofar as they had been known to me before the end of the war. But I referred, on the basis of countless examples, to the struggle conducted by the General Staff against orders that made a mockery of international law.

I no longer know how long my questioning lasted. At the time it seemed to me as though it had been hours. In reality it may have gone on for only an hour or so. During a pause I suddenly heard the English words: "Quite negative." Shortly after that, my interrogation was broken off. I returned to my cell bathed in sweat.

Later it seemed significant to me that I was never once asked about the Katyn affair, although that was still one of the prosecution charges at the time; and the prosecution representatives surely knew that nobody could give better information about that than I could. The western prosecutors apparently realized that if I were asked, I could prove the Soviet guilt for the crime. Nor was I ever listened to about Katyn later on. Instead of me, witnesses were called who, even with the best will in the world, could hardly give any substantive information.

My conduct during the nocturnal interrogation was obviously the reason why I was left off the witness list for the so-called "main trial" at Nuremberg. In 1948, however, I was summoned to Nuremberg as a witness once more. The prosecution tried to make me into one of their witnesses again, this time in the "southeast trial." After I had refuted the to-some-extent-ridiculous accusations and charges, the defense team for the accused German generals called me back to the stand. The attorney, Laternser, also questioned me about my resistance activity, to document once again that there had been resistance to Hitler's criminal orders on the part of the Wehrmacht, including by some of the generals who were defendants in this trial.

When I had plainly become uninteresting as a witness in 1946, I was supposed to be sent back to the Historical Division at Oberursel. When the items that had been confiscated from me during my admission to the prison were handed back, I immediately observed that my gold cigarette case was not among them. I protested vociferously, and then refused to get on a truck in which twenty-five SS men were already sitting. Finally the Americans forced me at gunpoint to climb aboard. After I had spent a bad night in the SS prison camp at Langwasser, the camp commandant, who was just as friendly as he was alcoholic, recognized that, once again, a mistake had been made. He saw to my transportation back to Oberursel.

Beginning in the summer of 1946, I found myself in the camp at Allendorf, near Marburg. Here, in the wooden barracks of a former munitions factory, the Americans had pulled together several hundred German generals and General Staff officers to begin systematically writing a history of the conflict. Along with the majority of the army and army group commanders, corps and division commanders, and senior General Staff officers of the German forces on the Western Front, both of the former chiefs of the General Staff—Colonel Generals Halder and Guderian—had also been summoned to Allendorf. Experts on particular topics had been brought there as well, such as the fighter pilot General Galland (for the conduct of the air war), or my cousin Count Hyazinth von Strachwitz, the so-called "Panzer Count" (for the tactical employment of tanks).[6] It seemed to matter to the Americans that both men were holders of the highest German decoration: the Knight's Cross with Oak Leaves, Swords, and Diamonds. It appeared to give them special satisfaction to have these men in their own custody: the Americans collected highly decorated German soldiers the way other people collect rare stamps.

Communities grew up within the camp—groups of regimental comrades, or of men who had served together during the war. Outside of such voluntary communities, there was only relatively slight contact among the imprisoned German officers. Some captive Waffen-SS enlisted men were assigned to us to do menial labor, but by an unspoken agreement we scarcely used them at all.

One day some time after our arrival at Allendorf, I was out walking through the camp streets. I was surprised to realize that scarcely any of the fellow-prisoners I encountered returned my greetings. A general standing in front of a barracks building called out to me, "Did you know you're in the newspaper?" When I answered "no," he asked me to step inside the barracks. There on a table lay a newspaper; an article on its front page had been marked. It concerned the book *Offiziere gegen Hitler* ("Officers Against Hitler"), written by Fabian von Schlabrendorff and published in Switzerland. The reviewer had repeated word for word the description of the assassination attempts of March 1943, in which my name was also mentioned; it must have seemed like sensational news to him. Up until then I had had no idea of the book's existence and publication. With the words "Yes, that's all quite correct," I took my leave of the still-silent officers who had gathered in the room.

Afterwards I was cut dead by the overwhelming majority of camp inmates. People no longer greeted me or offered me their hands to shake. Only my regimental and cavalry branch comrades stuck by me. I sought out the senior German officer in the camp, Colonel General Hollidt, to ask him to have a declaration I had drawn up—in which I completely admitted the veracity of Schlabrendorff's statements—read out at the next daily formation.[7] Hollidt roundly rejected this request, and he said to me, "Obviously you're not too clear about your actual situation. A short time ago a delegation of generals was here with me, and they requested your immediate removal from the camp. They told me that if that didn't happen, they would arrange to have you killed by the SS men here."

I responded that both the Americans and the SS troops, some of whom had belonged to the SS cavalry branch, had known all about me for a long time. No danger threatened me from that quarter. In fact I had often talked about the recent past with the SS men, with whom I played table tennis and handball, and in doing so I had been open with them about my views and my resistance activity. They had shown their understanding for my decisions, and would certainly never have been willing to carry out the monstrous request of some apparently unteachable individuals. My friends' attempts to mediate in the situation were unsuccessful. Since challenges to a duel were pointless in our situation as prisoners of war, settling the matter on the field of honor was also ruled out. So nothing else remained for me to do but to continue to walk through the camp with my head held high, and to burn my last bridges to the obviously still-convinced National Socialists.

A few days later at the daily formation, Colonel General Guderian stepped to the front and declared that the claims in Schlabrendorff's book were false concerning his role in the decision-making for future strategy in July and August 1941. In this connection he directed vehement attacks at Schlabrendorff. I countered by saying that as an eye- and ear-witness to the events of that time, I could corroborate the book's revelations in full. I reminded the general about particular details of events that had then taken place at the headquarters of Army Group Center. Guderian persisted in his attitude of denial, however.

The atmosphere in the camp grew more and more strained. Certainly I had never indulged myself in the delusion that our conspiracy would be approved of by everybody. But I had absolutely counted on our choices being understood by most people, and especially by most soldiers, as soon as the war crimes and the catastrophe of the war's outcome were finally known in full measure. In doing so, I had given too little consideration to the bad consciences of those men who, while in responsible positions, had avoided making the decision to resist tyranny, and who later went on the offensive in their search for excuses and explanations for their own failures.

But there were exceptions. During this period Colonel General Halder (with whom I had some long conversations in Allendorf) invited me to look up a certain *Herr* Böhm-Tettelbach in Wuppertal, to clarify a 1938 event with his assistance.[8] Shortly after Halder had become Colonel General Beck's successor as chief of the General Staff, he agreed to a suggestion from Colonel Oster to send Böhm-Tettlebach, whom Halder had known for a long time, to warn the British government about Hitler's war plans. Böhm-Tettelbach was a World War I officer who as a businessman in the postwar era had made good connections with important British people. Halder gave him the mission of getting in touch with members of the British government, if possible, and making it clear to them that only a determined attitude on Great Britain's part could prevent a world war. The Americans actually gave me a furlough and their permission to make the trip. When I visited Wuppertal, Böhm-Tettelbach told me that he had gone to London on 2 September 1938. There he had met with the Undersecretary of the Foreign Office, Sir Robert Vansittart, to whom he had transmitted Halder's message with full emphasis. Vansittart had thanked him with the words, "God bless you."

Just like the other warnings from Germany, this message from the chief of the German General Staff also could not prevent British Prime Minister Sir Neville Chamberlain from coming to Berchtesgaden on 15 September 1938—only a few days later—and sealing his deal with Hitler. The well-known British military author Basil Liddell-Hart had attempted to make public this important event in a major British newspaper. However, British officialdom prohibited this at the last minute. Nobody wanted to take responsibility for the failure at the decisive moment.

Another important event took place within the camp. After we had been transferred from the wooden barracks of Allendorf to solid accommodations in the nearby city of Neustadt, the Americans released many German generals and General Staff officers. These included Hitler's former military adjutant, General Gerhard Engel, who had, at least during his years of service in the *Führer-Hauptquartier,* been known as one of Hitler's faithful followers. Before the Ardennes offensive, I had gotten to know him as a division commander in my army's zone, and had observed that at the front his attitude toward National Socialism had clearly gone through a big change.

A few days later the American camp commandant, who bore a German Jewish name, had me summoned to his presence. He asked me what I had to say about Engel's release. I answered that I was happy for his freedom with all my heart; however, I was amazed that such proven resistance fighters as Colonel General Baron von Falkenhausen or myself, for example, had not at least been let go at the same time.[9] In response, the camp commandant said to me, "I asked for you to come and see me so I could explain it to you. You see, throughout his military career General Engel has demonstrated that he will always—and only—carry out the orders he has been given. He will put up no resistance to us in civilian life; therefore, he is of no danger to us. But you have shown that, if necessary, you'll follow your own conscience; and then, perhaps, you will not obey our decrees. Therefore people like you or General von Falkenhausen are dangerous to us. That's why we need to keep you in custody for a while longer."

The logic of his argument, just as persuasive as it was diabolical, left me dumbfounded. I could only reply to him that under those circumstances, it was an honor for me to remain in captivity.

My time as a prisoner of war gradually neared its end. The camp regime had been getting softer for a long time, and we had received some privileges. We could have visitors in the camp on Sundays and holidays, and beginning in the summer of 1947 we could take short furloughs on our word of honor. I was therefore able to see my ten-year-old daughter again for the first time, and to make contact with friends. Since I owned nothing but a few worn-out pieces of clothing, and needed to provide for my daughter and myself after my release, the most important thing to do was to establish myself in a civilian profession. At the time, nobody thought it likely that professional soldiers would ever be able to receive pensions.

At the end of November 1947, I was released from our camp with the last of the captive generals. Despite many negative experiences, I wouldn't have wanted to miss the years I spent as a prisoner of war. I learned much about human nature during this time. I had proven the value of my fundamental military attitude, and I was determined to preserve it on my journey into the uncertain future, in a civilian world that was strange to me.

VIII

Epilogue

Only after I had regained my freedom was I able to learn how and why I had escaped an otherwise probably certain death on the gallows. At the top of the list, I owe my life to Fabian von Schlabrendorff. After his own incarceration in the Gestapo prison on Prinz-Albrecht-Strasse in Berlin, he had assumed each day that I would be sent there as well. He was asked about me repeatedly in his Gestapo interrogations, during which he was tortured to the fourth degree. Despite the inhuman torments he suffered, he was able to hide my connection to the resistance circle. When things got very bad he saved himself by losing consciousness. To my knowledge he was the only person who withstood the Gestapo's medieval tortures without giving away a single name.

Trescow and my regimental comrade Freytag-Loringhoven had committed suicide, because they knew what lay ahead of them and they feared not being able to endure the anticipated torture sessions.

My other lifesavers, unquestionably, were Field Marshals von Kluge and von Manstein, who not only knew of my political attitude, but also about my assassination attempt and my other activities in the resistance. One word from them would have been enough to deliver me to the Gestapo.

Finally, I owe my life to the officers and NCOs of the *Abwehr* section at Army Group Center, from whom in 1942–43 I had received large quantities of explosives and fuses for which I had signed receipts. When it came out after 20 July 1944, that Stauffenberg had carried out his assassination attempt with the same type of materials, a tip from the *Abwehr* men would have sufficed, at the very least, to put me under grave suspicion.

During an interrogation by the notorious chairman of the People's Court, Roland Freisler, Schlabrendorff observed a file on his desk with my name on it. Perhaps this was destroyed with Freisler's other files when he was killed in a bombing raid.[1]

Counting Schlabrendorff, who was also able to save his own life through his remarkable steadfastness, only fifteen or twenty of us *active* members of the resistance were able to escape the massacre after 20 July and the meat hooks of Plötzensee prison. It has always been clear to me how small was my personal role within the active resistance. As one of the few survivors, however, I have felt obliged in the postwar era to guard the memory of the dead of 20 July, to respond against attacks on the resistance with all available means, and in this manner to carry on the spiritual struggle for the renewal of the German people that men like Beck, Oster, Tresckow, Stauffenberg, and Julius Leber inscribed on their banners.[2] I have therefore never passed up an opportunity, whether orally or in writing, and through the mass media of press, film, radio, and television, to stand up for a truthful depiction of events in the Third Reich and for the ideals of the German resistance in opposition to National Socialism.

It was my special mission in doing so to destroy the myth of the "genius" commander and Führer and to draw attention to the experience that had been gained so that nothing similar can happen again. Along with much support, I have also often encountered sharp disagreement in this work, and had to fight back against unjust accusations made against the resistance fighters.

At the end of 1951 the *Johanniterorden* (the Order of St. John) assigned me the mission of creating an organization to train people in giving first aid, the St. John Accident Assistance.[3] The Order, founded almost a thousand years earlier during the First Crusade, had since 1945 concerned itself only with other charitable activities. First aid training in Germany was the monopoly of the Red Cross.

The British Order of St. John, which sprang from the same roots as the German *Johanniterorden,* had always shared this task with the Red Cross in Great Britain. When certain British members of the Order had come to Germany after the war as occupation officers, they started up a first-aid training course in Lower Saxony. Then they got in touch with the German order, and asked it to provide several hundred trained people to carry on the educational work. The then-Master of the *Johanniterorden,* Prince Oskar of Prussia, decided to seize this opportunity to reactivate the Order's work. The Order (which had been the object of much defamation by the National Socialists) had lost the majority of its fifty-six institutions—hospitals, old-age homes, and orphanages—in eastern Germany. Its houses in the west were for the most part either destroyed or in use by the occupying powers. The leaders of the Order, working at that time from refugee quarters, exerted themselves to rebuild its organization and its charitable activities, despite the loss of its formerly extensive properties.

The task to organize a completely new charitable cause and build it up as quickly as possible seemed almost unachievable, but was uncommonly exciting to me. There was no money. I had to search for co-workers among members of the Order who were living in West Germany, mostly as refugees.

I had to decide whether to begin by creating a large organizational structure, or by starting in on the work immediately and accepting in advance the improvisation that would thereby become unavoidably necessary. I chose the latter course. With the strong support of the Order's chancellor, Count Wolf-Werner von Arnim, and using as our base the small nucleus in Hanover that we took over from the British, we carried on the work of training everywhere we found an opportunity, using very primitive means at first. Like a rolling snowball gaining in size, it spread with astonishing swiftness.

At the same time, I was striving to gain governmental financial support—which, however, would be a long time coming. The same was true of support from the Protestant church. The state and church authorities, as well as the other charity organizations, at first only watched our experiment with interest and reserve, without feeling that it had any chance of success.

It was clear to me from the outset that we had to address young people and captivate them with a burning ideal. The centuries-old mission of the Order, "to subdue Christ's foes, to help in sickness and need," had to be brought to life and made relevant to the modern world. In view of the overall situation in Germany in the first postwar years, there were many opportunities. What only a few people had thought possible came to pass. After only several years we had extended our project throughout almost all the states of the Federal Republic of Germany and West Berlin. But what was most important was that the young people came to us, and in such quantities that my initially small number of colleagues could barely manage them. After some initial difficulties, we had a good cooperative relationship with the Red Cross.

Working with these young people has been one of the most beautiful experiences of my life. Their enthusiasm and their willingness to serve are almost unbelievable.

In 1963 I had to give up the management of the St. John Accident Assistance: for professional reasons involving my career in publishing, I had to move from Cologne to Munich, but the organization's headquarters needed to remain near Bonn, the site of the Order of St. John's central office and of the national government. For me, my more than eleven years of honorable service to the Order, working against religious unbelief and for charity to neighbors, were the fulfillment of my last soldierly task.

I can consequently say that I was a soldier from my eighteenth year to my sixty-fifth, in an era of great political, technological, and military transition. In 1923, I stood in a barracks square in Silesia and did lance drills: thrust forward; thrust to the ground; cover right and left; cover over the head! Fifty years later I live as a refugee in West Germany and concern myself about ways to prevent a nuclear war. The contrast may appear immense; but the fundamental attitude of a soldier has remained the same.

Appendix
The Truth About "Katyn"

Document # 6032179 of the archives of the Institut für Zeitgeschichte (Institute for Contemporary History), *Munich, in the Rudolf-Christoph von Gersdorff papers.*

The document is a photocopy of a four-page, single-spaced, typewritten report, unsigned. On internal evidence it was written in German during the Nuremberg War Crimes Trials in 1946 for submission to the American and British authorities, and helpfully translated into English for that purpose, probably by an American. The text is here reproduced in its entirety, including typographical errors and other flaws; notes within square brackets are by the current translator.

The Truth About "Katyn"

Source: Genmaj. Rudolf von GERSDORFF, onetime G-2 of Central Army Group on Russian Front.

The Russian prosecution in the Nuremberg War Crimes Trial has stated that the 10,000 Polish corpses dug up in the Spring of 1943 in a wood near Katyn constitute a crime on the part of the German Army. As evidence depositions of Russian peasants and members of a German engineer battalion, apparently Russian prisoners of war, are offered.

It is not my purpose to cast the slightest doubt on the wealth of evidence against the Nazi terror which has been offered during this trial, since I have at all times been convinced of the guilt of the National Socialist regime. On the other hand it would depreciate the value of the evidence offered so far if an obvious untruth like the Russian account of Katyn were to remain uncontested. The Nuremberg Trial is too important an event to be burdened with an open lie.

I was G-2 of the Central Army Group from 1942 to 1943. At the beginning of September 1941 the HQ of the Army Group was moved from Borisov to Krasny Bor near Smolensk. A neighboring village to Krasny Bor is

Gniezdovo. In the beginning of 1943 a grave was accidentally discovered in
a forest about 2 Km away from Gniezdovo. Nazi propaganda later preferred
to refer to "Katny" [*sic*] as a name easier to remember, although Katyn is a
larger place some 4 to 5 Km away. It was also feared that the fact that there
were prehistoric Hunnic graves near Gniezdovo might provide material for
counter-propaganda as casting doubt on the facts. The little forest lay along
the bank of the Dnieper river. In it was a wooden villa which, according to the
statements of the local population, had been a rest home for political Commissars from Smolensk, and which, since September 1941, had been HQ of
the Army Group's Signals Regiment (commanded by Col. Ahrens). The HQ
of the Army Group was in occupation of the Gniezdovo area uninterruptedly
until the late summer of 1943. It is absolutely impossible for the crime to have
occurred during this period, as it would have been committed under the very
noses of our Group. Even if it had been committed during the short period
between the capture of Smolensk and the movement of the Army Group to
the Smolensk area, the commission of this crime could not have been kept
a secret from the supreme military authorities, especially if it had been the
work of a German Army unit, as the Russians claim. The so-called SS police
raiders (EINSATZKOMMANDOS) were, to my knowledge, withdrawn on
orders from the Army Group, at the time of the taking of Smolensk. The SS
and Police commander in the region of our Army Group was the then *SS-
Brigadefuehrer* Nebe, a former officer and criminal law official who had been
taken into the SS when all police functions were transferred to the SS and
whose antipathy to their methods and ideology appears from the fact that he
participated in the 20 Jul 44 plot against Hitler, after raising many objections
to SS atrocities. He was later dismissed from office. Nebe would never have
countenanced such a crime as the shooting of thousands of Polish officers. In
any case we should have had to hear about it.

In the spring of 1943, if I remember correctly, in March, the Secretary of
the Military Police (FELDPOLIZEISEKRETAER) Voss, who was responsible for the protection and counter-intelligence security of the HQ, reported
to me the following circumstances: Some Polish volunteer auxiliaries had
just arrived at the Eastern Front and marched through Gniezdovo. They
enquired of the Russian population, as they always did, about the fate of Polish prisoners-of-war from the 1939 fighting. Some inhabitants of Gniezdovo
then told them that early in April 1940 several trainloads of Polish prisoners-
of-war had arrived at Gniezdovo station and were marched by GPU men from
there to the woods along the Dnieper [the GPU, the Soviet secret police]. This
whole area was strictly barred to outsiders and was known as an execution
ground of the GPU. Shots were heard all day long and nothing was ever seen
of the Poles afterwards. The Polish volunteers went into the wood and dug

under the younger trees (about 3 year growth). They dug up a mass grave, full of corpses in the uniforms of Polish officers. As they had to proceed with their march they said prayers, threw the earth back into the grave and set up a tall birchwood cross.

I had the inhabitants then interrogated under oath. Their statements fully confirmed the date already received. I personally saw many of these Russians and they repeatedly described the affair in such a way that there was no question but that the GPU had been responsible for the shooting. The case was reported on through military channels and the Armed Forces High Command (OKW) decided that the mass graves should be opened in order to identify the dead and inform their relatives. The Polish Red Cross in Warsaw was to take the main part. If it turned out that the statements of the inhabitants were true then the case was to be exploited for its propaganda value. The Army Group entrusted the work of exhumation to the coroner (GERICHTSARZT) in the Supply Services (OBERQUARTIERMEISTER) Division, whose duty it was to investigate alleged violations of the Geneva Convention. I forget his name at the moment but he was a professor at Breslau University who was a leading physician in the Breslau Court Clinic before the war. His name can be discovered by questioning the then Army Group doctor, *Generalstabsarzt* Dr. Jaeckel, now in the PW camp at Allendorf in Hessen. This professor had an assistant and a commission of four or five people from the Polish Red Cross, including one or two doctors. The site was cordoned off and guarded by Polish volunteers. Then a mass grave was opened for inspection in which there were 5000 to 6000 corpses in 12 layers, one on top of the other. All the corpses had from one to three bullet-holes in the back of the head. There were bodies of two generals, a few staff officers and enlisted men (clearly orderlies) and all the rest were captains and lieutenants of the Polish Army. The corpses were all decomposed but because of the dry sandy soil and the uniforms they had held together and could be carefully exhumed, examined, and identified. The legal-medical examination showed beyond doubt that the cause of death must have occurred about three years earlier. This was confirmed by the tree-growth (BAUMWUCHS) which was established indisputably by Russian and German forestry experts as three years old. On the corpses were found all their papers and a large amount of money (zlotys). No valuables were found except amulets under some of the shirts, a general's cigarette-case, and a few rings. Among the papers discovered were letters from relatives which the officers had received during captivity, and numerous diaries. The letters dated from 1939 and the beginning of 1940. If the Nuremberg International Tribunal wants to question the relatives of the victims of "Katyn" they can ask them when their postal contact with the prisoners was interrupted. The diaries recounted the daily life of the dead in detail. All these papers were either preserved by the dry sand or made legible by the application of chemicals. From these diaries it appeared that these officers were the bulk of those taken by the Russians when they marched into Poland in 1939. After several intermediate stops they were brought to a former monastery in Kosiolsk where they seemed to have received correct treatment. They thought of nothing of course but their future release and return to Poland and thought their release was imminent when at the end of March 1940 they suddenly entrained and moved westward toward Smolensk. Some of the diaries continue until a few minutes before the shooting and state they stopped for a long time at a little station behind Smolensk (Gniezdovo), were discharged from the train, and taken in black closed vehicles to a nearby wood. They still did not suspect what was in store for them until their valuables were taken from them, when diary entries show they knew they were going to be shot. All these diaries end in the first April days of 1940.

Two more graves were discovered, also by looking for places where the tree-growth was three years old. In one grave many bodies were found with the hands tied behind their backs, and others with clothing pulled around their heads. These men were clearly people who had been guilty of resistance.

The propagandistic exploitation of the case was entrusted to the propaganda detachment under Major Kost, who came under the command of the commander of the communications zone behind the Center [*sic*] Army Group, General von Schenkendroff. Deputations and commissions came to Smolensk to view the sight, without any special explanation or accusation being given. Among the visitors were the Archbishop of Cracow; a commission of neutral news correspondents; a commission of neutral legal-medicine experts; a Red Cross commission; deputations of Polish PWs, officers, and EM [*sic,* for "enlisted men"]; and deputations of British and American PWs.

Special importance and evidential value attached to the visits of the legal physicians who voluntarily made dissections of the bodies. For all its horror the event was an opportunity never likely to be repeated, for scientific study. They all concurred that the deaths had occurred three years previously. The commission comprised members from Switzerland, Holland, Hungary, Norway, France, Finland, &c (*sic*) [*sic,* in original]. The only name I remember is that of the Swiss representative, who was called either Prof. Niville or Miville and came from Berne. The White Book published at the time by the German Foreign Office will give all the names. The Nuremberg Tribunal could at any time summon these foreign doctors to testify. Of the PW deputations I remember only that one of the Englishmen in Smolensk was member [*sic*] of the British football eleven.

All the visitors to "Katyn" were clearly impressed and completely convinced by the abundance of testimony that the shooting had occurred at the beginning of 1940 and was the work of the GPU. Even those who came forti-fied against being fooled by smart propaganda found it impossible to explain away the evidence as based on any possible trickery.

Everyone who saw the bodies and the moving documents of these men can have no doubt that the shooting of these Polish officers occurred long before the German invasion of Russia.

A total of 4000 to 5000 bodies were identified. The warmer weather made it imperative, for reasons of hygiene, to suspend the work, which was to be resumed in the fall. By that time circumstances on the front had changed, Smolensk was too near the enemy and the Army Group HQ was moved to the region of Orscha. The two generals were buried in two single graves. The rest of the bodies were properly interred in new graves. Meanwhile another mass grave was discovered about as large as the first, so that the estimation of 10,000 to 12,000 bodies is certainly not too high. The entire handling of the case was conducted along military and scientific lines. No National Socialist Party or SS authority had at any times any influence over the proceedings.

I repeat in closing that I am aware that the crime of Gniezdovo-Katyn has been surpassed many times by the murders of Jews and other Nazi crimes, but I am equally sure that the Polish officers were never shot by German hands, still less by members of the German army.

Notes

by Anthony Pearsall

Translator's Note

1. *In Cultural Amnesia: Necessary Memories from History and the Arts* (New York: W. W. Norton, 2007), 329.

Introduction

1. The Ashridge House of Citizenship, a finishing school for young ladies, existed from 1949 to 1958. Its head, a Miss Dorothy Neville-Rolfe, was remembered as "formidable" by another student of the school, and a few newspaper quotes from the era suggest a highly critical disposition.

Foreword

1. This unofficial motto had been used within the Prussian state since the reign of King Friedrich Wilhelm I in the eighteenth century, when the French language was frequently used at the royal court.

Preface

1. Constantin von Alvensleben (1809–1892): Prussian general who became a national hero for his leadership in the field during the war against France.

I. Background and Education

1. As of this writing, curious people may visit the website of the twenty-first century Gersdorffs: http://www.von-gersdorff.de.

2. Site of a medieval battle in what was later known as East Prussia, in which the invading Teutonic Knights—a German order of "warrior monks" sworn to religious vows of poverty, chastity, and obedience—were badly defeated by a Polish-Lithuanian army. The Polish victory at Tannenberg put an end to the Order's eastward expansion. The crushing German victory over Russian forces in the same neighborhood in 1914 was promptly dubbed the "battle of Tannenberg" and celebrated in nationalistic propaganda as a long-overdue vengeance on the Slavs.

3. Gersdorff's beloved home province of Silesia (in German, Schlesien) belonged to the kingdom of Prussia from 1742 onward, after its conquest by King Frederick the Great in a war against Austria. From 1918 to 1945 it was part of the federal state of Prussia. Silesia stretched along both banks of the upper Oder River and was centered on the city of Breslau, now Wroclaw. As the author notes, it was one of the most productive regions in all of Germany. During Gersdorff's childhood the population was some seventy-five percent German and twenty-five percent Polish; most cities, such as Breslau, were almost entirely German. After World War II Silesia was transferred to Poland, where it now forms the southwestern part of that nation, adjacent to the Czech Republic. Almost all of the German population died or fled at the end of the war, or were expelled in the aftermath. Gersdorff's hometown of Lüben, mostly destroyed in 1945, is now the small Polish city of Lubin.

4. Karl May (1842–1912): a prolific and fantastically popular German author of cowboys-and-Indians novels set in the American West—a place he never saw, ironically. His most famous characters, the Apache warrior Winnetou and his white blood-brother, Old Shatterhand, are still famous in Germany to this day. Both Adolf Hitler and Albert Einstein were proud, lifelong fans of Karl May's tales of adventure, as were millions of other German and Austrian boys of the era.

5. Hussars were a type of lightly armed cavalry troopers, celebrated for their speed and daring; *pandours* were Croatian soldiers in Austrian service during the eighteenth century, famed for their ferocity.

6. Warthegau: Reichsgau Warthe, a Nazi German administrative district along the Warthe (Warta) River from 1939 to 1945. As the author suggests, the Germans were a minority in Posen during his youth, perhaps less than twenty percent of the population.

7. Also known as Frederick I, Barbarossa ruled the Holy Roman Empire from 1155 to 1190. His exploits in peace and war made him a folk hero to the German people. The Piast dukes were a Polish noble house.

8. Hubertus von Gersdorff was born in 1909 and for most of his life worked as a corporate lawyer. While living in the west after World War II, he returned to concert stages and enjoyed some popular success. He died in 1964.

9. Needless to say, Gersdorff was correct about the predilection of horses for music. Experience has shown that they most prefer instrumental music that is upbeat and harmonious: what could be more so than a cavalry march?

10. A favorite destination for German vacationers since the eighteenth century, the picturesque Riesengebirge mountain range is now located within Polish and Czech national parks. Schneekoppe, the tallest summit, is some 5,200 feet high.

11. A once-popular German historical drama, first performed in 1888, *The Quitzows* told the romantic tale of Dietrich von Quitzow and his younger brother, archetypal German robber-barons of the late fourteenth century, and their doomed anarchistic struggle against an encroaching central authority. Ironically, the encroaching central authority was that of the Hohenzollern dukes, the rulers of Brandenburg and later of Prussia, from whom Kaiser Wilhelm II was directly descended.

12. A German port on the Baltic Sea for centuries, Danzig is now the Polish city of Gdansk.

13. Now the Polish city of Legnica.

14. Hartmannsweilerkopf, an elevation in the Vosges Mountains, was the scene of intense and prolonged close-quarters fighting between German and French troops, resulting in enormous casualties.

15. The Kapp Putsch was a short-lived attempt to overthrow the newly-elected democratic and socialist central government in Berlin in March 1920, under the putative leadership of a Prussian civil servant and German nationalist named Wolfgang Kapp (1858–1922). The real driving force, however, was Gersdorff's famous uncle, General Baron Walther von Lüttwitz (1859–1942), a leader of right-wing paramilitary *Freikorps* troops after World War I and a fervent monarchist.

II. Soldier in the Reichswehr

1. Johannes Friedrich ("Hans") von Seeckt (1866–1936), a brilliant General Staff officer before and during the First World War, was chief of the Reichswehr from 1920 to 1926 and created the very small, very professional, very "non-political" German army that Gersdorff, Henning von Tresckow, and their military contemporaries knew as junior officers. Seeckt was both a monarchist and traditionalist (it was his scheme to "match" companies and squadrons of the tiny Reichswehr with the "heritage" of disbanded regiments from the much larger old army) and a bit of a quirky progressive as well (for example, instead of having soldiers flogged for minor offenses, he preferred requiring them to lie beneath a cot and sing old Lutheran hymns).

2. By "East Prussian," Gersdorff is probably referring to the Trakehner breed developed in East Prussia, known for making superb cavalry and competition mounts. The Trakehners that are still bred in western Germany are descended from a small quantity of mares and stallions brought west by fleeing refugees in 1945.

3. Born in Paris in 1683, Antoine Pesne became the court painter of Prussia from 1710 until his death in 1757. Many of his rococo

paintings of the Hohenzollerns may still be seen in the art museums of Berlin or in the Charlottenburg Palace.

4. Paul von Kleist (1881–1954), a professional soldier and cavalry officer in the Kaiser's army, went on to command Panzer groups in Poland, France, Yugoslavia, Greece, and the U.S.S.R. during World War II, earning a marshal's baton and the Knight's Cross with Oak Leaves and Swords. He died in Soviet captivity.

5. Welfs: A nickname for the residents of the region centered on the city of Hanover in north-central Germany, originally the name of its medieval ruling family. In 1870 the reigning king of Hanover refused to join the confederation of German states led by Prussia in the Franco-Prussian War; after the defeat of France, the little kingdom was punished by abolition, and its territory was wholly absorbed (1871) into the state of Prussia. It may seem odd that the Cavalry School's leaders were still nervous about local hard feelings more than half a century later, but in Germany memories are long.

6. Born in 1894, the son of a career officer, the almost six-foot-five-inch Karl-Wilhelm von Schlieben was a World War I cadet and lieutenant. After serving in the postwar Reichswehr 9th Infantry Regiment (where he would certainly have met Henning von Tresckow in 1920), he transferred to the 7th Cavalry and served in it from 1924 to 1929. He and Gersdorff would also become distantly related by marriage when both men married women from the Kracker von Schwarzenfeldt family. Schlieben served with distinction in World War II, ending up as a much-decorated major general. As the last German military commandant of Cherbourg in Normandy, he surrendered to the Americans in June 1944. He died in West Germany in 1964.

7. Ebert, Noske: Pre-WWI trade-union leaders—Ebert had originally been a saddle maker and Noske a butcher—and Socialist politicians, who headed Germany's first democratically elected government after World War I. They entered into an uneasy alliance with the conservative, aristocratic military

men (personified by General von Seeckt) who still ran the army and most of the *Freikorps* paramilitary units as well, in order to stave off attempts by communist groups to launch a violent revolution and civil war on the Soviet model. Ebert perished in 1925, worn out by many crises; by dint of keeping an especially low profile, Noske managed to survive the entire Nazi era and World War II before dying of natural causes in 1946.

8. The 3rd Squadron of the 7th Cavalry Regiment was the heritage unit of the 4th Dragoon Regiment "von Bredow" (1st Silesian) of the Royal Prussian Army.

9. Thaer, Roeder, Felbert, Kressenstein, Gossler, Seherr-Thoss, Prittwitz: Albrecht von Thaer (1868–1957) was a cavalry officer who was only able to enter military service after satisfying his father's desire that he graduate from law school. He was famous for having ridden a horse from Berlin to Vienna in a record seventy-eight hours and forty-five minutes in 1892, when he was a second lieutenant in the Magdeburg Cuirassiers (7th Cuirassier Regiment "von Seydlitz"). Having quarreled with General von Seeckt, he left active service in 1921 and served for many years as the administrator of the Silesian estates of the former King of Saxony. At the end of World War II he was able to flee the Soviet onslaught and find refuge in Hanover.

Colonel von Roeder remains an obscure figure, but the Roeder clan could boast Prussian military heroes dating at least as far back as the Napoleonic Wars and the campaigns of Frederick the Great.

Friedrich von Felbert, regimental commander from 1925 to 1928, also remains otherwise obscure, but was related to Paul von Felbert, a prominent Wehrmacht general in the Second World War.

Franz Kress von Kressenstein (1881–1957), a Bavarian nobleman, finished his military career in 1938 as commanding general of the XII Army Corps.

Konrad von Gossler (1881–1939), was a career cavalry officer whose army career lasted until the year of his death; he ended with the rank of General of Cavalry.

Theobald von Seherr-Thoss (1882–1966), was a cavalryman from one of the grand old Silesian families. By 1933 he had been a soldier for thirty-one years, and had commanded a battalion in the 5th Guards Infantry Regiment late in World War I. He was simultaneously promoted to general rank and removed from active service in 1935.

Heinrich von Prittwitz und Gaffron (1889–1941) was killed near Tobruk in North Africa while commanding general of the 15th Panzer Division.

10. Borussia: The Latin translation of "Prussia" and the name of a student fraternity with chapters at several German universities. German fraternities of the day tended to be staunchly aristocratic preserves within universities, with elaborate uniforms, ceremonies, flags, and ritualized saber duels intended to result in conspicuous facial scarring; so it would only have been a short step from such a fraternity to a high-class German regimental mess, and the same type of young noblemen would have been found happily existing in either place. The Borussia fraternity chapter at Bonn University exists to this day: during Gersdorff's young manhood it was enormously prestigious, including among its alumni the former Kaiser Wilhelm II and four of his six princely sons. Two other Borussia-Bonn alumni were Count Peter Yorck von Wartenberg (1904–1944), an anti-Hitler conspirator who was hanged at Plötzensee prison after the failed 20 July coup, and his older brother Paul, one of Gersdorff's closest friends.

11. Count Adrian von Pückler, born in 1905 in Silesia. The "Fox Major" (*Fuchsmajor*) of a German student fraternity was the senior in charge of training new members, like the pledge master in an American fraternity. Prince Hermann von Pückler's famous estate in eastern Germany, its grounds and gardens fully restored, is now a public park and a destination for horticulturalists. As Gersdorff later remarks, this model cavalryman died as a Panzer leader in 1945. In Greco-Roman mythology, Castor and Pollux were semidivine twin brothers and legendary horsemen.

12. Wilhelm Heye (1869–1947), chief of the Reichswehr from the time of Seeckt's dismissal in 1926 until his own replacement by the incomparably more dynamic Kurt von Hammerstein-Equord in 1930. Heye is remembered, if at all, as a brave and competent soldier and a genial personality, but a virtual nonentity as the army's senior commander during the late 1920s. Plainly he liked to have a good time; photographs from the era depict a cheerful-looking man with not only the whiskers, but almost the physique, of a mature male walrus, a sharp contrast to the ascetic, whippet-thin soldier-scholar Seeckt.

13. Presumably Erich von Tschischwitz (1870–1958), an infantry general who was a senior Reichswehr commander as of 1927.

14. Senior Corporal Müller was probably otherwise unknown to history; but this NCO's joyful outburst—*ich kann nicht anders!*—were of course a parodic use of the famous words ("Here I stand, I can do no other") of the sixteenth-century German religious reformer Martin Luther when he publicly voiced his heretical opinions against the authorities of the Church, words that have been celebrated ever since as a statement of the supremacy of one's personal conscience. In mostly Lutheran Prussia, the brash corporal would have learned the phrase at school or in a confirmation class, like every other man at the party, presumably.

15. Mikhail Nikolayevich Tukhachevsky (1893–1937), a nobleman and Imperial Guards officer who nonetheless became one of the most ruthless (and successful) Bolshevik military commanders during the Russian Civil War. From 1925 to 1928 he was chief of staff of the Red Army. In 1937 Tukhachevsky, by then a marshal, was arrested, secretly court-martialed, and executed on blatantly false charges of anti-government conspiracy and spying for Nazi Germany. He was one of the most prominent of the countless thousands of victims of Stalin's political and military purges.

16. Presumably Lieutenant General Count Kuno von Moltke (1847–1923), who served

in his later life as adjutant to Kaiser Wilhelm II and military commandant of Berlin. His homosexual secret life led to him going down in history as a principal figure in the "Eulenberg Affair" of 1906/1907, a massive scandal revolving around allegations of homosexuality among some of the Kaiser's closest confidantes, replete with spectacular trials and feverish newspaper coverage. This ended his military career.

17. Eberhard von Schmettow (1861–1935), commander of the Life Guard Cuirassiers from 1906 to 1911. This scion of an ancient Silesian noble house was a distinguished commander in World War I, earning the *Pour le Mérite* with Oak Leaves.

18. Ludin and Scheringer were Reichswehr lieutenants who were dismissed from the service and tried for high treason in 1930 for allegedly spreading Nazi doctrines within the officer corps, and seeking the agreement of other officers not to fight against the Nazis in case that party seized power. Their Leipzig trial drew national attention and featured Adolf Hitler on the witness stand. The lieutenants were convicted but given very light sentences: Ludin actually converted into a fanatical communist while in prison, while Scheringer went on to become a high-ranking SS officer, and to be executed for war crimes in Czechoslovakia after World War II.

19. Born in Munich in 1887, Edmund Heines—handsome, blond, bold, and aggressive, a model Nazi street-fighter of the party's early, struggling years—served with distinction as a World War I infantryman, earned his way up from private to lieutenant, and then fought Bolsheviks and Poles as a member of various *Freikorps* units in the Baltic Sea region and Upper Silesia. He joined the National Socialist German Workers Party in 1925, and rose quickly through the ranks of the party's SA (or "brownshirts"). Heines was sentenced to death in 1929 for several murders arising out of his grassroots political work, but somehow obtained a pardon and freedom. By the early 1930s he was a Nazi member of the Reichstag and the head of the

Silesian SA, which the charismatic killer built up from ten thousand to over forty thousand members. After the Nazis took power, the brutal Heines attained his career apogee—as the chief of police in Breslau! However, he was purged during the "Night of the Long Knives" on 30 June 1934, and summarily executed. Heines, like the SA's top commander Ernst Röhm (1887–1934), was a surprisingly open homosexual; allegedly he was arrested while in bed with a much younger SA man, who was also dragged away and shot.

20. Gersdorff's older brother Ernst-Carl was born in 1902. He worked as an attorney at law in Breslau before World War II, and for a time was the legal representative of the former Prussian royal family. After the war he settled in Wiesbaden in western Germany, and died in 1977.

21. Treviranus, Schlange-Schöningen, Westarp: Gottfried Treviranus (1891–1971), a wartime officer in the Imperial German Navy, helped lead the German Nationalist Party during the interwar years, and rose to serve in the cabinet of Chancellor Heinrich Brüning from 1930 to 1932. He was a staunch conservative opponent of Hitler and the Nazis. He spent most of the Nazi era in England and Canada before returning to Germany in 1948.

Hans Schlange-Schöningen (1886–1960) was a Pomeranian agronomist and decorated World War I veteran who was active in Prussian politics and government as a Christian conservative during the Weimar Republic. From 1933 to 1945 he lived in "inner exile" on his estate. As a refugee in western Germany from 1945 onwards, he helped to found the CDU, the Christian Democrat party, which remains Germany's major conservative political party. From 1953 to 1955 he served as West Germany's ambassador in London.

Count Kuno von Westarp, born in the eastern province of Posen in 1866, was a jurist and politician, an important figure in German conservative circles during the 1920s and early 1930s. After the Nazi takeover in 1933 he withdrew from public life, and died in the ruins of Berlin shortly after the end of the war.

III. Soldier in Opposition

1. "Fräulein" Schmidt: Hans Walter Schmidt (1912–1934), an attractive, blond, Breslau-born youth. He joined the Nazi Party only in late 1932; but after being noticed by the flamboyant Edmund Heines, the handsome young man made a blindingly fast ascent in 1933–1934 from rank-and-file Hitler Youth to *SA-Obersturmbannführer* (SA-Lieutenant Colonel) and personal adjutant to Heines, who was by then Breslau's police chief as well as the leader of the Silesian SA. As Gersdorff indicates, their homosexual relationship was notorious, as were their drinking bouts and bullying. It was also rumored that Schmidt procured teenaged schoolboys for his boss and patron. Like Heines, Schmidt was arrested and summarily executed in the wake of the Nazi purge and score-settling called the "Night of the Long Knives" or the "Blood Purge."

2. Born in 1895 to an old family of Silesian landowners, Udo von Woyrsch was a nephew of Field Marshal Remus von Woyrsch, a World War I army commander. After fighting in World War I and as a *Freikorps* officer on the Polish border, he joined the Nazi Party and was among the first four thousand members of the SS, in which the ruthless, virulently anti-Semitic nobleman quickly reached the highest ranks. The anti-SA purge in Silesia, as conducted by Woyrsch "the Bloodhound" and described by Gersdorff, was more murderous than in any other German province. A personal friend to Heinrich Himmler and Himmler's sinister deputy Reinhard Heydrich, Udo von Woyrsch commanded the *SS-Einsatzgruppen* in occupied Poland in the fall of 1939, dealing out terror and murder to the local Jewish population until halted by the intervention of senior army officers. After serving a total of seven years as a British POW and a convict for crimes against humanity, the aristocratic war criminal was released in 1952 and died in West Germany in 1983.

3. Wechmar, Grolmann: Baron Carl von Wechmar, born in 1897, was a *Brigadeführer* (Brigadier General) in the Silesian SA. He was arrested and shot during the Blood Purge. Not long afterward, Hermann Goering telephoned the baron's family to apologize for the shooting, as a case of mistaken identity and a regrettable error. His nephew Rüdiger von Wechmar (1923–2007) would go on to become West Germany's ambassador to the United Nations during the 1970s.

Herr von Grolmann: Obscure, and not to be confused with Wilhelm von Grolman, an SA leader in Silesia at around the same time. Another *Herr* von Grolmann, perhaps the grandfather of Gersdorff's acquaintance, was a Prussian ambassador to Persia in the mid-nineteenth century.

4. Schleicher, Bredow. Kurt von Schleicher (1882–1934), a politically connected Reichswehr general who was Chancellor of Germany for a few months prior to Hitler's appointment to the office on 30 January 1933. Essentially a moderate conservative, Schleicher's hostility to Hitler, and apparent efforts to have the Hohenzollern family restored to some kind of constitutional monarchy, made him a target for assassination. Nazi gunmen killed him inside his house in Potsdam; his wife, who hurried into the room after hearing the noise, was also shot to death.

Ferdinand von Bredow (1884–1934), a friend and associate of Kurt von Schleicher, and his political ally. Like Schleicher, he would have preferred a military government, or even some form of "unity government" involving the Socialist Party, to Nazi rule. SS men arrested the general at his home in Berlin and allegedly he was dead on arrival at the detention center in nearby Potsdam, with two bullets in his head.

5. Blomberg, Fritsch: Field Marshal Werner von Blomberg (1878–1946), recipient of a rare *Pour le Mérite* medal for extraordinary valor in World War I, served as the Third Reich's Minister of Defense (later War) from 1933 to 1938. Pro-Nazi mostly in the sense that he believed that only a dictatorship could return Germany to glory, and that Hitler and

the Nazis would create the best dictatorship, the Pomeranian *Junker* general became a supine follower of the Austrian ex-corporal, going even further for Nazism than he was asked to do. On his own initiative, Blomberg caused all Jewish soldiers in the Reichswehr to receive immediate dishonorable discharges in 1934; in the same year, after the death of Hindenberg, he ordered all the soldiers in the Reichswehr to re-swear their allegiance not to *Volk und Vaterland,* but to Adolf Hitler personally, a most consequential event which Gersdorff experienced and described. The widower marshal married a pretty twenty-six-year-old typist in 1938, with Hitler as his best man. Goering and Himmler, both desiring to eliminate a rival for Hitler's favor, waited until after the wedding to "discover" that the young woman had previously posed for pornographic photos—taken by a Jewish lover! After refusing to have his marriage annulled, Blomberg was compelled to resign from the armed forces. He spent the war in obscurity, and died of natural causes while in custody at Nuremberg.

Colonel General Baron Werner von Fritsch (1880–1939) replaced Blomberg as Minister of War in January 1938; within a few days the lifelong bachelor was accused of homosexual activities by Himmler and Goering, who knew of his anti-Nazi leanings and wanted to get rid of him. The charges were completely false, but the scandal forced Fritsch to resign from the service in early February. In the wake of the "Blomberg-Fritsch Affair" Hitler replaced a number of other top commanders with more loyal men, and effectively made himself master of the Wehrmacht. Recalled to active duty at the outbreak of the war, the inconsolable Baron Fritsch appears to have sought and found his own death on the battlefield in Poland, becoming only the second of the hundreds of German general officers who would be killed in action during the next five and a half years.

6. Gerd von Rundstedt (1875–1953), scion of a Prussian noble family, entered military service in 1892 and served continuously until 1938, when he retired. Recalled to active

service in 1939, he commanded army groups in the east and west and finished the war as a field marshal. With forty-six years of active duty to his credit even before the war began, Rundstedt was, as Gersdorff notes elsewhere, the senior serving general in the entire Wehrmacht. Although an able and energetic commander and a master strategist, as well as a frank speaker in the old Prussian tradition, he also embodied the *nur-Soldat* ("just-a-soldier") attitude of all the Wehrmacht generals who managed to go along with just about whatever the Nazi leadership chose to do. The 20 July assassination attempt simply infuriated him, and afterwards he was a member (along with Guderian and Keitel) of the Court of Honor that expelled hundreds of officers from the service and turned them over to the tender mercies of the Gestapo. He was not tried at Nuremberg, however, due to his advanced age and his ill health. [For Guderian, see note 40 below; for Keitel, see Chapter IV, note 32.]

7. *"Ich hatt' einen Kameraden"*: The German soldiers' song that begins "Once I had a comrade/A better one you won't find," and is traditionally played at military funerals.

8. *Machtergreifung* ("seizure of power") is a term used in Germany for the Nazi Party's legal accession to national rule in 1933, which was followed by its uncompromising assertion of authoritarian power over almost all aspects of government and society.

9. *Kriegsakademie*: Literally the "Academy of War," this military staff college was founded in 1810 as the *Preussische Kriegsakademie* to provide advanced training in military science to promising officers after humiliating defeats at Napoleon's hands led to major reforms in the Prussian army. In Gersdorff's era the *Kriegsakademie* occupied a majestic building on the Dorotheenstrasse in Berlin and was open to up-and-coming young army captains from all parts of the Reich. Admission was competitive and the intensive two-year course concentrating on tactics and logistics was, if anything, more so. Graduation was the ticket to join the elite German General Staff, beyond question the best in the

world at the time; the *Kriegsakademie*'s basic "product" was supposed to be an officer at least theoretically capable of serving as chief of staff and operations officer at the division level. The German *Kriegsakademie* provided a principal model for the U.S. Army's Command and General Staff College and similar institutions in various other nations. The institution was abolished by the victorious Allies after the war.

10. Renata Kracker von Schwarzenfeldt, Matzdorf: The village of Matzdorf was overrun by the Red Army in 1945 and is now Maciejowiec in Poland. The palace and park were owned by the bride's grandmother, Emma von Kramsta, whose father, Karl Wilhelm Scheibler, had earned vast wealth as the founder of big textile mills in Lodz. Contemporary visitors to the old estate's grounds may still see the small, elegant, Greek-style mausoleum, weathered but still white, in which Gersdorff's sad and lonely wife was laid to rest in 1942. It is now almost overgrown by tall trees, down in a deep ravine that seems designed to be inhabited by fairies. The rare traveler to those parts may perhaps also hear the tale the Polish villagers tell nowadays to explain the curious place, a tale about a "princess" or "countess" who died when her horse stumbled and fell on the steep and slippery path that winds through the ravine, and for whom the tomb was built there. It seems to be a garbled folk-memory of the interment of the beautiful Baroness Renata von Gersdorff, in the dim olden days when grand German aristocrats were still the lords of the manor. So swiftly does history pass into myth.

11. Olympic equestrian events prior to 1952 were contested by cavalry officers from the armies of the various nations, all wearing their service uniforms. Gersdorff's friend Baron Konrad von Wangenheim (1906–1953) was one of the three officers selected to comprise the German three-day-eventing (dressage, cross-country, show jumping) team at the Berlin Olympics in 1936. He secured his team's gold medal and became a national hero with one of the most courageous individual performances in modern Olympic

history: after being thrown from his horse in the cross-country phase, he faultlessly completed that phase and the show-jumping phase the next day, overcoming dozens of difficult obstacles while in agony from a broken collarbone and with one arm in a sling, even managing to remount and continue when at one point his horse fell and landed on top of him. Taken prisoner on the Eastern Front in 1944, Wangenheim died in Soviet captivity, probably murdered in his cell by some of his jailers.

12. Several men of the noble family of von Wolff-Metternich zur Gracht served in the Wehrmacht during this era; the text leaves unclear with which one Gersdorff had dealings.

13. Brieg is now Brzeg in western Poland.

14. Christoph von Kospoth: A member of the old Silesian nobility; Red Army invaders left the family manor at Briese (now Brzekinka) in ruins at the end of World War II. In 1935 Reiter Regiment 7 became Panzer Regiment 2.

15. Sagan: Now the Polish town of Zagan.

16. Moritz von Faber du Faur (1886–1971), a Southwesterner who began his military career in 1904 as a cavalry cadet in the army of the kingdom of Württemburg, a small component of the German Empire near the French border. As a Wehrmacht general during World War II he commanded divisions or filled staff assignments on several fronts, competently but colorlessly. He was obviously a kinsman to Christian Wilhelm von Faber du Faur (1780–1857), a German professional soldier who is famed for his field sketches of the dire scenes he witnessed during Napoleon's winter retreat from Moscow in 1812.

17. Born in Silesia in 1896, Baron Heinrich von Lüttwitz fought in both world wars and rose to the rank of General of Panzer Troops, earning the Knight's Cross with Oak Leaves and Swords and the German Cross in Gold. Lüttwitz was the German commander who sent a courteous surrender request to the encircled American troops at Bastogne during the Battle of the Bulge in 1944, eliciting General Anthony McAuliffe's famous

one-word response, "Nuts!" Gersdorff would repeatedly cross paths with this military hero (and cousin), who survived the war and died in 1969.

18. An early member of the Nazi Party and a fanatical Hitler loyalist, Robert Ley (1890–1945), although notorious for his corruption, drunkenness, incompetence, and erratic behavior, served as head of the "German Labor Front," the toothless puppet organization that "represented" German industrial workers from 1933 to 1945 after the Nazi regime had eliminated independent trade unions. Ley's bitter jab at the "blue-blooded swine" may have owed something to his personal history as a younger son of a hopelessly impoverished farmer in the Rhineland, and to his youthful flirtation with genuine socialism. Ley hanged himself in his cell at Nuremberg before going on trial for war crimes.

19. Erich Marcks: A regular feature of elite formal dining in Europe during the nineteenth and early twentieth centuries was the parade of guests from the drawing room into the dining room, roughly in order of social rank and prominence, with each gentleman escorting a lady to the table; it was standard practice to partner a married woman with some man other than her own husband. Baroness von Gersdorff's dinner companion on this occasion was the future General of Artillery Erich Marcks (1891–1944), recipient of the Knight's Cross with Oak Leaves, a bespectacled, intellectual officer who would go on to lose one leg and two sons on the Eastern Front, and his life in Normandy a week after D-Day.

20. A General Staff ride was a trip through open country undertaken by a body of General Staff officers in order to practice terrain analysis and military planning in the field without troops. In Gersdorff's day such a ride was no longer necessarily on horseback, although it could be.

21. The future general Rudolf Schmundt (1896–1944), an Alsatian who served as an infantry lieutenant in World War I. After the war he was a regimental comrade and close friend of Henning von Tresckow, with whom

he served in the Reichswehr's 9th Infantry Regiment at Potsdam. Although highly intelligent and personally decent, Schmundt chose to become an enchanted follower of Adolf Hitler, serving as the dictator's military adjutant and also later as head of the Wehrmacht's personnel department. Ironically, he absorbed much of the blast from Stauffenberg's bomb on 20 July. Badly wounded and burned, Schmundt lingered on for more than two months before dying of his injuries. [For Stauffenberg, see Chapter V, note 37.]

22. General of Cavalry Günther von Pogrell (1879–1944), a longtime veteran of the Life Guard Hussars, one of the most glorious cavalry regiments of the old Royal Prussian Army. From 1936 to 1938, Pogrell was a regional inspector in the Wehrmacht's ever-dwindling horse cavalry branch when Gersdorff encountered him. During the war he retired from the army and died of natural causes.

23. The future Major General von Schmettow (1890–1970), a Silesian nobleman who spent the bulk of World War II in command of the German occupation forces on the Channel Islands. The good nature hinted at by Gersdorff is further evidenced by the facts that Count Schmettow tended to stroll around his British domain with no guards and with chocolate in his pockets for the children, that he received care packages from islanders after the war, and that he was welcomed back for a visit in 1963.

24. Hirschberg is now the Polish city of Jelenia Góra.

25. Georg Stumme (1886–1942), a cavalryman who commanded Panzer units in the early years of World War II; he died in North Africa at the beginning of the Second Battle of El Alamein, while serving as the acting commander of Panzerarmee Afrika in Rommel's absence. Much of his district as a cavalry inspector would not be German for much longer: Königsberg, the capital of East Prussia, is now the Russian city of Kaliningrad; the harbor town of Stettin is now Szcezin in Poland, and Breslau is now Wroclaw. [For Rommel, see Chapter V, note 42.]

26. *Kristallnacht,* the "Night of Broken Glass," took its name from the shards of broken plate-glass windows that littered the sidewalks in front of thousands of Jewish-owned shops all over Germany on the night of 9/10 November 1938. Almost three hundred synagogues also went up in flames. This nationwide anti-Semitic outrage was orchestrated by Propaganda Minister Josef Goebbels and carried out by mobs of SA and SS men and other Nazi supporters. History recounts that ninety-one Jews were murdered during this terrible night, while another thirty thousand Jewish men were arrested and sent to concentration camps in Germany, where some two thousand may have perished from mistreatment before the rest were released. *Kristallnacht* is rightly seen as a key inflection point in the Nazi persecution of Jews, which would become increasingly violent before climaxing in the "Final Solution."

27. Probably Richard-Heinrich von Reuss (1896–1942), who as a lieutenant colonel served as Ia of the X Army Corps in 1939–40, earned promotion to general rank, and died on the Eastern Front while commanding the 62nd Infantry Division near Stalingrad.

28. Hitler's architect and personal favorite, Albert Speer (1905–1981) joined the Nazi Party in 1931; his courtly manners and brilliant intellectual qualities immediately helped him to stand out among other party members. In 1938 he designed the gorgeous new Reich Chancellery to Hitler's specifications and then oversaw its construction in a blindingly fast nine months. (The Soviet occupiers later used stones from its ruins to construct their victory monument in the heart of Berlin.) Toward the end of World War II, Gersdorff would have personal dealings with Speer in the latter's new capacity as Reich Minister of Armaments and Munitions. Convicted as a war criminal at Nuremberg, Speer spent twenty years in prison and then published his best-selling and irreplaceable memoirs of life in Hitler's inner circle.

31. General Alfred Jodl: Born in 1890, this Bavarian officer, a modest and decent man, became Chief of the Operations Staff of the Wehrmacht in August 1939, and served in that function until May 1945, when he personally signed Germany's unconditional surrender agreement. He was convicted and hanged as a "war criminal" at Nuremberg in 1946, a fate that has remained controversial.

30. Heinrich-Hermann von Hülsen (1895–1982), was commander of the reconnaissance section of the 44th Infantry Division during the Polish campaign. He was in command of the 21st Panzer Division when the German forces in North Africa surrendered in May 1943, and spent the rest of the war in British captivity.

31. General von Morawski: Obscure; but there seems to be little to add to the portrait Gersdorff paints of a decent professional soldier of the old school, bedeviled by the tides of twentieth-century European history.

32. The Potocki (pronounced "Pototski") family was one of the oldest and most prominent aristocratic clans in Poland, and one of the wealthiest, too, as Gersdorff's account makes clear. Count Alfred Antoni Potocki was born in 1886. His principal inherited estate at Lanczut, or Lancut, comprised a magnificent palace and a park of some five thousand acres, as well as thousands of acres of the surrounding farmland and forests; his industrial holdings elsewhere in Poland also helped to make him one of the richest men in Europe between the wars, with a fabulous private art collection and a deluxe international lifestyle that included an Oxford education, African safaris, and innumerable friends among the rich and famous. It is no surprise to read that the passionate hunter Hermann Goering had been one of his guests. Seeing the writing on the wall in mid-1944, the astute Count Potocki was able to use his excellent German connections to ship *eleven freight-car loads* of his most precious possessions all the way west across the Reich to the Grand Duchy of Liechtenstein (the Potockis being related by marriage to the ducal family), preserving them from the pillaging Red Army hordes that duly arrived at Lancut on 26 July 1944. The artworks were joined in the west by their owner, who died in Geneva

in 1958. The palace and grounds of Lancut where Gersdorff dealt with the count in 1939, monumental symbols of Polish income inequality in former times, are now a popular tourist attraction.

33. Lothar Rendulic (1887–1971), an Austrian professional soldier who fought for the Habsburg monarchy in World War I, and joined the Austrian Nazi Party as early as 1932. Obviously a believer in the concept of Greater Germany, and something of a scholar (he earned a law degree while in his thirties), Rendulic was welcomed into the Wehrmacht and the General Staff with open arms after Austria became part of the Reich in 1938. The future Colonel General Rendulic had a busy and ruthless wartime career that brought him army and army group commands as well as the Knight's Cross with Oak Leaves and Swords. *Soldier in Falling Empires* was the appropriate title of his postwar military memoirs.

34. The future Field Marshal Wilhelm List (1880–1971) commanded armies or army groups in the invasions of Poland, Greece, Yugoslavia, and in the fighting for control of the oil-rich Caucasus region in the Soviet Union. Relieved of command in late 1942 after failing to capture Rostov and Baku (mostly the result of fuel shortages, and lack of air support which had been diverted to the battle of Stalingrad), he sat out the rest of the war in retirement.

35. Brauchitsch, Halder: Field Marshal Walther von Brauchitsch (1881–1948) was commander-in-chief of the army from 1938 to 1941, when he was relieved after the failure to capture Moscow. His supine behavior toward Adolf Hitler was not much respected within the service.

Colonel General Franz Halder (1884–1972), a soft-spoken Bavarian artilleryman in a high command dominated by bristling Prussian *Infanteristen,* served as Chief of the General Staff at OKH from 1938 to 1942, when he was relieved by Hitler after disagreeing with the Führer once too often about the conduct of the war. After the 20 July coup he was arrested on suspicion of involvement,

and spent time in concentration camps before being liberated by U.S. troops. Gersdorff got to know him well when they were both American prisoners of war.

36. Presumably Bernd von Pezold (1906–1973), a well-connected General Staff officer who, like Gersdorff, was a member of the cavalry fraternity. By coincidence Pezold had served before the war in the same elite cavalry regiment as the future Colonel Claus von Stauffenberg, a family friend. [For Stauffenberg, see Chapter V, note 37.]

37. Günther Blumentritt (1892–1967), a future General of Infantry and recipient of the Knight's Cross with Oak Leaves. The affable and friendly Bavarian was, in addition, a formidable strategist who played major roles in planning the invasions of Poland and France. During much of the war he was a right-hand man to such famed commanders as Gerd von Rundstedt and Erich von Manstein, but he also distinguished himself as a fighting general. After the war he published several interesting books and helped to create the new army of the Federal Republic of Germany, the Bundeswehr.

38. The brilliant, handsome, suave and charismatic son of a Prussian cavalry general, the future Brigadier General Henning von Tresckow (pronounced "TREZH-ko"; 1901–1944) joined the super-elite 1st Guards Infantry Regiment in 1917 and became perhaps the youngest lieutenant in the entire German army by the spring of 1918, barely seventeen years old. He led a machine-gun platoon on the Western Front and earned the Iron Cross. In 1921 he left the Reichswehr to be a university student, work as a banker, and travel through much of the world, before returning to the service in 1926. First in his class at the *Kriegsakademie* in 1934–36, the supremely well-connected and personally impressive Tresckow was obviously destined to reach the highest ranks in the army. However, his attitude toward the Nazi Party had changed from initial lukewarm support to an ever-growing hostility, even as he played key roles as a General Staff officer in the invasions of Poland, France, and the U.S.S.R.

Following the failure of the 20 July bombing and coup d'état—he was fighting in Poland at the time—Tresckow killed himself with a hand grenade.

39. Heinz Guderian (1888–1954), one of the architects of "Blitzkrieg" warfare, a superb tank commander and a difficult and temperamental subordinate. He was of most importance during the invasions of France and the Soviet Union, when he personally commanded Panzer groups in fast-moving campaigns.

40. Count Merveldt: It is unclear to which of several contemporary Count von Merveldts Gersdorff here refers.

41. From 1831 until the 1950s, spahi light cavalry regiments in the French army consisted primarily of Arab and Berber troopers and NCOs from France's North African colonies (modern Algeria, Tunisia, and Morocco) commanded by white French officers. The spahi regiments were renowned for their colorful Arab-influenced uniforms, white Arabian horses, and bold fighting in half a dozen wars. (The word itself is derived from the Ottoman Turkish *sipahi,* a mounted soldier.) The last remaining so-called spahi regiment in the contemporary French army is an armored unit and its soldiers are recruited from within France, but they still wear Arab-style white capes when marching in parades.

42. The immensely likeable Philippe Pétain (1856–1951) became a French national hero during the First World War for his dogged tenacity and strategy during the monstrous, months-long Battle of Verdun in 1916. After retiring from the army in 1931, he entered politics and served as a minister in one or two of the revolving-door French governments of the period. At the time of France's defeat in 1940, the conservative military man blamed what he perceived as the moral laxity of the interwar years for the disaster and gloomily agreed to become the head of state and pursue "the way of collaboration" with Germany; he was then eighty-four years old. After the war Pétain was convicted of treason in a kind of show trial and sentenced to death, but the sentence was commuted to life imprisonment,

which he served for the most part in a condition of senile dementia. He may have owed his life to the fact that General (later, President) Charles de Gaulle had been his protégé as a young officer.

43. The future Major Baron Phillip von Boeselager (1917–2008) stemmed from Rhineland nobility. Like his brother Georg, he was a veteran of hard combat on the Eastern Front as well as the fighting in France described by Gersdorff. He became the aide-de-camp to Field Marshal von Kluge at Army Group Center HQ in Russia. Henning von Tresckow recruited him for the conspiracy. He managed to escape detection in the wake of the failed coup on 20 July 1944, and served until the end of the war. To the end of his long lifetime he was a constant advocate for the memories of his fellow conspirators and their cause; he welcomed this writer into his home in Germany in 2006, still as vigorous as a much younger man, and spent an afternoon talking about the men of the German resistance. [For Georg von Boeselager, see Chapter V, note 2; for Kluge, see Chapter IV, note 38.]

44. The dynamic French politician and statesman Pierre Laval (1883–1945), who after France's defeat in 1940 reached the reasonable conclusion that Nazi Germany was destined to beat Great Britain next and win what was still a purely European war, and that France needed to make the best of her situation in the new international order. He became the "minister of state" in Marshal Pétain's collaborationist government. In a controversial trial soon after the war, Laval was convicted of treason and executed, a scapegoat for millions of French citizens who had collaborated along with him. The journey that Gersdorff describes was to the village of Montoire-sur-le-Loir in north-central France, where Adolf Hitler met with Pétain and Laval in late October 1940 to discuss the future relationship between victorious Germany and defeated France.

45. Major von der Groeben: By coincidence the same officer would also replace Henning von Tresckow in 1943 when the

latter rotated out of his assignment as Ia of Army Group Center in Russia.

46. Friedrich-Wilhelm von Mellenthin was born in Breslau in 1904 to a Pomeranian cavalry officer and a Silesian noblewoman, and enlisted in the 7th Cavalry one year after Gersdorff. His thrilling experiences as a General Staff officer on various fronts produced two significant postwar books, *Panzer Battles* and *German Generals of World War II*. After emigrating to South Africa in the 1950s and serving as a manager of Lufthansa's African operations, Mellenthin died in 1997.

IV. Soldier
in the Resistance

1. Lieutenant Colonel Berndt von Kleist, born in 1896, was a World War I comrade of Tresckow's from the 1st Guards Infantry Regiment and one of his trusted counselors in World War II, which Kleist actually managed to survive unscathed. "Rock of bronze" is a translation of *rocher de bronze,* which although worded in French is a Prussian phrase that describes a man who is steady and solid as a rock. An "O-4" was a staff member with undefined duties, available for any special task.

2. An attorney in civilian life, Fabian von Schlabrendorff (1907–1980) entered active service as a reservist in 1939 and saw action in France in 1940. During the summer of 1939 he had met Henning von Tresckow and the two had mutually confided their anti-Hitler, anti-Nazi beliefs. Tresckow saw to Schlabrendorff's assignment to Army Group Center as his personal aide. Arrested soon after 20 July, Schlabrendorff survived intense torture and various mortal dangers without cracking, until he was liberated by American troops in the spring of 1945. Having returned to legal practice after the war, he ended his career as a judge on the Federal Constitutional Court, the German supreme court.

3. Tall, lean, pale, and austere, with an intense gaze and frosty expression, Field Marshal Fedor von Bock (1880–1945) was Tresckow's wife's uncle. He was famous for exhorting troops that their greatest honor was to die for their country. As Gersdorff describes, Tresckow was free to call this intimidating man *Onkel Fedi* without rebuke, even in staff meetings. Just as Tresckow had hand picked most of his own subordinates on the staff, he had been hand picked himself by von Bock to help mastermind the invasion of Russia, and there could be few stronger testimonies to Tresckow's reputation on the General Staff. A *Pour le Mérite* recipient in World War I, von Bock spearheaded the Wehrmacht's peaceful entry into Vienna and the invasion of Czechoslovakia, before successively commanding Army Group North in the invasion of Poland, Army Group B in the invasion of France, and Army Group Center in the invasion of the Soviet Union. Relieved "for health reasons" after the defeat at Moscow, he commanded another army group in southern Russia in 1942 before being removed from that command as well, and permanently retired. He was mortally wounded a few days before the war ended in May 1945, when a low-flying Allied plane strafed the civilian car in which he was a passenger.

4. Wittenau, Knigge, Conrad: The text allows us to know no more than that Gersdorff's assistant, Major Schach von Wittenau, was of the noble Prussian family of Schach von Wittenau.

Major Baron Andreas von Knigge: Born in 1900, this pillar of the Lower Saxon nobility survived the war and died in 1977 on his estate in the village of Leveste.

First Lieutenant Conrad: It has not proved possible to learn more about this individual. A certain *Dr. Iur.* (that is, doctor of law) Conrad served as the chief judge in the German wartime inquiry into the Katyn Massacre, but if it was the same man it seems likely that Gersdorff would have mentioned the fact.

5. Canaris, Herrlitz, Oster: Wilhelm Canaris (1887–1945), head of *Abwehr* (German military intelligence) since 1935, had been steadily plotting against Hitler and the Nazi regime since before the war. He was executed in 1945.

Colonel Herrlitz is historically obscure.

Brigadier General Hans Oster (1887–1945), a career soldier, served in the *Abwehr* from 1933 to 1943. He was involved in plotting a coup attempt in 1938 and worked closely with Henning von Tresckow during the war. General Oster was executed alongside Admiral Canaris in 1945. Fabian von Schlabrendorff wrote of Oster that he was "a man such as God meant men to be, lucid and serene in mind, imperturbable in danger."

6. Hess, Karl Haushofer, Albrecht Haushofer: On 10 May 1941, the Deputy Führer Rudolf Hess (1894–1987) flew an airplane across the English Channel and parachuted over Scotland, where he was immediately taken prisoner. He was apparently hoping to negotiate a peace agreement with Great Britain, which Churchill (who had no interest) generously described after the war as "a completely devoted and frantic deed of lunatic benevolence." Like many other observers, Churchill came to believe that Hess was mentally ill. He spent the remainder of his long life behind bars, finally as the last inmate of Spandau Prison in Berlin.

Karl Haushofer (1869–1946) and Albrecht Haushofer (1903–1945), a fascinating father and son academic team, were longtime associates of Rudolf Hess, who had studied world geography and geopolitics (then a rather new term) under their tutelage. The Haushofers were both professors of geography and proponents of grandiose, and sometimes rather zany, geopolitical explanations of world history and programs for German expansion; they were also steadily involved with behind-the-scenes German diplomacy, both before and during the Nazi era. A German patriot but no Nazi, the younger Haushofer was secretly in contact with anti-regime conspirators during the war, was imprisoned after 20 July, and was shot by an SS executioner in late April 1945, when the Red Army was already smashing through the suburbs of Berlin. His heartbroken father and (half-Jewish) mother committed suicide not quite a year later. A poem by Albrecht Haushofer, in which he could have been speaking for thousands of his countrymen, was in one of his pockets when he died. It read as follows:
I am guilty
But not in the way you think.
I should have earlier recognized my duty;
I should have more sharply called evil evil;
I reined in my judgment too long. . .
I did warn,
But not enough, and not clearly;
And today I know what I was guilty of.

7. Günther Gericke: It is possible to confirm that this officer's name was *von* Gericke and that he attended the conference in question as the Ib of Army Group Center, but he has not left much more of a historical record.

8. Hans-Georg Schmidt von Altenstadt (or von Schmidt auf Altenstadt; 1904–1944), at the time chief of the War Administration (*Kriegsverwaltung*) section in the Quartermaster General's department at OKH. He died of wounds received while serving as chief of staff of XIV Panzer Corps in northern Italy. With his death the German line of his noble family became extinct; their castle at Gattendorf in Bavaria is now a hotel.

9. The anti-Hitler co-conspirator Arthur Nebe (1894–1945) is the most morally ambiguous of them all; objectively, he would have qualified as a major war criminal (his successor in command of *Einsatzgruppe B* was in fact hanged at Nuremberg), but Nebe's true thoughts and motivations must always remain obscure as we have no first-hand testimony from the man; he was of necessity very secretive. A First World War veteran and a very successful police detective in Berlin during the turbulent 1920s, Nebe joined the Nazi Party and the SS in the early 1930s. Following the *Machtergreifung* he played an increasingly dangerous double game, running the national criminal police (*Kriminalpolizei,* or *Kripo,* responsible for the investigation of ordinary non-political crimes) while secretly consorting with anti-Nazi individuals, working and socializing with Himmler and Heydrich while allegedly despising them. As early as 1938 Nebe was willing to participate in a coup d'état to overthrow Hitler. Under

his command *Einsatzgruppe B* was not as "active" as groups run by more committed SS officers to the north and south, and even its lower total of reported victims may have been deliberately inflated to satisfy Himmler's insistent demands for "results"; but tens of thousands of Jews, Gypsies, and others nonetheless died under its guns. On the other hand, Nebe proved to be a most faithful and helpful member of Tresckow's grand conspiracy, and the tough and cynical arch-conspirator Fabian von Schlabrendorff, a tried-and-true Nazi-hater if ever there was one, respected him and spoke up for his memory forever after. Nebe put in only five months in the war zone and then was able to return to Berlin. He played an active personal role in the attempted coup d'état on 20 July 1944, and was put to death the following year.

10. Blitz Girls: *Blitzmädchen* was the popular term for young women who had volunteered to serve as uniformed female auxiliaries to the German armed forces. They filled numerous clerical, signals, and logistical jobs in rear areas and in the Reich, as more and more men were dispatched to the front lines. But by late in the war about 450,000 *Blitzmädchen* were also serving in antiaircraft batteries across Germany, along with many adolescent boys too young for the army. Presumably the Blitz Girls assigned to the Luftwaffe's conference guests were especially attractive hostesses in well-fitting uniforms.

11. The American journalist William Shirer ate a meal with some German officers at this deluxe dining establishment less than a year before Gersdorff uncomfortably dined there, and wrote, "We stuffed [ourselves] on hors d'oeuvres, steak, mountains of vegetables, and fresh strawberries and cream, washing it all down with two bottles of quite good Chateau Margaux." In wartime Europe, with food rationing already commonplace, this qualified as a remarkable meal even by 1940. The German officers with Shirer delighted in having such a feast before returning to the Reich.

12. Kesselring, Sperrle, Richthofen: Albert Kesselring (1885–1960), a Bavarian officer

who became involved with the Luftwaffe at its birth during the 1930s (although he only learned to fly at age forty-eight), and who was one of Germany's most popular military commanders during World War II. Fighting bravely and tenaciously on several different fronts, Kesselring earned the respect of both friends and foes, as well as the Knight's Cross with Oak Leaves, Swords, and Diamonds, Nazi Germany's highest military decoration. The conversation that Gersdorff recorded accurately reflects the field marshal's modest personal style.

Field Marshal Hugo Sperrle (1885–1953) and General of Aviators (later Field Marshal) Baron Wolfram von Richthofen (1895–1945), who both commanded major Luftwaffe formations at the time.

13. The Luftwaffe fighter pilot Werner Mölders, born in 1913, amassed a total of 115 aerial victories in the Spanish Civil War (as a member of the German "Condor Legion") and during the early years of World War II, and was the first man ever to earn the Knight's Cross with Oak Leaves, Swords, and Diamonds. Removed from combat duty and appointed inspector general of fighter aircraft in mid-1941, the national hero died in November of that year, ironically as a mere passenger aboard a transport plane that crashed near Breslau.

14. Night and Fog Decree: Adolf Hitler was an extraordinary devotee of the operas of Richard Wagner; in *Das Rheingold,* the malevolent dwarf Alberich dons a cloak of invisibility, while saying, *Nacht und Nebel, niemand gleich* ("Night and fog, resembling no one"). The Night and Fog Decree specified that if not put to death, civilians in occupied lands who committed acts of resistance were to "vanish" by being removed to concentration camps in Germany, while their families received no further information about their whereabouts or fate. Although Gersdorff mentions it at this point in his book, Hitler did not issue the decree until 7 December 1941.

15. Leeb: Field Marshal Wilhelm *Ritter* von Leeb (1876–1956), commander of Army

Group North in the invasion of the Soviet Union until January 1942, after his troops had encircled Leningrad but failed to capture it.

16. Hardenberg, Lehndorff-Steinort: Reserve Major Count Carl-Hans von Hardenberg (1891–1958), who served in the 1st Guards Infantry Regiment with Henning von Tresckow during 1917–1918, was a wealthy landowner near Berlin. At his estate during the war he hosted many meetings of anti-Hitler conspirators. Arrested after the coup had failed, Count Hardenberg was sent to Sachsenhausen concentration camp, where he came close to death. He and his family escaped in the postwar era to West Germany, where he resettled.

Reserve Lieutenant Count Heinrich von Lehndorff-Steinort (1909–1944), an East Prussian landowner, served as one of Field Marshal von Bock's aides-de-camp and later as a staff officer in East Prussia. He was one of the members of the conspiracy whom Henning von Tresckow attracted to the cause. Arrested after 20 July 1944, Count Lehndorff was hanged at Plötzensee prison less than two months later.

17. General Eugen Müller: Major General (at the time) Müller (1891–1951) commanded the *Kriegsakademie* from 1 April to 1 September 1939. Working thereafter for General Halder as the army's Quartermaster General, he was responsible among other things for legal affairs in occupied territories. Tresckow's pointed question—"What exactly can General Müller say to Gersdorff?"—reflects his clear understanding of Müller's comparatively minor importance within the supreme command; he was a skillful administrator, but by no means a policymaker. He spent the entire war at his desk in Berlin, until the war had finally come to him.

18. General Hans von Greiffenberg: The then-Brigadier General von Greiffenberg (1893–1951), a Pomeranian nobleman, was chief of staff of Army Group B (later Army Group Center) from May 1941 to April 1942. Promoted to major general in the latter year, the colorless professional spent most of the rest of the war as a Wehrmacht functionary in Budapest. He looms small in all histories of Army Group Center, put in the shade by the Bock-Kluge-Tresckow trio and the fascinating assortment of top generals who passed through the group during the war. [For Kluge, see note 38, below.]

19. SS-Colonel Schulz: Karl Schulz, like Arthur Nebe a career police detective and a pre-war member of the *Reichskriminalpolizeiamt* (RKPA), Nazi Germany's criminal investigation department. In the post-war years he headed the criminal investigation department for the police force of the city-state of Bremen in the Federal Republic of Germany.

20. Richard Sorge, a half-German, half-Russian communist born in 1895 in Baku (then in the Russian Empire) but raised in Germany, spied brilliantly for the Soviet Union for some twenty years under the cover of a freelance journalist and completely committed Nazi. From 1933 to 1941 he operated from Tokyo, where he could gather information from indiscreet German embassy personnel and Japanese sources. Unmasked by Japanese counterintelligence in late 1941, Sorge was hanged in 1944. Years later he received a posthumous "Hero of the Soviet Union" award and appeared on Soviet and East German postage stamps. Historians of espionage consider him one of the master spies of modern times.

21. Hermann Hoth (1885–1971), commander at the time of Panzergruppe 3, which captured Minsk and Vitebsk along the road to Moscow. He was soon transferred to command an army in Ukraine.

22. Borissov, now in Belarus, is a small industrial city about forty miles northeast of Minsk, on the Moscow-Minsk railroad line and highway; Napoleon's retreating troops fought a desperate battle here in 1812 while trying to get across the icy Beresina River. In 1941 it probably had about 50,000 inhabitants.

23. Moscow Forward Command: Officially a sub-unit of *Einsatzgruppe B,* in the zone of Army Group Center. Given the date, Gersdorff's visitor was probably SS-Brigadier

General Professor Dr. Franz Six (1909–1975), a Ph.D. in sociology, a professor at the university of Berlin, and a so-called "150 percent" Nazi ever since his undergraduate days. Reinhard Heydrich appointed Dr. Six to the ideological department of the Reich Main Security Office, where his paranoid fantasies about Jews, Freemasons, Jehovah's Witnesses, the Boy Scout movement, and other insidious enemies were able to run riot. Had the conquest of Great Britain actually occurred, Dr. Six was set to establish *Einsatzgruppen* in several major cities, with the aim of hunting down and eliminating all Jews and anti-Nazi elements from Winston Churchill on down. Although his big plans for the city of Moscow came to naught, little *Vorkommando Moskau* under Six's leadership managed to liquidate at least 144 civilians, most but not all of them Jews. After a few post-war years in prison, Dr. Six lived quietly in West Germany—working in Porsche's marketing department!

24. SS-General von dem Bach-Zelewski (1899–1972), a stocky, friendly-looking fellow, essentially spent the war remorselessly directing the slaughter of civilians on the Eastern Front, trying and failing to control anti-German partisan activity. In the summer of 1944 he would be responsible for putting down the Warsaw Uprising, during which another 200,000 civilians, more or less, died. In exchange for serving as a prosecution witness against his former superiors, he never faced charges at Nuremberg or extradition to Poland or the U.S.S.R.; although he died in prison, it was for the murder of some German political opponents during the 1930s. It was said that some of his animosity against Jews stemmed from the fact that three of his sisters had married Jewish men.

25. The future Major General Adolf Heusinger (1897–1982), a smooth and brilliant General Staff man with a rare talent for survival. After fighting heroically in World War I and being wounded several times, he soldiered on in the Reichswehr and the Wehrmacht. By the summer of 1941 he was chief of the operations section at OKH, working under Halder while maintaining contacts with

Tresckow's circle. While serving as acting chief of the General Staff on 20 July 1944, Heusinger was actually standing next to Hitler when Stauffenberg's bomb exploded, but survived yet again. While recuperating from his injuries he was arrested and interrogated about his many contacts with known plotters, but even the Gestapo could not pin anything on him, and he survived this crisis as well. In the 1950s he helped to create the Bundeswehr and served as one of its senior generals; and finished his career as chairman of NATO's "Military Committee" in Washington, D.C., from 1961 to 1964. Heusinger was probably the only man entitled to wear both a Hitler-era Iron Cross and a 20 July "Wound Badge," and the U.S. military's Order of the Legion of Merit—although he surely never wore them all at the same time. [For Stauffenberg, see Chapter V, note 37.]

26. Krassny Bor: This suburb of Smolensk is not to be confused with the identically named suburb of Leningrad at which a major battle took place in 1943.

27. Manfred von Heydebrand: Historically obscure, although given Gersdorff's preoccupation with equestrian arts, he may well have been an offspring of the Prussian aristocrat Leopold von Heydebrand und der Lasa, who in 1898 published an astonishingly detailed and comprehensive instruction book for training horses in dressage. The sturdy Ju-52 aircraft on which he traveled was the workhorse cargo plane of the Wehrmacht, transporting men, supplies, and mail: the troops affectionately called it *Tante* ("Aunt") *Ju*.

28. *Einsatzkommando 8,* one of *Einsatzgruppe B*'s sub-units, "cleared" the Borissov ghetto on 20/21 October 1941, killing an estimated 6,500 Jews in the manner described. The *Aktion* at Borissov was only one of many large and small massacres going on behind the German lines at the same time, in the process that some have dubbed the "Holocaust by bullets."

29. Lithuanian SS: The Soviet Union invaded and occupied the little trio of "Baltic States"—Latvia, Lithuania, and Estonia—in

1939. The "bourgeois" local populations became the victims of the commissars and secret police from Russia, who were not tender with them. After the Germans invaded and occupied the Baltic States from the other direction in 1941, thousands of Lithuanians volunteered for service in the Wehrmacht or the SS; they served mostly in rear areas in the U.S.S.R. Some of them—motivated partly by traditional anti-Semitism, partly by a hasty indoctrination in stamping out the "Jewish Bolshevism" that had harmed their own country, and no doubt in some cases by innate cruelty—joined the ranks of the *Einsatzgruppen*'s traveling executioners and worked enthusiastically.

30. *Kube, Koch:* Wilhelm Kube (1887–1943), Gersdorff's unloved fellow-Silesian, joined the Nazis in the early 1920s and was one of the party's earliest Reichstag members in 1924. A former theology student and a professing Christian in a party that at least encouraged irreligion, he was a leader during the 1930s of the "German Christian" movement, which sought to "Nazify" the Protestant church in Germany. Kube was assassinated in Minsk by a maid who placed a bomb inside a hot-water bottle in his bed. (She escaped and was awarded the Hero of the Soviet Union medal).

Erich Koch (1896–1986), a Nazi since 1922 (the member number on his party card was 90), served as *Reichskommissar Ukraine* until mid-1943. After the war he was extradited to Poland and imprisoned for life.

31. The later General of Artillery Johann Sinnhuber (1887–1974), commander of the 28th Infantry Division (later the 28th Jäger Division) from May 1940 to July 1943. For part of 1944 he was commander of the LXXXII Army Corps in France with Gersdorff as his chief of staff.

32. *Keitel, Bormann:* Field Marshal Wilhelm Keitel (1882–1946) served as chief of OKW from early 1939 until the end of the war, largely due to the subservient attitude toward Hitler that led to his army nickname of "Lakeitel," a play on his name and on the German word *Lakei,* a lackey. Although he

was a desk-bound officer for the duration of the conflict, orders that he willingly signed—including, but not limited to, the Commissar Order and the Night and Fog Decree—led to his trial and execution at Nuremberg, where he advanced the classic "I-was-only-following-orders" defense to no avail.

Martin Bormann (1900–1945), who joined the Nazi Party in 1925, by mid-wartime had become Hitler's private secretary and head of the Party Chancellery. As such he sat at the bureaucratic center of the Nazi Party and was the dictator's right-hand man on a day-to-day basis, controlling access to Hitler and managing his paperwork, appointments, and personal finances. To a large extent he also seems to have called the shots for the extermination of Jews in occupied lands. Despite persistent rumors to the contrary over the years, the sinister Bormann appears to have died in the ruins of Berlin while attempting to escape from Soviet forces after Hitler's suicide.

33. *Politruk* is an abbreviation for "political leader," the title that replaced "political commissar" in 1942. As Gersdorff suggests, in practice the main day-to-day business of a small-unit commissar or *politruk* was to spread inspiring propaganda and help to sustain the morale of the troops, sometimes with games, contests, or treats, although in theory the principal task was to monitor the unit commander for any signs of anti-Soviet opinions.

34. Smolensk Cathedral, or the Cathedral Church of the Assumption, has occupied a dominating hilltop since 1101. The gorgeous present-day structure was built between 1663 and 1772, and is now a place of worship once again. Not to be confused with Smolensk Cathedral in Moscow.

35. Count Yorck, born in 1902, was the eldest of several brothers, two of whom were killed in action during the war. A third, Peter Yorck von Wartenburg, was executed in the wake of 20 July as an anti-Hitler conspirator; he was a member of the so-called *Kreisauer Kreis* (Kreisau Circle), intellectuals who met in secret to discuss the possible contours of a post-war, post-Nazi Germany. Gersdorff's

remarkable friend Paul Yorck was a university-trained agronomist who could read Latin and Greek about as well as German. In 1932 he gave in to temptation and joined the Nazi Party, but quit it again a year later, *after* Hitler had come to power (the opposite of the normal pattern). During the 1930s he was a stalwart of the *Bekennende Kirche* (Confessing Church), a Protestant movement intended to peacefully resist Nazi policies by opposing them with Christian teachings. Count Yorck sheltered Jews on his estate, including one family that hid there for the entire war. Badly wounded on the Eastern Front in 1943, Count Yorck was invalided out of the army and lived at Klein-Öls until his arrest after 20 July. He was an inmate at Sachsenhausen concentration camp outside Berlin until Red Army troops liberated the camp in May 1945. Paul Yorck von Wartenburg became a ranking diplomat in the foreign service of the Federal Republic of Germany, a prominent Christian leader, a founder of Bavaria's conservative Christian Social Union party, an officer of France's prestigious *Legion d'Honneur,* and lived to be one hundred years old.

36. Wilhelm Dilthey: An important German philosopher (1853–1911), for some years the senior professor of philosophy at the University of Berlin.

37. It has been said that one or more German reconnaissance patrols in early December 1941 got close enough to the center of Moscow to glimpse the spires of the Kremlin on the far horizon. But they got no farther.

38. Günther von Kluge (1882–1944), born in Posen, entered the Prussian army in 1901 and stayed on active duty for the rest of his life. He endured the battle of Verdun in 1916 and served ably in the Reichswehr and prewar Wehrmacht. After leading armies in the invasions of Poland and France he attained field marshal rank in 1940. The following year he commanded the 4th Army in Operation BARBAROSSA, before taking over Army Group Center. He killed himself with a cyanide capsule in 1944, after events that Gersdorff describes elsewhere in the book. The curious nickname *der kluge Hans* or "Clever

Hans" was the name of a horse that became famous in Germany, around the time von Kluge became a soldier, for seeming able to do basic arithmetic. How or when it became applied to von Kluge (none of whose given names was Hans) is a small mystery.

39. Colonel General Erich Hoepner: A Prussian cavalry officer since 1906, Erich Hoepner (1886–1944) became a Panzer leader during the interwar years and eventually commanded the Wehrmacht's 4th Panzer Group, which came within fifteen miles of Moscow in December 1941. Having withdrawn his exhausted troops in the face of the mighty Red Army counterattack, contrary to Hitler's "stand fast" orders, Hoepner was relieved of command in the most humiliating fashion, even being dismissed from the Wehrmacht. Fervently anti-communist and anti-Soviet but no fan of the Nazis either, Hoepner had been involved with anti-Hitler conspiracies since the 1930s and entered into the Operation VALKYRIE conspiracy as well. After participating in the 20 July coup d'état attempt in Berlin, Hoepner was arrested, tried, and executed within a few weeks.

40. Field Marshal Erich von Manstein: Perhaps the Wehrmacht's greatest strategist, the intellectual commander Erich von Manstein (1887–1973) had entered the Prussian army in 1906 and gone on to serve in the Reichswehr and the Wehrmacht. His exploits as a wartime General Staff strategy planner, army commander, and army group commander earned him the Knight's Cross with Oak Leaves and Swords. However, persistent disagreement with Hitler over military strategy led to his dismissal from active service in mid-1944, and he was still living in retirement when he surrendered to British forces the following year. Some measure of the international respect that Manstein enjoyed is evidenced by the fact that Sir Winston Churchill donated money to his defense fund when the field marshal was tried in 1949 for war crimes committed by German troops in Russia. He was found guilty of some charges and served four years in prison. In later life Manstein advised the new Bundeswehr of

the Federal Republic of Germany, published best-selling memoirs, and was buried with full military honors.

41. Count Friedrich von Oberndorff: A nobleman from the Rhineland (1890–1970); not prominent in the history of the war or apparently of anything else.

42. The Commander of XII Army Corps was General of Infantry Walter Schroth (1883–1944). As Gersdorff wrote, Schroth never received another promotion or front command. After vegetating in various low-profile general officer postings within Germany for the next two and a half years, he died in an automobile accident somewhere near his then-current headquarters in Wiesbaden.

43. *Rollbahnen*: Highways that the Wehrmacht had designated as main supply routes in the occupied territory for the transport of troops and materiel between cities. By inference the situation was even worse for less well-maintained and well-guarded routes.

44. Kromyadi, Sakharov: Konstantin Kromyadi, or Constantin Kromiadi (1893?–1991), was a Greek national who enlisted in the Imperial Russian Army during World War I, presumably motivated by the desire to fight Turks and uphold the Orthodox faith; he then fought against the Bolsheviks in the Russian Civil War. During the 1920s and 1930s he lived in Western Europe. At the end of World War II he settled in West Germany, later working for Radio Free Europe. The old anti-Communist crusader died in the United States in the same year that the Soviet Union died.

Igor Sakharov was presumably Igor Konstantinovich Sakharov, the son of a Tsarist general. His father had been a top commander in World War I and on the "White" or anti-Bolshevik side in the Russian Civil War, and later an émigré in Berlin.

45. Zhilenkov, Boyarski: Apparently, General Georgi Nikolaievich Zhilenkov was Nikolai Georgievich Zhilenkov (1910–1946), and not the other way around. The former commissar of the Soviet 32nd Army was captured on 14 October 1941, as he tried to escape through German lines after the army's destruction. He succeeded for a time

in masquerading as a simple truck driver; after being unmasked in 1942, he eventually agreed to join the anti-Stalin forces. He was captured by Americans at the end of the war but repatriated to the U.S.S.R., where he was tried and executed for treason in 1946.

Colonel Boyarski was presumably Colonel V. I. Boyarski, commander of the Soviet 42nd Infantry Division when he was captured near Kharkov on 3 August 1942. He went over almost immediately to the anti-Stalin Russian forces in German service. Czech partisans captured and hanged him on 7 May 1945.

46. General Belov: The future Colonel General Pavel Alexeivich Belov (1897–1962), Hero of the Soviet Union, commanded I Guards Cavalry Corps during 1941–1942.

47. General Vlasov: Andrei Andreyevich Vlasov (1900–1946), a heroic Soviet general whose army was nonetheless surrounded and destroyed in June 1942. As a prisoner of war, he agreed to lead Russian troops against the Soviet regime, under German sponsorship. He was tried and hanged for treason in the U.S.S.R. in 1946. The tragic fate of the Russian anti-communist volunteer forces is that some four million of their number, having succeeded in surrendering to the British and American forces in central Europe at the end of the war in 1945, were returned to Stalin's clutches under a shameful provision of the Yalta accords that provided for the repatriation to the U.S.S.R. of anyone who had been a Soviet national prior to August 1939. The senior officers were mostly executed; the junior officers and enlisted men went straight into the Gulag system of labor camps, where their treatment was the harshest of all. As Alexander Solzhenitsyn wrote in *The Gulag Archipelago,* the Soviet regime was uniquely bad (among other ways) in that no other war in Russia's long history had resulted in Russians changing sides to fight for a foreign invader of their homeland.

48. Reinhard Gehlen: In spring 1942, the future General Gehlen (1902–1979), a soldier since 1920, became chief of OKW's Foreign Armies East section (*Fremde Heere Ost*), in which he was already a senior intelligence

officer. The brilliant and enterprising future spymaster graduated from the *Kriegsakademie* in 1935, meaning that he overlapped for one year the academy superstar Henning von Tresckow (class of 1936), whom he probably met at that time if not earlier. He surrendered to American military intelligence at the end of the war and shrewdly parlayed his vast knowledge of the U.S.S.R.'s internal workings (and his even more vast hidden collection of microfilmed intelligence files) into freedom and the chance to work for the U.S. Army and eventually the CIA as the Cold War got started—targeting the Soviet Union and its new satellite states. From 1956 to 1968 he was the first head of the *Bundesnachrichtendienst,* the intelligence service of the Federal Republic of Germany. Gersdorff's daughter remembers her father writing reports for Gehlen in the 1950s, presumably concerning Soviet issues. This may have been when General Gehlen was still running the *Organization Gehlen* as a private spy agency sponsored by U.S. intelligence agencies, prior to 1956.

49. Piekenbrock, Lahousen, Bentivegni: The future Major General Hans Piekenbrock (1893–1959), chief of *Abwehr I* from 1936 to 1943, when he left to command an infantry division on the Eastern Front.

Erwin von Lahousen (1897–1955), an Austrian officer who transferred into the Wehrmacht after the unification of Austria and Germany in 1938; he was chief of *Abwehr II* (Sabotage) from 1939 until mid-1943, when he took a regimental command on the Eastern Front. Badly wounded by a bursting artillery shell, Lahousen was an invalid in Germany when the war ended. He had the honor, as a volunteer witness, of being the first person to testify for the prosecution in the so-called Main Trial at Nuremberg, in which the defendants were Hermann Goering and twenty-one other high-ranking officers and senior civilian officials.

The future Major General Franz von Bentivegni (1896–1958). He left *Abwehr III* in 1943 and eventually commanded a division on the Eastern Front. Like his colleague Piekenbrock, he dodged arrest and execution

after 20 July but spent the years from 1945 to 1955 as a Soviet prisoner of war before being repatriated to West Germany.

V. Soldier and Traitor

1. Lieutenant Colonel Hotzel: Historically obscure.

2. The future Colonel Baron Georg von Boeselager (1915–1944) was the older brother of Philipp von Boeselager. A friend and admirer of Henning von Tresckow, he was heavily involved in the 20 July plot, but like Tresckow was far away on the Eastern Front when the bomb went off. Less than six weeks later he died in action against Red Army troops. He posthumously received the Swords to his Knight's Cross with Oak Leaves, for extreme gallantry in his last action. His gallantry was so extreme (standing erect on top of a tank in broad daylight, waving his troops on to attack an enemy machine-gun nest that had the entire area under fire) that it is almost possible to see it as a deliberately sought death on the part of Boeselager, a devout Catholic for whom suicide would have been a mortal sin. The sport of modern pentathlon in which he competed during peacetime had become an Olympic sport in 1912, and was designed to test five skills a theoretical cavalry officer of that time might need if stranded behind enemy lines: riding an unfamiliar horse, swimming, running cross-country, pistol shooting, and fencing. If Georg von Boeselager was good at this soldierly game, he was certainly at least an expert pistol marksman, possibly world-class. As of this time the modern pentathlon has managed to survive as an Olympic sport, although this formerly important competition is now considered one of the oddest and most obscure on the Summer Games schedule. *Autre temps, autre moeurs!* (Other times, other standards!)

3. Gersdorff's Silesian cousin, the "Panzer Count" Strachwitz von Gross-Zauche und Camminetz (1893–1968), a superb equestrian and sportsman, served in an imperial guards regiment during World War II and as a reserve officer in the Reichswehr 7th Cavalry

Regiment between the wars. In contrast to Gersdorff he was apparently fascinated by tanks at first sight and volunteered for active service in the new 2nd Panzer Regiment in 1935. He was also a member of the Nazi Party and the *Allgemeine-SS*. During World War II he proved to be an aggressive and phenomenally successful armored commander, so that he ended up as a major general and a recipient of the Knight's Cross with Oak Leaves, Swords, and Diamonds. His last but certainly not least achievement in the war was a successful breakout from a Soviet encirclement in Czechoslovakia, so that he and his surviving troops could reach Bavaria and surrender to the Americans instead.

4. The Rzhev-Vyazma Salient was the site of a year-long series of meat-grinder operations slugged out between Smolensk and Mozhaisk, the last important town west of Moscow. All but unknown in the West, the monstrous Rzhev battles ate up 300,000 to 450,000 Wehrmacht soldiers and anywhere from 500,000 to 1,000,000 Red Army men. After holding off the enemy in the salient for just over a year, the Germans withdrew from it in March 1943. Gersdorff's description of fresh regiments climbing off their trains just in time to be sent into the line and decimated reflects an even bigger wastage on the other side; but the Soviet Union had manpower to spare, and Germany did not.

5. The capital of Georgia, Tbilisi, has also been historically known as Tiflis. As Gersdorff notes, the Wehrmacht was no longer remotely capable of reaching the place after the defeat at Stalingrad.

6. Friedrich Paulus (1890–1957) commanded the German 6th Army before and during its gruesome encirclement by Soviet forces in the city of Stalingrad. Promoted to marshal rank over the radio on 30 January 1943, he surrendered his surviving forces a day later. (Over ninety percent would die in Soviet captivity, however.) After 20 July 1944, the captive marshal became a major figure in the Soviet-sponsored "National Committee for a Free Germany" and made radio broadcasts urging German surrender. Released from

Soviet captivity in 1953, he settled in East Germany.

7. Hans Krebs (1898–1945) served as an officer in World War I and then in the Reichswehr and Wehrmacht. He spent almost his entire career in staff assignments, where his professional abilities, ingratiating manners, and humorous wit endeared him to multiple commanders. Having served in the Moscow embassy before World War II, he spoke Russian, and understood Russian conditions better than most of his contemporaries. By March 1945 he had become a colonel general and the German army's last chief of staff; after unsuccessful armistice negotiations with the Russians in the ruins of central Berlin, he committed suicide in the *Führerbunker*, a day or two after Hitler's death.

8. Blücher, Yorck, Moltke: Household names in the Prussia these men had all grown up in; the first two commanded armies during the Napoleonic Wars, and the last-named in the Franco-Prussian war of 1870–71.

9. Theodor Morell (1886–1948): Hitler's unsavory doctor, notorious for dosing the Führer with methamphetamines and many other narcotics, and with secret quack remedies of his own.

10. Heinz Brandt (1907–1944), an Olympic equestrian gold medalist (show jumping, 1936) was on the OKW General Staff. He could not escape his fate in the end; on 20 July 1944, he was the officer at the conference table at Rastenburg who moved the absent Stauffenberg's briefcase behind a thick wooden table leg. This saved Hitler's life, but the blast mortally wounded Colonel Brandt. [For Stauffenberg, see Chapter V, note 37.]

11. The future Brigadier General Helmuth Stieff (1901–1944), chief of the Organization section at OKW, a pre-war military acquaintance of Henning von Tresckow, became an enemy of the regime after witnessing some of the atrocities that took place in Poland in 1939. Tresckow recruited him as a co-conspirator during the war. After the 20 July events Stieff was arrested and later executed.

12. Berlin Arsenal: The *Zeughaus* on Unter den Linden, central Berlin's main ceremonial

avenue, is a Baroque structure built between 1695 and 1730 as a field artillery arsenal building. In 1875 it became a Prussian military museum. It now houses the German Historical Museum and is a major tourist attraction. Visitors may walk through the spacious *Lichthof* where these events took place and view a wall plaque in Gersdorff's honor, placed there after the reunification of Germany.

13. Walter Model, born in 1891, served in World War I and in the Reichswehr and Wehrmacht as an infantry officer. During World War II this pro-Nazi military man proved to be among the most talented and energetic of all German generals and led armies on both the Eastern and Western Fronts, earning a reputation for repairing collapsing front lines, and also earning the Knight's Cross with Oak Leaves, Swords, and Diamonds as well as his field marshal's baton. "Hitler's Fireman" is believed to have committed suicide on or about 21 April 1945, while retreating from American forces in western Germany, although his body was never identified.

14. Hotel Eden: Across the street from the entrance to the Zoo, in the western part of Berlin.

15. "Twilight of the Gods": A reference to Richard Wagner's morose tragic opera *Götterdämmerung,* about the downfall of the gods of Valhalla. In Germany the reference would require no explanation.

16. Grand Admiral Karl Dönitz (1891–1980) had recently become the commander-in-chief of the German navy, a long-time submariner for what had basically become a submarine-dominant naval arm. In 1945 he would become Nazi Germany's last head of state, for the week or less that it took him to sign Germany's unconditional surrender agreement on 8 May 1945.

17. Metropolitan of Moscow: "Metropolitan" in this sense is a high prelate of the Russian Orthodox Church, like a Catholic archbishop, and refers in this case to Sergius, then the Metropolitan of Moscow and Kolomna (1867–1944). As one of a minority of priests and prelates who survived vicious atheistic persecution and remained on duty from the Bolshevik revolution until the German invasion, Sergius (a prison survivor himself) was the principal churchman with whom Stalin cynically dealt to obtain church support for the war effort (such as the public declaration in the museum exhibit) in exchange for some concessions and a lessening of persecution. Among the concessions was agreement to Sergius's election in 1943 as "Patriarch of Moscow and all Russia"—this highest post had been vacant since the death of Sergius's predecessor in 1925. Goering's mirth was no doubt at the irony of a Christian churchman calling for support of the intensely godless Soviet regime, since he and Hitler cared almost as little for clergymen as they did for Communists. Patriarch Sergius I died of natural causes in the spring of 1944.

18. Union Club: A very elite men's club in Berlin, whose members were wealthy aristocrats and big businessmen. It also owned and operated the Hoppegarten racetrack and stables complex on the outskirts of the city, a major stop on the European flat-racing circuit before World War II. It seems quite natural that Gersdorff was a member. The club occupied a most elegant building in the heart of Berlin, between the Arsenal and the Brandenburg Gate, and a short walk from either.

19. Descended from the eighteenth century Jewish banker Salomon Oppenheim, Jr., the wealthy and elegant Baron Waldemar von Oppenheim (1894–1952) ranked in Nazi Germany as a *Mischling 2. Grade* (hybrid of the 2nd degree), a person with one Jewish and three non-Jewish grandparents. As such he faced certain legal restrictions but was allowed to survive and keep much of his property, although he had had to sign his bank over to a fully German employee. Back in the family's possession since the end of the Second World War, Bank Sal. Oppenheim Jr. & Cie is one of the few German private banks with unbroken familial ownership since its foundation (in 1789). As one of the most prominent German racehorse owners before the war, Baron Oppenheim was clearly already well acquainted with the

horse-mad Baron Gersdorff, his fellow Union Club member.

20. The expression does not sound strange in German, as military commanders not infrequently addressed their troops familiarly as *Kinder,* also using (as here) the informal mode of address used by parents to their offspring.

21. General Ludwig Beck (1880–1944) was Chief of the General Staff from 1935 to 1938, when Hitler replaced him with Halder. Beck's fault had been resisting Hitler's plans for aggressive war. The much-admired general went into retirement. A leading member of the anti-Hitler conspiracy, he was to have served as president of the Reich in the transitional regime. Instead he shot himself on the night of 20 July and was finished off by a sergeant.

22. Hans-Alexander von Voss (1907–1944), Tresckow's one-time subordinate for operations planning (Ia/op) at Army Group Center, went undetected for a few months after 20 July. Tipped off to his imminent arrest by the Gestapo, he chose to shoot himself.

23. Georg Schulze-Büttger (1904–1944), one of Henning von Tresckow's most reliable subordinates and co-conspirators. As of 20 July 1944, he had parted ways with Manstein and was serving as chief of staff of 4th Panzer Army on the Eastern Front. The Gestapo arrested him a month later, and he was hanged at Plötzensee prison later in the year. He had been General Beck's adjutant from 1935 to 1938.

24. Goerdeler, Popitz: Carl Goerdeler (1884–1945), the former *Oberbürgermeister* (Chief Mayor) of Leipzig, was perhaps the most prominent civilian in the resistance movement built up by Beck, Tresckow, and the other soldiers. Like them he was a conservative and traditionalist Prussian of his time, but the excesses of Nazi rule were abhorrent to him. He was executed after the failure of the plot; had it succeeded, he would have served as chancellor of the transitional regime.

Johannes Popitz (1884–1945), a former senior civil servant in the Ministry of Finance

and a civilian member of the grand conspiracy; like Goerdeler, with whom he was hanged in 1945, he was a staunch conservative who would probably have liked to bring back the monarchy, but was opposed to Nazism, especially as the movement's crimes piled up.

25. General of Infantry Theodor Busse (1897–1986), was at the time chief of staff of Manstein's Army Group South on the Eastern Front; this brave and highly competent officer was nonetheless yet another of the just-a-soldier generals with whom Tresckow's circle apparently never even bothered. After the war, Busse was for a time the director of civil defense in the Federal Republic of Germany during the Cold War years when a Soviet attack was always a strategic possibility.

26. Alexander Stahlberg (1912–1995) was one of Tresckow's cousins. After Stahlberg had endured hard combat on the Eastern Front during 1941 and 1942, Tresckow brought him to Army Group Center in Smolensk with the aim of attaching him as an aide-de-camp to Field Marshal von Manstein, knowing his younger cousin to be adept at both classical violin playing and the game of bridge, two of Manstein's private passions. Stahlberg stayed with Manstein for the rest of the war and negotiated the marshal's personal surrender to the British in May 1945. Afterwards he became a businessman in West Germany.

27. Seydlitz, Yorck: Major General Baron Friedrich Wilhelm von Seydlitz (1721–1773), Frederick the Great's best cavalry general, and General Count Ludwig Yorck von Wartenburg (1759–1830), a commander in the Napoleonic era. Both honored Prussian generals disobeyed their sovereigns in wartime for the good of the nation.

28. Operation CITADEL: An enormous German offensive, an enormous German defeat, otherwise known to history as the Battle of Kursk in July/August 1943. Excellent Soviet intelligence and German delays in launching the attack allowed the Red Army, a much-improved version from that of the summer of 1941, time to prepare massive in-depth defenses, on which waves of Wehrmacht forces were caught and broken, despite the

typically massive casualties on the Soviet side. After CITADEL, the strategic initiative on the Eastern Front passed definitively to the Soviet side.

29. The German discovery of this Soviet war crime, here described by Gersdorff, took place in early April 1943. It is known to history as the "Katyn Massacre," the name Gersdorff gave it shortly after its discovery. (See also "The Truth about Katyn," in the appendix, page 160, a document Gersdorff wrote as a witness and expert consultant to the Nuremberg war crimes trials.)

30. Not to be confused with the regular military police (*Feldgendarmerie*), the Wehrmacht's *Geheime Feldpolizei* (Secret Field Police) was responsible for security work in the field, including counterespionage, countersabotage, and detection of treasonable activity.

31. This non-commissioned officer is perhaps otherwise unknown to history.

32. The NKVD, (Gersdorff referred to it as the GPU in his post-war report, see also the appendix, page 160, "The Truth about Katyn"), was the frightful Stalin-era governmental agency that was responsible for, among other things, espionage, secret police work, internal repression, and the Gulag labor-camp system.

Gerhard Buhtz, M.D. (1896–1944), who directed the exhumation at Katyn, was in civilian life a professor of forensic medicine and criminology at Breslau University. His 1943 investigation at Katyn, whatever else it was, was a classic early example of a mass-burial exhumation and forensic inquiry, moreover in very difficult circumstances: a real professional triumph. He died in an accident in Minsk the following year.

33. Marko Antonov Markov, a professor at the Medico-Legal Institute of Sofia University during and after the war. By the time of his Nuremberg testimony, Bulgaria and the professor were under Soviet control, and Markov testified under questioning from a Soviet prosecutor that the Katyn body he dissected could not have been dead for more than a year and half, thus making the corpse,

by inference, a victim of the Germans and not of the Russians.

34. Führer-Reserve: The administrative "assignment" for officers who were temporarily between duty assignments. For some out-of-favor generals it became "cold storage" for indefinite periods of time up to and including the end of the war.

35. Hans von Sierstorpff: Presumably a member of the Silesian branch of the von Francken-Sierstorpffs, an aristocratic family.

36. General of Infantry Karl Brennecke (1891–1982), who from the spring of 1943 until the end of the war superintended the training courses for new division commanders, corps commanders, and senior members of the General Staff.

37. Colonel Count Claus Schenck von Stauffenberg (1907–1944), Catholic aristocrat and veteran of the Reichswehr 17th Cavalry Regiment, was both a brilliant young General Staff officer and one of the leading figures in the anti-Hitler conspiracy—the man who carried the bomb to Hitler's sanctuary at "Wolf's Lair" at Rastenburg in East Prussia on 20 July 1944, and left it in a briefcase a few feet away from Hitler's legs. After attempting to make the coup d'état succeed in Berlin, he was arrested and shot the same night. An intellectual—he was one of the "disciples" of the renowned mystical poet Stefan George (1868–1933) and a deeply moral man, equally handsome and heroic—Stauffenberg ranks alongside such men as Henning von Tresckow and Hans Oster as driving forces in the German resistance.

38. Baron Wessel von Freytag-Loringhoven (1899–1944), a career soldier since 1922 and an active member of the German resistance, joined Canaris's staff at *Abwehr* in 1943 after combat service on the Eastern Front. After the failure of the 20 July plot, he committed suicide to avoid arrest and interrogation at the hands of the Gestapo.

39. The broadcast journalist Hans Fritzsche (1900–1953), head of the Radio Division of the Propaganda Ministry, was already working for German government radio before the Nazis took power; he opportunistically joined

the party only later in 1933. A mid-level functionary and news commentator and by no means a policy maker or even a very serious National Socialist, Fritzsche was nonetheless a defendant in the main war crimes trial at Nuremberg in 1946, although as the American journalist William Shirer wrote, "No one in the courtroom, including Fritzsche, seemed to know why he was there—he was too small a fry—unless it were as a ghost for Goebbels. . . ." Josef Goebbels had, of course, committed suicide a year earlier. Unlike most of his fellow defendants, Fritzsche was acquitted of all charges against him. As Gersdorff indicates, the professional radio talker seems at least to have had a lively sense of humor.

40. General of Infantry Hermann Reinecke (1888–1973): the National Socialist Leadership Officers were Nazi military officers assigned the duty of spreading party propaganda within the Wehrmacht, in partial imitation of the Red Army's successful (from the regime's viewpoint) political-commissar program. In contrast to most senior military men, Reinecke had become a passionate Nazi Party member in the 1930s, to the extent that he was sometimes derisively referred to behind his back as *Hitlerjunge* ("Hitler Youth") Reinecke.

41. Lüttwitz, Rothkirch, Krüger, Choltitz, Schwerin-Schwanenfeldt: General of Panzer Troops Baron Smilo von Lüttwitz (1895–1975). At the time of this course in early 1944 he was in command of an armored division and preparing to become a corps commander later in the year.

General von Rothkirch: General of Cavalry Count Edwin von Rothkirch und Trach (1888–1980), another of Gersdorff's fellow Silesian cavalrymen.

General Krüger: General of Panzer Troops Walter Krüger (1892–1973).

General von Choltitz: General of Infantry Dietrich von Choltitz (1894–1966); as the last German military commandant in Paris in August 1944, he avoided compliance with Hitler's repeated demands to destroy the French capital and fight to the death in the rubble as in Stalingrad or Berlin. Choltitz

surrendered The City of Light to the Allies intact, in spite of the impatient question he received from Hitler as the Allies approached, "Is Paris burning?" For this, he became a good guy in the postwar book and film that take their titles from Hitler's question. To this day, grateful French tourists pay their respects at his grave in western Germany.

Count von Schwerin-Schwanenfeld: Presumably Count Ulrich-Wilhelm Schwerin von Schwanenfeld (1902–1944), an anti-Nazi aristocrat who was called up as a reserve officer when World War II began. He belonged to the conspiracy against Hitler with heart and soul and died on the gallows after its failure.

42. Erwin Rommel (1891–1944) earned the *Pour le Mérite* as an infantry junior officer in World War I and, having switched to tanks in the interim, earned his marshal's baton and deathless fame as "the Desert Fox," commander of the Afrika Korps—the one Wehrmacht army that was never even accused of committing any war crimes—in the North African campaign. A man of great personal honor and dignity, Rommel was apparently willing to support a coup d'état after Hitler's death. When this became known after 20 July 1944, Hitler allowed Rommel the opportunity to commit suicide by poison, and had him buried with full military honors as a "heart attack" victim, in order to avoid the blow to civilian morale that the national hero's arrest and trial would have caused. Curiously, Field Marshal Rommel, one of the ultimate "nice guys" among World War II top commanders, shared with Field Marshal Ferdinand Schörner, one of the meanest on any side, the very rare distinction of being awarded the *Pour le Mérite* in the first world war and the Knight's Cross with Oak Leaves, Swords, and Diamonds in the second. [For Schörner, see Chapter VI, note 42.]

VI. Soldier in the Downfall

1. Whatever history knows or is likely to know of Gersdorff's brave and faithful orderly Paul Kühn is probably within the pages of this book.

2. Sven von Mitzlaff (1914–1992), a Mecklenburg nobleman and former member of the Reichswehr 4th Cavalry Regiment, the Potsdam-based aristocratic counterpart to Gersdorff's beloved 7th Cavalry at Breslau. What Gersdorff does not mention, but what must have helped endear Mitzlaff to him, is that in the 1930s the major had been a famous flat-track racer, who had won Germany's amateur-jockey championship three times. After the war he earned over a thousand racetrack victories as one of the top horse trainers in West Germany.

3. La Roche Guyon: This spectacular hilltop chateau between Paris and Normandy is now a tourist attraction, and visitors may stroll in the same ornate French-style garden on the banks of the Seine where Gersdorff encountered the German field marshal strolling with the French duke.

4. Speidel, Gehrke, Elfeldt: Major General Hans Speidel (1897–1984), after fighting heroically in World War I, entered the Reichswehr. In his spare time during the 1920s he studied history and economics and earned a Ph.D. During World War II he was a brilliant General Staff officer in the east and the west. Jailed for suspicion of involvement in the grand conspiracy, he remained in custody from September 1944 until almost the end of the war. In the postwar years this soldier-scholar taught history and entered the Bundeswehr; a fluent speaker of English and French, he was commander of NATO ground forces in Central Europe from 1957 to 1963.

General Gehrke is historically obscure.

Major General Otto Elfeldt (1895–1982), commander at the time of the 47th Infantry Division. He became a prisoner of war while attempting to break out of the Falaise Pocket later in the year.

5. Colonel von Tempelhoff: Hans-Georg von Tempelhoff (1907–1985).

6. Paul Hausser (1880–1972), dubbed by some "the father of the Waffen-SS" had been in uniform ever since entering one of the royal Prussian military academies at the age of twelve. After retiring from the Reichswehr as a general in 1932, he entered the SS in 1934 and helped develop its military arm. In the interim he had been a member of the right-wing *Stahlhelm* paramilitary organization. He led 2nd SS-Division *"Das Reich"* in Operation BARBAROSSA and lost his right eye to a grenade splinter late in 1941, but returned to command II SS-Panzer Corps on the Eastern Front during 1942 and 1943. Gersdorff had probably met him at least by that time. In 1951 he and Sepp Dietrich were among the co-founders of a lobbying group, which this tireless old soldier successfully directed until his death, for the interests of former SS men in the Federal Republic of Germany.

7. The future Major General Max Pemsel (1897–1985), a Bavarian professional soldier, endured this career nadir and went on to receive the Knight's Cross as a division commander in Finland later in 1944. Taken prisoner in northern Italy in 1945, he spent time as a prisoner of war and served as a Bundeswehr general from 1956 to 1961.

8. *Stahlhelm* organization: During 1932 and 1933, following his retirement from the Reichswehr, Hausser had become a leader in the big right-wing paramilitary organization of war veterans whose name meant "Steel Helmet." Informally it was the fighting arm of the DNVP, the German National People's Party, during the Weimar Republic. After the Nazis came to power, the *Stahlhelm* was compulsorily affiliated with the Nazi Party's SA, before being abolished altogether in 1935. By this time, of course, Hausser had already moved over to the SS.

9. Prior to 20 July 1944, the army had maintained the traditional military salute rather than use the *Hitlergrüss,* the famous stiff-armed Nazi salute and simultaneous *"Heil* Hitler" cry. The latter salute became mandatory after the failed coup.

10. General of Aviators Alfred Bülowius (1892–1968), then the commander of the Luftwaffe's 2nd Fighter Corps. Although the support he promised was not forthcoming, in fairness, it must be said that by this time in the war the far-outmatched Luftwaffe barely had air superiority in the skies above its own airfields, let alone anywhere else.

11. General of Panzer Troops Heinrich Eberbach (1895–1992), received the Knight's Cross with Oak Leaves for service on the Eastern Front, was captured in a village near Amiens on 31 August 1944, as described by Gersdorff. It may have come as a relief to him. During his previous twelve months of service he had rotated through the command of four separate Panzer corps and two numbered armies and suffered a severe wound requiring a recuperation period in Germany.

12. The Bavarian hard man Josef "Sepp" Dietrich (1892–1966) had been a simple field artillery sergeant during World War I, and afterwards struggled for a decade to earn a living as a waiter, a farm laborer, and a police constable, as well as working other lowly jobs. He was a petrol-station attendant in Munich, fueling cars and washing windows, when his boss first told him about Nazism. Beginning in 1928 Dietrich made a career in the Nazi Party and the SS, enjoying intimate access to Adolf Hitler as his personal chauffeur and bodyguard commander in the years of struggle, and was ready as well to kill when needed. During World War II he earned the Knight's Cross with Oak Leaves, Swords, and Diamonds, for he was a brave warrior if no great strategist. Seven thousand former comrades attended his funeral, certainly a sign of his personal popularity. Calling stiff aristocrats with pedigrees seven-centuries long *"du"* (as Gersdorff describes) may have been a private pleasure for this proletarian by birth and background, but the historical impression left by the rough-edged Waffen-SS chieftain, essentially a throwback to the swashbuckling and casually brutal German mercenaries of the Thirty Years' War, is of a man somehow hard not to like; and Gersdorff, a stiff and pedigreed aristocrat if ever there was one, obviously liked him well enough.

13. Reserve Major Count Friedrich-August von Brühl (1913–1981) commanded a battalion of the 16th Panzer Regiment and was a Knight's Cross recipient.

14. The decoration is formally known as the Knight's Cross of the Iron Cross, and was intended for men who had already earned the Iron Cross, 1st Class. As Gersdorff notes, the *Ritterkreuz* could therefore be traced back to the original Iron Cross award created by King Friedrich Wilhelm III of Prussia in 1813. During World War II, out of millions of German servicemen in all branches, only 7,365 received the Knight's Cross; out of these, only 890 also received the Oak Leaves, 160 the Swords, and 27 the Diamonds, all embellishments to the basic Knight's Cross for additional qualifying deeds. A decoration worn on a ribbon around the collar, the hard-to-get *Ritterkreuz* was as such the Third Reich replacement for the *Pour le Mérite* of the Royal Prussian Army.

15. Major General Alfred Gause (1896–1967), a long-time staff officer for Rommel.

16. Presumably Hans-Joachim Hirche, a General Staff major who was Ic of 7th Army at the time.

17. Wilhelm Bittrich (1894–1979) was one of the decent and honorable Waffen-SS commanders and would probably have gone along with a coup d'état and brought his troops with him if Hitler had died on 20 July 1944. As commander of II SS-Panzer Corps that summer, Bittrich did more than any other single person to ruin the British Operation MARKET GARDEN flanking maneuver; he lived long enough to consult with Cornelius Ryan, the author of the most famous book about the operation, and then to see himself played by Maximillian Schell in the movie of the same name, *A Bridge Too Far.* [See note 19, below.]

18. General of Panzer Troops Erich Brandenberger (1892–1955), a fine commander who earned the Knight's Cross with Oak Leaves during the war. Despite the conflict with Field Marshal Model that Gersdorff describes, he finished the war as commander of the 19th Army on the Western Front.

19. Montgomery's plan was Operation MARKET GARDEN, an attempt to use principally British armored and American and British airborne forces to outflank the Germany army and push into northern Germany. The fighting took place all along the single principal route north ("Hell's Highway") in Holland, notably in the areas around Nijmegen and Arnhem.

Historians will never finish debating whether or not the operation and the associated halt of the Allied advance was a good idea or "grossly wrong" as Gersdorff opines.

20. The future General of Panzer Troops Count Gerhard von Schwerin (1899–1980), a recipient of the Knight's Cross with Oak Leaves and Swords, left a surrender note behind in the ancient and culturally rich city of Aachen as Gersdorff describes, not wishing to see the place destroyed. Instead of reaching General Courtney Hodges of the U.S. 1st Army, the note fell into Nazi hands, with almost fatal consequences for Count Schwerin. He later commanded the LXXVI Army Corps in northern Italy until April 1945, when he and his command went into British captivity. After the war he was a business executive in West Germany.

21. *SS-Standartenführer* Przybilski: This SS officer with a Polish surname seems to have left no mark in history. An *SS-Standarte* was on paper a unit of three hundred men, and the *Standartenführer* rank corresponded to that of a Wehrmacht colonel.

22. Colonel Wiese: A certain Hubert Wiese; not to be confused with a general named Hubert Weise.

23. General of Cavalry Siegfried Westphal (1902–1982), at the time that Gersdorff here describes, was chief of staff to OB-West. He entered the Prussian army as an officer cadet on 10 November 1918; World War I ended the next day. He soldiered on in the Reichswehr and Wehrmacht cavalry and served during the war in North Africa and France, mostly on senior staffs. He seems to have been the last man ever to be promoted to General of Cavalry, on 1 February 1945; at the time of this incident he was still a major general. After a couple of years as a prisoner of war, he was active as an author and as a leader of veterans' associations in West Germany.

24. Josef Grohé (1902–1988), a Nazi Party member since 1922, was the *Gauleiter* (regional party leader) of the Rhineland from 1928 to 1945.

25. The future Major General Gerhard Engel (1906–1976), at that time the commander of the 12th Volksgrenadier Division (formerly the 12th Infantry Division) on the Western Front, and a recipient of the Knight's Cross with Oak Leaves.

26. Erwin Fussenegger (1908–1986) was an Austrian army officer taken into the Wehrmacht in 1938. During the war he served in the invasion of Norway and on the Eastern Front before transferring to France to become Quartermaster General of 7th Army. He headed the post-war Austrian army from 1956 to 1970. He had attended general staff courses in both Austria and Germany.

27. Schloss Schlenderhan, Manteuffel: Schlenderhan, an estate and stud farm, had been taken over by the German armed forces for the duration of the war. It lies some twenty miles west of Cologne. Schlenderhan continues to routinely turn out champion thoroughbreds after more than a century. It is still owned by a descendant of Baron Eduard von Oppenheim, who founded the stud farm in 1869.

General of Panzer Troops Baron Hasso-Eccard von Manteuffel (1897–1978), recipient of the Knight's Cross with Oak Leaves, Swords, and Diamonds. He was an outstanding commander in North Africa and on the Eastern and Western Fronts. After the war he played a significant role in West German politics.

28. Waldenburg; Prince of Holstein: Brigadier General Siegfried von Waldenburg (1898–1973), a Silesian cavalryman, was the last commander of the 116th Panzer Division, nicknamed the "Greyhound Division." By coincidence Gersdorff's second wife, during the 1950s, was also one of the Silesian Waldenburgs.

Major in the General Staff His Highness Prince Friedrich-Ferdinand of Schleswig-Holstein-Sonderburg-Glücksberg (1913–1989) was the 116th's operations officer at the time of the Hürtgen Forest battle. The unlucky American unit on this day was the 28th Infantry Division (the "Keystone" Division), and specifically its 112th Regimental Combat Team, both from the Pennsylvania National Guard.

29. Literally "People's Grenadiers," pieced-together infantry units of reduced personnel strength and enhanced automatic-weapons and anti-tank armament compared to earlier formations, used in the Wehrmacht in 1944–45 as an answer to the challenges of diminishing manpower and almost purely defensive combat.

30. The future Brigadier General Alfred Toppe (1904–1971). After the war he did extensive work as an advisor to the U.S. Army's military historians.

31. The *Führerbegleitbrigade,* assembled in November 1944, included infantry elements of Hitler's Wehrmacht guard detachment, the mobile artillery from his East Prussian compound *Wolfsschanze*; and units drawn from Panzer Corps Grossdeutschland.

32. Then Colonel, later Brigadier General Otto Remer (1912–1997), wounded and much-decorated on the Eastern Front, was the major in command of the Wehrmacht unit responsible for security in central Berlin as of 20 July 1944. He was ordered to arrest Josef Goebbels and went to do so, but Goebbels (with Hitler on the telephone) convinced him that the officers giving the orders were conspirators and traitors. He then employed his unit to break up the coup d'état. In gratitude, Hitler promoted him to full colonel on the same night. He proved to be an unsuccessful senior commander, leading his units to appalling casualties on both major fronts. Ever proud of his role on 20 July, he became a postwar hero to neo-Nazis, anti-Semites, and Holocaust deniers, all of which he remained to his dying day.

33. Schloss Merkeshausen: As Gersdorff notes, this is a rural area of the Rhineland near the city of Bitburg.

34. General of Infantry Hans-Gustav Felber (1889–1962).

35. Werner Voigt-Ruscheweyh had served as the 7th Army's Ia under the chief of staff Gersdorff ever since 1 September 1944. The bombing of Schloss Merkeshausen occurred on 21 February 1945.

36. Kloster Himmerod is a Cistercian abbey located near the city of Trier. Abbot Vitus Recke (1887–1959) was the monk who owed Gersdorff a favor for some unspecified reason.

37. General Fäckenstedt: Major General Ernst Felix Fäckenstedt (1896–1961).

38. Irmgard von Opel (1907–1986), of the family of wealthy industrial tycoons who made Opel automobiles, was probably the world's best equestrienne in the 1930s in cross-country and show jumping. In 1934 she had been the first woman ever to win the German Spring-Derby, one of the most renowned hunter-jumper contests in Europe. Her family's estate of Schloss Westerhaus is near the town of Ingelheim am Rhein on the left (western) bank of the Rhine River.

39. General of Infantry Hans von Obstfelder (1886–1976), who earned the Knight's Cross with Oak Leaves and Swords after battles in Russia and in the Normandy campaign. Gersdorff's last army commander was a man who did a lot of fighting and lived an unusually long life, while leaving scarcely any personal traces in the history of his era.

40. The Hammelburg Raid: An American survivor later said that when the Task Force Baum armored column, while still finding its way to Hammelburg, drove straight past a group of German soldiers doing morning calisthenics, he thought, "Well, it's not a secret mission any more." As Gersdorff makes clear, it was already no secret before then. The German officer with whom Gersdorff spoke over the phone was presumably a certain Colonel Hoepple. The raid was doomed from the start through over-hasty planning, poor intelligence (the task force got lost on the German country roads it had to navigate), and very inadequate forces and equipment. The whole operation stands in stark contradiction to Patton's dictum that a mediocre plan violently executed today is better than a perfect plan executed next week. (But Gersdorff seems to have made at least one minor error in this recounting, in that thirty-five Americans are said to have made it back to their own side.) The commanding officer of Combat Command B was Lieutenant Colonel Creighton Abrams (1914–1974), much later

the commander-in-chief of U.S. forces in Vietnam from 1968 to 1972, and then the U.S. Army's chief of staff.

41. Fritz Sauckel (1894–1946), the *Gauleiter* of Thuringia, a Nazi Party member since 1923. He was hanged at Nuremberg as a war criminal. In fairness to Sauckel, it is difficult to see what he could have contributed as a leader in the last-ditch defensive battles, as he had no military experience whatsoever.

42. Field Marshal Ferdinand Schörner (1892–1973), "Bloody Ferdinand," a pro-Nazi career soldier from Bavaria, was a brutal disciplinarian notorious for the summary execution of soldiers under his command. One of Hitler's favorite generals, he was the last-promoted of the German field marshals (April 1945), and was designated in Hitler's fantasy-filled "political testament" to take over command of the armed forces. Captured by the Americans but almost immediately handed over to the Russians, he spent a decade in Soviet prison camps, and then another several years in a West German prison for the murder of his own soldiers.

43. Teplitz-Schönau: A Sudeten German community, now Teplice in the Czech Republic. The Austrian princely family of Clary-Aldringen had been the local nobility for about three hundred years, but 1945 was the end of all that. In previous centuries, Goethe, Chopin, Liszt, and even Casanova had all been guests of the Clarys at Schloss Teplitz.

44. Hostau: General Patton and other equestrian officers in his command—and in the first few decades of the twentieth century, it was still normal for professional officers to be horsemen of fair-to-excellent quality—wanted to save the precious horses at Hostau from the Red Army, especially since it was feared that the Russian soldiers might slaughter all the animals for meat. The 3rd Army did manage to transport over a thousand prize stallions and mares into Germany in a maneuver lightheartedly dubbed "Operation Cowboy." Among other equines they saved 375 horses of the famed white "Lippizan" breed that provides the mounts for the Spanish Riding School in Vienna, the mecca of dressage.

A heavily fictionalized version of the event was the subject of *Miracle of the White Stallions,* a little-remembered 1963 Walt Disney film starring Robert Taylor and Lilli Palmer. See 2nd Cavalry on: www.lipizzaner.com/lipizzaner_frameset.asp.

45. Major von Mutius: A certain Albrecht von Mutius, last Ic of the 7th Army.

46. Elbogen, Karlsbad: Now Loket and Karlovy Vary in the Czech Republic.

47. Von Deichmann, Gescher: These two junior officers are historically obscure.

48. Lieutenant General Hobart R. "Hap" Gay (1894–1983), the 3rd Army's chief of staff from February 1944 onward, a quietly efficient subordinate to the most flamboyant and outspoken general in the U.S. Army.

49. Natzmer, Alpine Redoubt: Major General Oldwig Otto von Natzmer (1904–1980), a career soldier who seems to have hated his last commanding officer "Bloody Ferdinand" as much as anyone else could. At the 1957 West German trial during which Natzmer testified against his former boss, another ex-military witness stated that whenever Schörner left his headquarters on inspection tours, the warning telephone calls would go out— *Schörner in the field!*—and that was worse than when the Russians attacked." Perhaps Gersdorff was lucky not to have met the bloodthirsty Bavarian at Teplitz while accompanied by a terrier.

Alpine Redoubt: The *Alpenfestung* was believed by many to be a vast and well-fortified zone in the mountains of southern Bavaria and western Austria where Hitler and his remaining forces would be prepared to hold out indefinitely with stockpiled food and supplies. In reality it did not exist, but during early 1945 many Germans and the western Allies both gave the story credence.

VII. Soldier in Captivity

1. Dulles, Solz, Gisevius: Allen W. Dulles (1893–1969), a corporate lawyer and U.S. diplomat before the war, was the station chief in Bern, Switzerland, for the Office of Strategic Services, a wartime precursor to the

Central Intelligence Agency. As such he had steady contacts with the anti-Hitler resistance inside Germany. From 1953 to 1961 Dulles was the director of the CIA.

Adam Trott zu Solz (1909–1944), a well-connected attorney and former Rhodes Scholar at Oxford University, was a member of the anti-Nazi Kreisau Circle and was arrested and executed after the 20 July attempt.

Hans Bernd Gisevius (1904–1974), also a lawyer by trade, was a wartime member of Admiral Canaris's *Abwehr* and a most persistent anti-Hitler conspirator. Canaris arranged for his appointment as vice-consul in the German embassy in neutral Switzerland, which allowed him to stay in touch with Allen Dulles. After the failure of the conspiracy he succeeded in making a daring escape over the Swiss border, and survived to testify for the prosecution at Nuremberg. In the postwar years he authored two books: *To the Bitter End,* about his experiences in the covert anti-Nazi movement from 1933 to 1945; and *Where Is Nebe?* a tribute to his close friend and co-conspirator, the enigmatic Arthur Nebe.

2. Horthy, Schwerin-Krosigk, Lindemann, Bonin, Epp, Reitsch. Miklós Horthy (1868–1957) rose to the rank of admiral in the Austro-Hungarian navy, and after World War I became an admiral without a fleet in a country without a coastline, Hungary. From 1920 until 1944 the ultra-conservative nationalist directed Hungarian affairs as the "Regent of the Kingdom of Hungary" although the kingdom had no king either, and no intention of getting one. He allied Hungary with Germany in World War II, hungry to regain lands that had been lost to Hungary's neighbors in the treaty that ended World War I. The Germans used military force to remove him from power and arrest him after he had sought to work out a separate peace deal with the Allies. He died in Portugal, an exile from Hungary under communist rule.

Count Lutz von Schwerin-Krosigk (1887–1977), a non-political budget technocrat who became Germany's Minister of Finance in 1932, before the Nazis came to power, and stayed on in the job until the end of the war.

Colonel General Georg Lindemann (1884–1963) had commanded a division in the invasion of France and armies on the Eastern Front. By the end of the war he was in command of German troops in occupied Denmark.

Colonel in the General Staff Bogislaw von Bonin (1908–1980) was chief of operations at OKH when in January 1945, he gave the German "defenders" of Warsaw permission to withdraw rather than put up a militarily senseless and suicidal battle for the city. This was against a direct order from Hitler, and the Gestapo arrested Bonin within a few days. He spent the rest of the war in concentration camps, expecting to be executed, before falling into the hands of American troops in May. He became a journalist.

Brigadier General Franz *Ritter* von Epp (1868–1946), a Bavarian World War I hero and famed anti-communist *Freikorps* commander in 1919 and 1920, facilitated the Nazi Party's growth in its early days in Munich, and served continuously as a Nazi member of the Reichstag from 1928 to 1945. From 1933 he was the Nazi leader of Bavaria, increasingly only a figurehead. Already an ailing old man when arrested by the Americans in 1945, he died in captivity of natural causes.

Hanna Reitsch (1912–1979), a Lutheran pastor's daughter from Silesia, was a superb aviator and glider pilot and the only woman ever awarded the Iron Cross, 1st Class. As a civilian test pilot for the Luftwaffe, she was also the first woman ever to fly a helicopter, a rocket-propelled aircraft (1943), and a jet fighter (1944). A Nazi true believer, she worshipped Adolf Hitler and piloted the last German airplane in and out of Berlin before the Soviets closed in, to visit Hitler in his bunker. She remained an unrepentant admirer. Near the end of her life she candidly told an American journalist, "And what have we now in Germany? A land of bankers and car makers. Even our great army has gone soft. Soldiers wear beards and question orders. I am not ashamed to say I believed in National Socialism. I still wear the Iron Cross with diamonds Hitler gave me. But today in all Germany you can't find a single person who voted Adolf Hitler into power. . . . Many Germans feel guilty about the war. But they don't explain the real guilt we share—that we lost."

3. The compassionate American major was Howard Penn Hudson (1914–2005), the Deputy Chief of the Operational History (German) Section of the U.S. Army Historical Division in 1945–47. A warm and outgoing Chicago native and University of Chicago graduate, Hudson had been a professional journalist before the United States entered World War II; he was assigned to Patton's 3rd Army as a combat historian and then to the USAHD after the war. As deputy chief of the section charged with collecting the commentaries of German former commanders and General Staff officers, he was effectively in charge of the care, feeding, and movement of several hundred other captive generals and colonels besides Gersdorff. Hudson left the army as a lieutenant colonel, and went on to civilian success as a renowned expert in public relations and newsletter publishing for many years.

4. The son of a West Point graduate and professional soldier, Burton C. Andrus (1892–1977) entered the U.S. Army's commissioned ranks through the back door in 1917 as a World War I reserve officer, and persisted in a classic time-serving dud officer's career as undistinguished as it was long; incredibly, he was still only a colonel in 1945 despite already being a Regular Army lieutenant colonel in 1940. (By way of comparison, Dwight D. Eisenhower traveled from lieutenant colonel to five-star general in the same time span.) Assigned to the 2nd Armored Division in early 1942 as G-3 (Air), Andrus was culled out and left behind when the division shipped out to North Africa later that year. His brief wartime command in Europe in 1944 was over a unit called the 10th Traffic Regulation Group. In 1946 a *Time* magazine reporter at Nuremberg

described Andrus in cold print as a "pompous, unimaginative . . . officer who wasn't up to his job. . . . Every morning his plump little figure, looking like an inflated pouter pigeon, moved majestically into the court, impeccably garbed in his uniform and highly shellacked helmet." When Hermann Goering managed to commit suicide by poison despite all of Andrus's elaborate security measures, the other prisoners, every man of whom appears to have despised Andrus just as heartily as Gersdorff did, rejoiced no matter what their individual opinion of Goering was. He retired in 1952—still a colonel.

5. Hans Laternser (1908–1969) specialized in tax law before the war. Since he had never joined the Nazi Party, he was one of the first attorneys allowed to reopen a practice after the war's end. He became the chief defense attorney for the German General Staff and the OKW high command at the Nuremberg trials, for the most part quite successfully. Later he defended other men accused of war crimes.

6. Adolf Galland (1912–1996), a flamboyant Luftwaffe fighter pilot and recipient of the Knight's Cross with Oak Leaves, Swords, and Diamonds. The Americans were interested among other things in his experience flying and fighting in Me-262 jet planes, an innovation that came along too little and too late to turn the war in Germany's favor, but was clearly the technology of the future.

7. Karl-Adolf Hollidt (1891–1985), commander of the 6th Army (a new one formed after the original 6th Army had been annihilated at Stalingrad) on the Eastern Front in 1943–44.

8. Hans Böhm-Tettelbach, an industrialist and former lieutenant colonel.

9. General of Infantry Alexander von Falkenhausen (1878–1966), a *Pour le Mérite* recipient during World War I, had retired from the army before World War II began. Recalled to active duty, he became the military governor of Belgium from 1940 to 1944. A personal friend of Carl Goerdeler, Falkenhausen detested the Nazi regime and supported the grand conspiracy. After its failure

he was arrested and spent the rest of the war in concentration camps, but survived.

VIII. Epilogue

1. President from 1942 of the *Volksgericht-hof* ("People's Court"), a special tribunal that tried people accused of political offenses, including many of the 20 July conspirators, the Nazi attorney Roland Freisler (1893–1945) was sadistic, brutal, and hysterical even by the standards of Third Reich justice. He was one of the participants, as the representative for the Ministry of Justice, in the so-called Wannsee Conference in 1942, which gave the seal of approval to the extermination of the Jews of Europe. Freisler was killed in an American bombing raid on Berlin in February 1945, but not before he and his kangaroo court had handed out some 2,600 death sentences in less than three years.

2. A Socialist newspaper publisher and Reichstag member before the Nazis came to power, Dr. Julius Leber (1891–1945) spent the years 1933 to 1937 in a concentration camp and thereafter worked as a coal dealer. He was an active secret opponent of the Nazi regime who came in contact during the war with Stauffenberg and other conspirators.

Had the coup d'état succeeded, he was to have become the minister of labor in the transitional government. The Gestapo arrested Leber fifteen days before Stauffenberg's bomb went off. After a trial in Freisler's courtroom, he was sentenced to death and executed.

3. *Johanniterorden*: The Bailiwick of Brandenburg of the Chivalric Order of St. John of the Hospital at Jerusalem is a German Protestant "descendant" of the medieval order of Knights Hospitaller, founded in 1099 to provide care for Christian pilgrims to the Holy Land. The German order is connected to the English Order of the Hospital of St. John of Jerusalem and the Catholic Knights of Malta, both of which also trace their organizational ancestry to the Knights Hospitaller. The *Johanniterorden* is an important Christian provider of medical and rescue services in the Federal Republic of Germany; as Gersdorff describes, one of its major projects since World War II has been the provision of first-aid training to volunteers. It was largely due to his service with the St. John organization that in 1979 the German government granted Gersdorff its Grand Cross of the Order of Merit, one of the highest civilian awards for outstanding public service.

Index

Other Titles by The Aberjona Press . . .

Defending Fortress Europe: The War Diary of the German 7th Army, June–August 1944
by Mark J. Reardon
352 pages. 19 Maps. 41 Photos. Index.
Paperbound. ISBN 13: 978-0-9717650-3-0.

Swedes at War: Willing Warriors of a Neutral Nation, 1914–1945
by Lars Gyllenhaal and Lennart Westberg, translated by Carl Gustav Finstrom
394 pages. 4 Maps. 134 Photos. 3 Illustrations. Index.
Paperbound. ISBN 13: 978-0-9777563-1-5.

Victory Was Beyond Their Grasp: With the 272nd Volks-Grenadier Division from the Hürtgen Forest to the Heart of the Reich
by Douglas Nash
412 pages. 22 Maps. 88 Photos. 3 Illustrations. Index.
Paperbound. ISBN 13: 978-0-9777563-2-2.

Sledgehammers: Strengths and Flaws of Tiger Tank Battalions in World War II
by Christopher Wilbeck
272 pages. 35 Maps. 42 Photos.
Paperbound. ISBN 13: 978-0-9717650-2-3.

Slaughterhouse: The Handbook of the Eastern Front *edited by Keith E. Bonn*
520 pages. 9 Maps. 88 Photos. Extensive 16-page bibliography. Paperbound. ISBN 13: 978-0-9717650-9-2.

Waffen-SS Encyclopedia
by Marc J. Rikmenspoel
300 pages. 82 Photos. Extensive 20-page bilbiography.
Paperbound. ISBN 13: 978-0-9717650-8-5.

Seven Days in January: With the 6th SS-Mountain Division in Operation NORDWIND *by Wolf T. Zoepf*
312 pages. 37 Maps. Index.
Paperbound. ISBN 13: 978-0-9666389-6-7.

Into the Mountains Dark *by Franklin Gurley*
256 pages. 40 Photos.
Paperbound. ISBN 13: 978-0-9666389-4-3.

Black Edelweiss: A Memoir of Combat and Conscience by a Soldier of the Waffen-SS
by Johann Voss
224 pages. 8 Maps. 22 Photos.
Paperbound. ISBN 13: 978-0-9666389-8-1.

The Final Crisis
by Richard Engler
368 pages. 25 Maps. 20 Illustrations. Index.
Paperbound. ISBN 13: 978-0-9666389-1-2.

The Good Soldier: From Austrian Social Democracy to Communist Captivity with a Soldier of Panzer-Grenadier Division "Grossdeutschland"
by Alfred Novotny
160 pages. 62 Photos.
Paperbound. ISBN 13: 978-0-9666389-9-8.

Audio CD, 6-disc set, 6.5 hours.
ISBN 13: 978-0-9777563-0-8.

Victims, Victors: From Nazi Occupation to the Conquest of Germany as Seen by a Red Army Soldier
by Roman Kravchenko-Berezhnoy
300 pages. 6 Maps. 26 Photos.
Paperbound. ISBN 13: 978-0-9717650-6-5.

American Illiad: The History of the 18th Infantry Regiment in World War II
by Robert Baumer
424 pages. 17 Maps. 45 Photos.
Paperbound. ISBN 13: 978-0-9717650-5-4.

Odyssey of a Philippine Scout: Fighting, Escaping, and Evading the Japanese, 1941–1944
by Arthur Kendal Whitehead
304 pages. 6 Maps. 20 Photos. Paperbound.
ISBN 13: 978-0-9717650-4-7.

Five Years, Four Fronts
by Georg Grossjohann
218 pages. 28 Maps. 30 Photos. Index.
Paperbound. ISBN 13: 978-0-9666389-3-6.

THE ABERJONA PRESS Setting the highest standards . . . in *History*
P.O. Box 629, Bedford, PA 15522; **toll free: (866) 265-9063;** www.aberjonapress.com